W9-BPJ-134

MAIL ORDER SELLING

WILEY SMALL BUSINESS EDITIONS

Jeffrey G. Allen, *Complying with the ADA*

Kim Baker and Sunny Baker, *How to Promote, Publicize, and Advertise Your Growing Business*

Irving Burstiner, *Mail Order Selling: How to Market Almost Anything by Mail,* Third Edition

Fred Hahn, *Do-It-Yourself Advertising*

Daryl Allen Hall, *1001 Businesses You Can Start from Home*

Daryl Allen Hall, *1101 Businesses You Can Start from Home*

Herman Holtz, *How to Start and Run a Writing and Editing Business*

John Kremer, *The Complete Direct Marking Sourcebook: A Step-by-Step Guide to Organizing and Managing a Successful Direct Marketing Program*

Gregory and Patricia Kishel, *How to Start, Run, and Stay in Business*

Gregory and Patricia Kishel, *Build Your Own Network Sales Business*

Gregory and Patricia Kishel, *Cashing In on the Consulting Boom*

Gregory and Patricia Kishel, *Start, Run, and Profit from Your Own Home-Based Business*

Christopher Malburg, *Business Plans to Manage Day-to-Day Operations*

Harry J. McLaughlin, *The Entrepreneur's Guide to Building a Better Business: A Step-by-Step Approach*

Patrick D. O'Hara, *How to Computerize Your Small Business*

Richard L. Porterfield, *Insider's Guide to Winning Government Contracts*

M. John Storey, *Taking Money Out of Your Corporation*

L. Perry Wilbur, *Money in Your Mailbox: How to Start and Operate a Successful Mail-Order Business,* Second Edition

MAIL ORDER SELLING

How to Market Almost Anything by Mail

THIRD EDITION

Irving Burstiner, Ph.D.

John Wiley & Sons, Inc.

New York • Chichester • Brisbane • Toronto • Singapore

Dedicated to my wife, Razel,
for her patience and encouragement

This text is printed on acid-free paper.

Copyright © 1982, 1989, 1995 by Irving Burstiner
Published by John Wiley & Sons, Inc.

All rights reserved. Published simultaneously in Canada.

Reproduction or translation of any part of this work beyond
that permitted by Section 107 or 108 of the 1976 United
States Copyright Act without the permission of the copyright
owner is unlawful. Requests for permission or further
information should be addressed to the Permissions Department,
John Wiley & Sons, Inc.

This publication is designed to provide accurate and
authoritative information in regard to the subject
matter covered. It is sold with the understanding that
the publisher is not engaged in rendering legal, accounting,
or other professional services. If legal advice or other
expert assistance is required, the services of a competent
professional person should be sought.

Library of Congress Cataloging-in-Publication Data:

Burstiner, Irving.
    Mail order selling : how to market almost anything by mail /
Irving Burstiner. — 3rd ed.
        p.   cm. — (Wiley small business editions)
    Includes index.
    ISBN 0-471-09791-8 (cloth : alk. paper). — ISBN 0-471-09759-4
(pbk. : alk. paper)
    1. Mail-order business.   I. Title.   II. Series.
HF5466.B88   1995
658.8′72—dc20   94-48372

Printed in the United States of America
10 9 8 7 6 5 4 3 2 1

Preface

Welcome to this thoroughly revised, updated, and expanded *third* edition of *Mail Order Selling!* I've added six new chapters; each is packed with dozens of useful facts:

- *Chapter 1—"Exploring the Exciting World of Direct Marketing."* Reviews direct marketing's expanding role in our economy, introduces the field of mail order selling, accents the contributions of direct response advertising, and describes the phenomenal growth of at-home shopping via TV.

- *Chapter 7—"Automation Alert: Go on Computer as Soon as You Can."* Focuses on the benefits of computerizing your new mail order business, offers advice about the kinds of hardware and accessories you'll need, and recommends appropriate software for the direct marketing firm.

- *Chapter 8—"Promotion: Your Master Key to Sales Growth."* Offers many insights into the promotion mix, the tools and techniques of sales promotion, effective public relations programs, and publicity.

- *Chapter 19—"Telemarketing."* Provides specifics on the value of adding a telemarketing operation to help you increase your sales volume and on the training of skilled telemarketers.

- *Chapter 20—"How to Manage Company Finances More Effectively."* Shows you how to improve your mail-order operation by monitoring closely certain financial ratios, how to avoid cash flow problems, the value of budgets as planning and control devices, and the tax obligations you face as a business owner.

- *Chapter 21—"Planning Your Organization."* Discusses approaches to organizational planning including recruiting and selecting personnel, pay plans, the training and development of employees, motivation, and supervision.

The third edition is designed to help those among you who fit any of the following brief descriptions:

- You have the courage and initiative to dream about starting a business of your own, even though you're not sure of the type of business to go into.
- You prefer to keep your present job for the time being, so you can continue to buy food and clothing, pay the rent, and take care of other necessities, but you need to earn more.
- You're struggling to keep abreast of inflation, cope with a sluggish economy, and live with high tax rates.
- You've been looking for ways to convert your idle time into extra dollars.
- You would like to know more about the potential of a mail order enterprise.
- You're becoming increasingly dissatisfied at your place of business, perhaps because you're paid much less than you believe you're worth or because you realize that your chances of being promoted are rather slim.
- You haven't enough capital to warrant investing in machinery and a plant or a new store and its opening inventory.
- You find you must stay at home, yet you would like to bring additional income into your household.
- Although retired, you know you need to earn more so that you can pay for an occasional vacation, a new car, or some other luxury.

My intent was to write a comprehensive, practical, and easy-to-follow guidebook for starting and running a successful mail order operation. I planned to remove much of the mystery that seems to surround this field and to expose those "secrets of the trade" that are presumed to be known to only a few. At the same time, I studiously sought to tone down those exaggerated visions of potential, untold wealth that reputedly hypnotize the aspiring mail order entrepreneur.

I won't promise to set you squarely on a fast, sure track to riches. The truth of the matter is that mail order selling isn't a quick, certain, no-sweat path to wealth. To succeed in this field, just as in any other kind of business, you need courage, know-how, innovativeness, and dogged perseverance. You must also have some money to invest. Even with these requirements fulfilled, you still face a great deal of hard work—and uncertainty.

Yet, mail order does have its attractive features. Some of them are unique. For example, there's no need to commit yourself at the outset to renting business premises. Nor do you have to leave your present job. Moreover, you can launch your own business with a much smaller investment than is typically required for other types of enterprise.

Yes, you can earn an excellent, full-time livelihood selling by mail. You may even succeed in making a lot of money; many people do. But perhaps the most rewarding payoff in this business is the fun and excitement you'll enjoy all along the way.

Many of the mail order books and manuals currently on the market are weak in specifics, or bog down in trivial details, or are unrealistic in their appraisal of eventual rewards. Few offer more than a cursory treatment of "prestart" activities, so important in securing a foothold in this field. Two or three are much too technical, too advanced—and designed to serve primarily as texts for advanced courses in direct marketing. They're not for the beginner, but rather for the larger, well-established operation.

This third edition of *Mail Order Selling* is organized into five parts:

- *Part I* introduces you to the exciting field of direct response advertising in general, and mail order selling in particular, and then discusses the phenomenal growth of at-home shopping via TV. After reviewing the more significant advantages and disadvantages of starting one's own business, you're offered a thorough grounding in the fundamentals of launching a mail order operation and provided with a detailed outline to help you prepare your business plan.

- *Part II* begins by furnishing insights into buyer behavior and demonstrating how to target both consumer and organizational markets. You're shown where to look for, and how to select, goods and/or service(s) to sell by mail. You discover how to locate the financing you need to start a successful business. You learn all about balance sheets and income statements—and how to set the selling prices for your offerings. Following a discussion of the advantages and disadvantages of the three legal forms of ownership, you're shown how to set up your operations center, told about patents and copyrights, advised on the kinds of insurance coverage to seek and on which records to keep (and how long to keep them). You're also advised to computerize your operation just as soon as you can. A thorough treatment of promotion then follows. You learn about the tools and techniques you need to convey the story of your new mail order enterprise to potential customers and how to get free publicity. An entire chapter about the selling process concludes this part.

- *Part III* focuses on print advertising and the print media. It delves into the intricacies of print production, discussing such aspects as composition, art and photo reproduction, the use of color, and hints for reducing production costs. Subsequently, you're shown how to create effective print advertisements, devise compelling headlines, and write order-pulling ad copy.

A detailed overview of direct mail selling follows. This describes the "basic direct mail package" and shows you how to schedule your direct mail campaigns, key your mailings, convert inquiries into orders, save on postage, and much more. A chapter on mailing lists addresses important topics such as list maintenance, the testing and evaluation of purchased lists, and how to make more money by renting your house list. It also offers a sampling of list brokers and compilers, along with their names, addresses, and telephone numbers.

The final two chapters in Part III are devoted to the print media. You learn of the different types of newspapers and magazines, review the attractions and drawbacks of these media for direct-response advertisers, and are shown how best to buy space. Also provided are comparisons of advertising rates among a variety of magazines.

- *Part IV* explores the broadcast media. It examines the advantages and disadvantages of advertising on radio and TV and, among other topics, describes how to purchase air time and how to prepare results-getting radio announcements and TV commercials. A chapter on telemarketing completes Part IV. You learn why this method of selling has been growing so fast as well as how to develop your telemarketing program, hire and train telemarketers, and other useful information.

- *Part V* contains three chapters, each of which offers more advanced information for the growing mail order firm. You learn how to run your business better by monitoring certain financial ratios— and are given a simple procedure that will stave off cash-flow problems. You're shown how proper budgeting can help you plan and control your operation. You're also made aware of your responsibilities regarding taxes and your company.

The topics of organizational planning, personnel administration, motivation, and employee supervision are then addressed. The final chapter in this book centers on the future of your new mail order business. After discussing both growth and expansion, it explores other opportunities—in wholesaling, manufacturing, and retailing.

- *The Appendix* contains examples of filled-out federal tax forms to help you in preparing your income tax returns for your new business.

Contents

PART IV: THE BROADCAST MEDIA AND TELEMARKETING

PART V: ADDITIONAL INFORMATION FOR THE GROWING FIRM

PART

1

INTRODUCTION

Exploring the Exciting World of Direct Marketing

Over the second half of this century, a vast explosion of scientific knowledge has transformed much of the American scene—hopefully for the better! Among the more memorable technological innovations are the jet-liners that crisscross our skies; lunar modules, satellites, space probes and shuttle voyages; robot-controlled assembly lines; and the rapidly developing science of genetic engineering.

In the business sector, changing technology has also impacted marketing activity in general and mail order selling in particular.

A few of the technological contributions that affect direct marketing companies include:

- Advances and refinements in television including, among others, stereophonic sound, remote controls, cable television, satellites, and the proliferation of transmission channels.

- The invention and rapid mass acceptance of such home/office equipment as tape decks and cassettes, personal computers, camcorders, VCR recorders and tapes, compact disks, CD-ROM players, and so on.

- The distribution of 800 and 900 telephone numbers; inventions such as beepers, portable and cellular phones; and other accomplishments in telephone technology.

- The accelerated evolution of room-sized data-processing equipment, culminating in the proliferation of diminutive yet power-packed

desk-top and laptop computers with all their wizardry and multime-dia capabilities.
- Ongoing experimentation with advanced interactive electronic systems and the development and continuing expansion of the information superhighway.

Over the past few decades, we've also witnessed substantial change within the American population. Among the features of singular interest to direct marketers are:

- An increasing life expectancy.
- Vigorous growth in nonfamily, one-, and two-member households.
- A large number of married women now in the workforce.
- Increasing per-capita income.
- A higher level of education.
- More leisure time.
- Widespread interest in proper diet, physical exercise, and maintaining good health.
- Sharp growth in the "Over 65" age segment of the population.
- The near-universality of credit-card usage.

THE EXPANDING ROLE OF DIRECT MARKETING

During the past half-century, major changes have also taken place in the mail order/direct marketing arena.

The leading publication in its field defines direct marketing as:

> An interactive system of marketing that uses one or more advertising media to effect a measurable response and/or transaction at any location, with this activity stored on database.[1]

Mail Order and Direct Marketing

Along with tremendous growth in this field over the past few decades, the phrase *mail order selling* has been supplanted by the term *direct market-ing*. We should, however, distinguish clearly between these two terms. Strictly speaking, mail order refers more to a specific *method* of selling than anything else. It entails *selling by mail* either through:

1. Mailing out circulars, brochures, sales letters, flyers, catalogs, and/or other advertising literature (we give the name *direct mail* to this advertising medium) or
2. Using newspapers, magazines, radio, television, and/or other media to bring in orders or inquiries.

---

[1] *Direct Marketing*, September 1994, p. 4.

Selling by mail then fills those orders or requests for information via the U.S. Postal Service or, perhaps, an alternate carrier such as United Parcel Service (UPS).

On the other hand, *direct marketing* is a much broader concept, although that began with mail order selling. It is a complex marketing system characterized by an interactive, multimedia approach. Not only does it make use of the more traditional advertising media (direct mail, magazines, newspapers, radio, and television) but also it often employs inbound and outbound telemarketing, home shopping programs and infomercials, computer services, relationship-building databases, and other electronic approaches.

A number of major corporations, among them Motorola, AT&T, and Hewlett-Packard, are presently developing "complete interactive communication centers—a combination of television, computer, telephone, and database for every home around the globe."[2]

The Internet

Often referred to as the electronic or information superhighway, the Internet or Net is a vast global web of computer networks into which as many as 22 million people can now tap through home and office computers. The number of Internet "travelers" grows at the rate of a million more each year.

The roots of this information freeway go back nearly three decades to a loosely organized network of computers used by government agencies, university researchers, and a few large corporations to share information.

On the Internet, all kinds of information can be retrieved from thousands of databases around the world. You can also send and receive electronic mail (E-mail), shop for goods and services, play games or converse with other people along the highway, post notices on electronic bulletin boards, and both receive and forward news items from and to just about anywhere. With the exception of the telephone charges that can accumulate rapidly, you'll find that Internet usage is free—and open to one and all.

Incidentally, posting a notice on one of the bulletin boards expressing your readiness to mail information free of charge to interested parties may bring in many hundreds of replies. One caution, though: Before tapping into this electronic superhighway be sure to learn all you can about the Internet itself, user etiquette, and the politically correct way to proceed.[3]

---

[2] Robert McKim, "The New Interactive Marketing Opportunities," *Direct Marketing,* September 1993, p. 31.

[3] For helpful insights into the electronic superhighway, see: Jill H. Ellsworth and Matthew V. Ellsworth, *The Internet Business Book* (New York: Wiley, 1994); Paul Gilster, *The Internet Navigator,* 2d ed. (New York: Wiley, 1994); John R. Levine and Margaret Levin Young, *More Internet for Dummies* (San Mateo, CA: IDG Books, 1994); Mary Ann Pike, *Using the Internet,* 2d ed. (n.p.: Que Corporation, 1995).

You can gain access to the Internet through CompuServe, Prodigy, Delphi, GEnie, America Online, and other service networks.

MAIL ORDER SELLING: THE CORNERSTONE OF DIRECT MARKETING METHODS

To many of us, an enchantment surrounds the two words mail order. Mail order selling seems to be the kind of money-making business that offers great potential and yet doesn't call for very much in the way of capital investment. Moreover, you can start it up without endangering, or leaving, your present job.

Mail Order: Myth and Reality

We're fascinated with the dream of making a big score, of being inundated with orders, of mail bulging with checks and money orders, of firmly stepping out on the road to riches, of financial independence and self-sufficiency. It all seems so easy, too. Find a unique product, prepare and place an advertisement, and the orders soon begin to arrive. All you then need do is address labels, cart off packages each day to the post office, and, of course, make your daily deposits at the local bank.

Most of us believe we can do all this on little more than a shoestring. We can do it in our spare time. We need no office, no place of business; a table in the basement or the kitchen should suffice.

This widespread, positive, and exciting attitude is encouraged by the many books, pamphlets, and manuals that are available. Many of them preach how easy it is for you to make a fortune in next to no time at all.

Although people can and do strike it rich in the mail order field, overnight successes are extremely rare. Despite what you may have been led to believe, you probably won't get rich by the end of your first six months of operation. Nor in a year's time. It may take you five, ten, or more years—or you may never become rich at all. What you most likely can do is earn a living, a good living. Eventually, too, you may become most comfortable.

The purpose of this book is to help show you how to attain that objective.

The Mail Order Dilettante

Many of you may have already experimented once or twice with marketing merchandise by mail. A typical scenario runs something like this:

You come across an interesting product. You believe you can sell it for perhaps three times its cost or even more; this gives you the kind of markup that makes the item "workable" for selling by mail. From the manufacturer or other source, you obtain a glossy 8 × 10 photograph of the product. You prepare copy and suggested layout for a small advertisement, then schedule space in a forthcoming issue of a magazine. The advertisement is published—and you await the results.

Then you discover that the orders you have received don't even cover your advertising cost. Chastened, you pull back, considering yourself lucky to have gotten out of the mail order business with such a small loss.

Or, you may have tried to play it smart. Instead of springing for the cost of a magazine display advertisement, you composed a small classified one. You ran it for three days, or for a full week, or in the Sunday edition of a large metropolitan paper. This way, you almost recouped your advertising expense. You may have even earned a bit of profit. But then you decided it wasn't worth all the effort, and you gave up entirely on mail order selling.

Some among you may have succumbed to the attractions of those frequently published advertisements that offer ready-made catalogs for sale. The companies that distribute these beautiful, four-color, professionally prepared, order-pulling catalogs promise all sorts of glowing rewards. They remind you that you could never hope to duplicate such catalogs for even twice their cost, or more. You can buy them by the thousand, and have your firm's name and address imprinted on the covers. You then address them to your list of names and addresses, affix postage, and mail them. The catalog companies will handle all your orders on a "drop ship" basis.

Even as you and I and many others have discovered, you then found out the profit on the merchandise you sold was insufficient to cover even your postage costs. By way of consolation, however, you should realize that you weren't in the mail order marketing business at all. You simply dabbled your toes in the stream, gambling and losing. You had done no serious planning. Few first advertisements or direct mail efforts turn a profit. You have to place many ads, realizing that some may produce losses, several may break even, and an occasional one will prove profitable. All along, you need to keep careful records so that you can determine your *cost per order* or *cost per inquiry.* You need to build, however slowly, a mailing list of customers who buy from you. The healthy mail order business is built on *repeat sales*—and on a *line* of products, rather than a single product.

Above all, you need to study the basics, learn how to write copy that "pulls" inquiries and orders, do your homework, and prepare a comprehensive business plan long before you start your operation.

DIRECT-RESPONSE ADVERTISING: PATHWAY TO PROFIT FOR INDUSTRY AND COMMERCE

Direct-response advertising attracts attention, delivers sales presentations designed to arouse interest, tells prospective buyers how to respond to the offer, and aims at inducing responses from prospects most often in the form of an actual order. Business organizations of all kinds are relying more and more on direct-response approaches to increase their sales revenues and reduce their operating expenses. Wherever they may advertise—in the print media, on radio or television, in their direct mail campaigns, or through inbound or outbound telemarketing operations—they encourage immediate feedback by indicating the toll-free telephone numbers to call, offering coupons, and even by providing instructions as to which keys they must tap on their computers to complete electronic transactions.

Growth of At-Home Shopping via Television

For many years, a wide variety of products have been sold successfully and are still being marketed through television commercials between 30 and 120 seconds in length; music records and tapes, books, cutlery, magazine subscriptions, exercise equipment, and movies on VCR tapes are some examples. Although television is high on the list among the many advertising media used by the larger direct marketing companies, small-scale mail order firms tend to avoid this avenue of promotion. Air time can be expensive—and professionally produced TV commercials are costly.

An infomercial is a much extended TV commercial, one that may run for 30 minutes, a full hour, or even longer. It's a professionally-made, thoroughly detailed, and televised sales presentation about a product. It's an excellent form of persuasive communication and the next best thing to a personal visit by a top-performing sales representative.

Infomercials elicit an immediate response from many of its viewers, usually in the form of a telephone call to a toll-free 800 number, to place an order or, less often, to make an inquiry. A single showing of a 30-minute infomercial may bring in $50,000 or more in sales within half an hour after it has been televised.

In the early 1980s, a new television network formed expressly for the purpose of selling goods directly to consumers, began broadcasting. This Florida-based retailing organization was the Home Shopping Network (HSN). Its approach was simple; it displayed and offered a whole series of items at attractive prices to the viewing public. A firm money-back guarantee assured consumer satisfaction. Toll-free numbers were provided for interested shoppers to call in their orders. (The network could easily handle thousands of incoming calls per hour.)

HSN was an immediate success. Its audience began to grow at a fantastic rate. Manufacturers and retailers converged in droves on the network to sign contracts for showing their products on TV. Sales of jewelry, apparel, cosmetics, giftware, and electronics boomed. By 1994, HSN's nationwide reach extended to more than 60 million households.

A second home-shopping network, originating in Pennsylvania, began transmitting in 1986. This was QVC; the initials stand for Quality, Value, Convenience. As of now, more than 50 million households can tune in to it—and the network sells well over $1 billion worth of merchandise each year. Expansion continues: in a cooperative venture, QVC has begun broadcasting to millions of people in Mexico.[4]

---

[4] *Direct Marketing,* January 1994, p. 13.

Hoping to emulate the successes of these two pioneers, other networks have been developing ever since. Already in operation are such entities as The Fashion Channel, ValueVision, and ViaTV. Additional home shopping ventures are currently in the testing stage, among them Catalog 1, S (The Shopping Channel), and TV Macy's. Even existing cable companies are experimenting with the genre; Nickelodeon and MTV are examples. The area of interactive television shopping is currently under active study by corporations such as Time-Warner, Viacom, Tele-Communications Inc., and Bell Atlantic.

Although few mail order companies can afford to promote their offerings via home shopping programs, the future nevertheless still looks bright for these and other direct marketers. As one writer puts it, we can look forward to "a sharp increase in mail order purchases through on-line computer databases, on computer disk and CD-ROM, video, and through interactive television."[5]

SOURCES OF ADDITIONAL INFORMATION

Bacon, Mark S., *Do-It-Yourself Direct Marketing: Secrets for Small Business.* New York: Wiley, 1994.

Gosden, Freeman F., Jr., *Direct Marketing Success: What Works and Why.* New York: Wiley, 1989.

Gross, Martin, *The Direct Marketer's Idea Book.* New York: AMACOM, 1989.

Katzenstein, Herbert and William S. Sachs, *Direct Marketing,* (2d ed.). New York: Macmillan, 1992.

Lewis, Herschell Gordon, *Direct Marketing Strategies and Tactics.* Chicago: Dartnell, 1993.

Nash, Edward L., *The Direct Marketing Handbook,* (2d ed.). New York: McGraw-Hill, 1992.

Simon, Julian L. and Julian Simon Associates, *How to Start and Operate a Mail Order Business,* (5th ed.). New York: McGraw-Hill, 1993.

Stone, Bob, *Successful Direct Marketing Methods,* (3rd ed.). Lincolnwood, IL: National Textbook, 1993.

Wilbur, L. Perry, *Money in Your Mailbox,* (2d ed.). New York: Wiley, 1992.

---

[5] Caryne Brown, "The Future of Mail Order," *Income Opportunities,* March 1994, p. 71.

Starting a Mail Order Business

How often have you thought about starting a business of your own? Of the opportunity to be your own boss, answering to no one but your own conscience? Of pursuing the vision of an eventual fortune?

You're not alone. Each year, millions of people have the same thoughts and desires—and hundreds of thousands do try their hand at launching a small enterprise. Some succeed, others fail.

No one knows the exact number of new businesses that are initiated during any one year. However, it is generally assumed to be somewhere around 500,000.

One fact seems certain: Launching a new business typically represents a considerable gamble on the entrepreneur's part.

What holds most people back from trying? Perhaps the realization that most types of businesses require a sizable investment. Perhaps not knowing how to go about opening a business. Or being too comfortable and not open to change. Or the fear of failure. Or too little self-confidence.

WHAT YOU MAY GAIN BY LAUNCHING A BUSINESS OF YOUR OWN

Launching a business of your own is no easy, automatic road to riches and independence. As in any new course you might chart during your lifetime, this avenue has both benefits and drawbacks. Before arriving at that go/no-go decision point, you owe it to yourself to study the pluses and the minuses of this move.

What Are the Benefits?

Some of the more attractive aspects to starting your own business are:

- You'll have an opportunity to earn more money than you ever could by working for someone else.
- As the owner, you'll report to no one else; nor will anyone order you around.
- You'll reap the psychic benefits that accrue to putting your own education, training, and capabilities to use for yourself rather than for someone else.
- You need never fear that you may someday be fired by an employer.
- You'll enjoy the perks that other business owners do. You'll be able to deduct certain expenses from your tax liabilities: the cost of operating the car or truck you need to use in your mail order enterprise, the premiums for group health insurance, and so on.

What Are the Drawbacks?

Here are the drawbacks to starting a business:

- You'll find yourself working longer and harder than when you were employed by another firm.
- In making decisions, you'll have to rely on your own judgment far more often than you needed to when you were working elsewhere.
- More likely than not, you won't be able to count on a decent, regular income for quite a long time.
- You'll have little or no time for fun, for vacationing, or even for relaxing with your family and friends.
- There is, of course, the possibility that you may fail, and lose your entire investment.

On average, you are likely to gain from going into any type of business of your own. There are, however, some additional advantages to starting a mail order enterprise. Here's a list of some of the benefits:

- You can start in your spare time, without conflicting with your regular job.
- You have a chance to supplement your income, to earn extra dollars to buy some of the luxuries you cannot now afford.
- You experience the joy and challenge of running your own small business.
- Your eventual success is not related to age, sex, race, creed, or handicap.
- If you're already retired, this business gives you an opportunity to add to your social security and/or pension.

- Location's never a problem; you can work from your home in any section of the country.
- If you operate on a full-time basis, you'll save costs of transportation to and from a job, and you'll not need to worry about proper office or work clothing.
- Your overhead expenses will be minimal; additional labor might be supplied by your spouse and children.
- You can work at your own pace.
- You have the potential for eventual expansion, perhaps into wholesaling to stores or through agents—or even into store retailing.
- If your business meets with success, you'll be able to set up your own retirement plan, life and health insurance coverage, and other benefits.

FACTORS THAT INFLUENCE YOUR SUCCESS

The statistics on new business ventures are always disheartening. Year after year, they show that a substantial percentage of new starts go out of business within the first two or three years of operation. This attrition rate is variously attributed to the owner's lack of know-how or experience, inadequate financing, insufficient sales volume, weak management ability, or—in the case of store retailing—poor location.

Your chances of succeeding in mail order will be affected by many of the same factors. As would be true in any other type of enterprise, you not only need knowledge, adequate financing, and management talent, but also the courage to take chances—and the sense to plan thoroughly. People enthused by the entrepreneurial spirit tend to rush ahead precipitously. Be cautious. Proceed slowly. Learn all you can before giving yourself the go signal. Don't become a statistic in the failure column.

Here are the elements that make for success, the major topics with which you should become familiar (all are covered in subsequent chapters):

- Customer knowledge.
- Merchandise and/or service(s) to offer.
- What selling is all about.
- Money and its management.
- Details of starting up and record keeping.
- Making your business plan.
- Direct mail advertising.
- Print production and advertisements.
- Developing and maintaining a mailing list.
- Direct marketing through print and broadcast media.

- Other vital management areas (legal aspects, taxation, management basics, and so on).
- Business growth and expansion.

Good luck to you—and to your new business.

WHERE TO GET INFORMATION AND ADVICE

If you're like the majority of people who go into business for the first time, you have had little or no prior management experience, management training, nor do you know where to go for advice or to ferret out information you may need. Several resources are discussed in the next section.

The U.S. Small Business Administration

In your new role as mail order entrepreneur, you'll find the Small Business Administration (SBA) to be a valuable source of facts and assistance. Created by Congress in the 1950s, this federal agency exists to serve the needs of, and encourage the growth of, small enterprises in America.

If you were a manufacturer, or in a wholesale business, the agency could help you with government procurement assistance and in subcontracting. Since you are in direct marketing, however, their most important contributions will be in the areas of providing management advice and, perhaps, financial help. More than 90 field offices of this agency are located throughout the country (Exhibit 2–1). You can make an appointment by telephone to see one of their SCORE or ACE counselors. (SCORE stands for Service Corps of Retired Executives; ACE, for the Active Corps of Executives.) You'll get worthwhile advice from former business owners.

At these offices are management assistance officers who set up management courses, workshops, conferences, and business clinics in their areas. They also work with small business institutes at many colleges and universities.

Printed materials are also available. For an order form and copies of these publications, write to:

U.S. Small Business Administration
P.O. Box 30
Denver, CO 80201-0030.

Most people in small business think of the SBA in terms of the financial assistance it can render. The agency may provide loans for a variety of purposes: construction, expansion, the purchase of machinery, even working capital. It may loan money to a business directly, or, more commonly, enter into a participation agreement with a bank. There are also special SBA programs for disaster, physical damage, and economic

EXHIBIT 2-1   Field offices of the U.S. Small Business Administration

Albany, NY	Little Rock, AR
Albuquerque, NM	Los Angeles, CA
Anchorage, AK	Lubbock, TX
Atlanta, GA	Madison, WI
Augusta, ME	Marquette, MI
Bala Cynwyd, PA	Marshall, TX
Baltimore, MD	Miami, FL
Birmingham, AL	Milwaukee, WI
Boise, ID	Minneapolis, MN
Boston, MA	Montpelier, VT
Casper, WY	Nashville, TN
Charlotte, NC	Newark, NJ
Chicago, IL	New Orleans, LA
Cincinnati, OH	New York, NY
Clarksburg, WV	Oklahoma City, OK
Cleveland, OH	Omaha, NE
Columbia, SC	Phoenix, AZ
Columbus, OH	Pittsburgh, PA
Concord, NH	Portland, OR
Corpus Christi, TX	Providence, RI
Dallas, TX	Richmond, VA
Denver, CO	Rochester, NY
Des Moines, IA	Sacramento, CA
Detroit, MI	St. Louis, MO
Eau Claire, WI	Salt Lake City, UT
Elmira, NY	San Antonio, TX
El Paso, TX	San Diego, CA
Fargo, ND	San Francisco, CA
Fresno, CA	Santa Ana, CA
Harlingen, TX	Seattle, WA
Harrisburg, PA	Sioux Falls, SD
Hartford, CT	Spokane, WA
Hato Rey, PR	Springfield, IL
Helena, MT	Syracuse, NY
Honolulu, HI	Tampa, FL
Houston, TX	Tucson, AZ
Indianapolis, IN	Ventura, CA
Jackson, MS	Washington, DC
Jacksonville, FL	West Palm Beach, FL
Kansas City, MO	Wichita, KS
King of Prussia, PA	Wilkes-Barre, PA
Las Vegas, NV	Wilmington, DE

Source: Minority Business Development Agency, *Franchise Opportunities Handbook.* (Washington, DC: U.S. Department of Commerce, June 1991), xvi–xviii.

injury loans, as well as loans for the handicapped and the economically disadvantaged. Other SBA programs include lease guarantee, surety bond, and minority enterprises. The agency also licenses small business investment companies (SBICs) to work with small firms and makes loans to state and local development companies. Visit the nearest field office for full details.

Other Government Agencies

Help is available for the new business owner from other government agencies besides the SBA, not only at the federal level, but also often at state and local levels. Among the federal agencies, the Bureau of the Census of the Department of Commerce is probably the nation's biggest supplier of information. In addition to the *Census of Population, Census of Business,* and other major publications, they issue the annual, information-laden *Statistical Abstract of the United States.* The Department of Labor publishes, among other reports, the *Survey of Consumer Expenditures* and the *Survey of Current Business;* the Federal Reserve System distributes the monthly *Federal Reserve Bulletin;* and so on.

Business Organizations and Periodicals

A number of organizations can be useful in helping you manage your fledgling enterprise. In addition to those of interest to business in general, such as the American Management Associations (135 West 50th Street, New York, NY 10020) and the American Marketing Association (250 South Wacker, Suite 200, Chicago, IL 60606), you might consider contacting one or more of the following organizations for advice and assistance:

Advertising Mail Marketing Association
1333 F Street, N.W.
Washington, DC 20004
202/347-0055

Carolinas Direct Marketing Association
P.O. Box 40523
Raleigh, NC 27629
919/990-1441

Direct Marketing Association
11 West 42nd Street
New York, NY 10036
212/768-7277

Direct Marketing Association of North Texas
4020 McEwen, Suite 105
Dallas, TX 75244
817/640-7018

Direct Marketing Club of New York
224 Seventh Street
Garden City, NY 11530
516/746-6700

Direct Marketing Club of Southern California
2401 Pacific Coast Highway, Suite 102
Hermosa Beach, CA 90254
310/374-7499

Florida Direct Marketing Association
1951 N.W. 19th Street
Boca Raton, FL 33431
407/347-0200

Midwest Direct Marketing Association
800 Hennepin Avenue
Minneapolis, MN 55403
612/339-8141

National Association of Private Enterprise
232 Precinct Line Road
Hurst, TX 76054
800/223-6273

National Federation of Independent Business
600 Maryland Avenue, S.W., Suite 700
Washington, DC 20024
202/554-9000

Small Business Network
P.O. Box 30220
Baltimore, MD 21270
410/581-1373

Several publications oriented toward small business contain valuable information in most issues. These include:

Entrepreneur Magazine
2392 Morse Avenue
Irvine, CA 92714

In Business
JG Press, Inc.
419 State Avenue
Emmaus, PA 18049

Inc.
38 Commercial Wharf
Boston, MA 02110

Income Opportunities
1500 Broadway
New York, NY 10036

There's also the all-important *Direct Marketing,* at least for everyone involved in selling products or services via the mails or through the mass media. Reading a number of issues is a must, just as an introduction to the field of mail order selling. And it's even more vital for you to know this publication if you're intent on succeeding in the business. Every issue yields valuable insights into direct marketing. List brokers, compilers, and managers advertise in the book; so do service organizations and manufacturers of the kinds of supplies you'll need in your operation. This is the Bible for the field. The address is:

Direct Marketing
224 Seventh Avenue
Garden City, NY 11530
516/746-6700

UNLOCK THE DOOR TO SUCCESS WITH THOROUGH PLANNING

Let's talk about planning. Unhappily, we're not taught how to plan in school. It's something we learn by doing. And it's an activity most of us tend to shy away from and leave to others to do, partly because planning requires time, deep concentration, and lots of energy. It's also because we're more attuned to doing rather than thinking and because we're intuitively suspicious about things beyond our control. Like the future—and luck.

So we avoid planning for the most part, except for really important issues. Going into your own business is, of course, one of those really important issues. Before jumping into the water and risking the capital, hard work, and months (if not years) of time needed to establish your mail order enterprise, doesn't it make sense to do some intensive planning?

You should carefully examine why you're getting into business in the first place and what your immediate and long-range goals are. You need to scan the entire field in which you intend to operate, so that you know what you're doing. For when you plan properly, you take in the whole picture: your own business, your competition, the media you'll advertise in, the state of the economy, government constraints, and so forth. Not to do so exposes you to the danger of overlooking one or more significant aspects, the absence of which may have a profound effect on your plan's outcome.

You can't, of course, foresee all eventualities; no one can predict the future with any meaningful degree of certainty. Yet, by forcing yourself to think things through at the outset, and committing your thoughts to paper, you can develop a detailed *business plan.* This most useful guide will see you onto the pathway to success. It won't be infallible. Neither will it be, nor should it be, inflexible; plans need to be adjusted all along the way.

The Planning Process

Planning is a three-step process. It consists of (1) setting specific objectives, (2) working out methods, techniques, programs, and timetables to reach those objectives, and (3) assessing progress being made and making the necessary adjustments.

It's helpful to adopt the systems approach when planning; this involves breaking down the entire picture into segments. A good technique is to draw diagrams of these segments on paper, then study them. Ask yourself the same one-word questions that the reporter uses to get at all the facts in a news story. They are the Five W's: Who? What? Where? When? Why? (and a sixth: How?).

YOUR GUIDE: THE BUSINESS PLANNING WORKBOOK

The rest of this chapter contains what is in effect a mini planning workbook to assist you in developing a comprehensive plan for your new mail order business. Answers to many of the questions will require considerable thought on your part. It will be well worth it, however. Go at it slowly, in between your day-to-day activities, and when your head is clear. Seek a quiet room, with a good lamp and a table to work at. Take along several well-sharpened pencils and some extra sheets of writing paper for figuring, or for doodling, when you're temporarily stuck.

The planning workbook is divided into the following sections:

1. Preliminaries.
2. My Customers.
3. My Place of Business.
4. My Financial Plan.
5. My Merchandise/Services Plan.
6. My Promotion Plan.
7. My Personnel Plan.

Section 4 is critical: it will help you determine how much money you need to start up in business. It will also give you an overview of what your company's financial status should look like at the end of your first year of operation.

MY PLANNING WORKBOOK

I. PRELIMINARIES

    A.   The name of my business is:

    B.   A brief description of my business is:

    C.   Address from which I plan to operate:

    D.   Length and type of lease (if any):

    E.   Local regulations to comply with:

    F.   I have chosen this legal form:

    G.   Have I accomplished the necessary paperwork?

         (Filed certificate? Made partnership agreement? Set up corporation?)

    H.   Other principals involved in the business (if any):

MY PLANNING WORKBOOK (Continued)

I. Names and addresses of the professionals I plan to work with:

ACCOUNTANT _____

LAWYER _____

INSURANCE REP _____

J. Bank information

1. I intend to use this bank:

2. Number of my business checking account:

K. My objectives

1. Immediate goals:

2. Goals to reach by end of first year:

3. My long-term objectives (next five years):

MY PLANNING WORKBOOK (Continued)

II. MY CUSTOMERS (Complete either IIA or IIB.)

A. I'll be selling directly to the consumer rather than to other firms.

1. A profile of the "typical" customer I plan to sell to is:

    SEX

    MARITAL STATUS

    AGE (RANGE)

    LEVEL OF EDUCATION

    NUMBER OF CHILDREN

    TYPE OF RESIDENCE

    KIND OF AUTOMOBILE

    SPORTS, HOBBIES

    OTHER RECREATIONAL ACTIVITIES

    ADDITIONAL INFORMATION

2. Some of the things my customers like are:

3. Some of the things my customers dislike are:

4. When my customers shop by mail, they expect:

B. On the other hand, I plan to sell merchandise or services by mail to industry (manufacturers, wholesalers, retailers, service firms, and so on) and/or to other types of organizations.

1. A profile of the "typical" company or other organization I have in mind is:

    TYPE OF FIRM/ORGANIZATION

    SIZE OF FIRM/ORGANIZATION

    APPROXIMATE ANNUAL SALES VOLUME

    TITLES OF PERSONS TO BE CONTACTED

MY PLANNING WORKBOOK (Continued)

SOME OF THE THINGS THESE PERSONS LIKE

SOME OF THE THINGS THESE PERSONS DISLIKE

WHAT THESE PERSONS EXPECT WHEN THEY SHOP BY MAIL

III. MY PLACE OF BUSINESS

A. For my first year of operation, I'll need:

1. _____ square feet for workroom space

2. _____ square feet for storage space

B. Other needs (for first year):

1. Lighting

2. Ventilation

3. Heating

4. Air conditioning

5. Remodeling

6. Shelving

MY PLANNING WORKBOOK (Continued)

7. Furniture and equipment needs

DESCRIPTION OF ITEM	QUANTITY NEEDED	ESTIMATED COST/UNIT	TOTAL COST

8. Supplies needed

DESCRIPTION OF ITEM	QUANTITY NEEDED	ESTIMATED COST/UNIT	TOTAL COST

9. Names, addresses, and other pertinent information of suppliers of needed furniture, equipment, and supplies:

MY PLANNING WORKBOOK (Continued)

IV. MY FINANCIAL PLAN

A. My expected sales volume for the first year is:

I believe the following sales projections for my new business are as sound as I can make them:

For my first three months of operation   _____

For my second three months   _____

For the third quarter   _____

For the fourth quarter   _____

Estimated sales for my first year   _____

B. My insurance program

A summary of my planned insurance program

C. Needed capital

1. This is how I have calculated the amount of capital I need to start this business:
   a. I worked with the aid of Worksheet No. 2 (Exhibit 2–2).
   b. Where indicated at the top of column 1 on the worksheet, I entered my estimate of first-year sales volume.
   c. I completed all entries in column 1, under Estimated Monthly Expenses—from Salary of owner-manager down to Miscellaneous. (I used pencil, because I sometimes needed to re-work a figure.)
   d. Using the suggestions given in column 3, I came up with estimates for each expense and then showed these in column 2.
   e. I tackled the section that reads "Starting Costs You Only Have to Pay Once." I followed all suggestions provided in column 3 for these Starting Costs, and then completed column 2.
   f. I added all entries in the second column; this yielded the figure I needed.

EXHIBIT 2–2   Worksheet no. 2 (U.S. Small Business Administration)

ESTIMATED MONTHLY EXPENSES			
Item	Your estimate of monthly expenses based on sales of $_____ per year	Your estimate of how much cash you need to start your business (See column 3.)	What to put in column 2 (These figures are typical for one kind of business. You will have to decide how many months to allow for in your business.)
	Column 1	Column 2	Column 3
Salary of owner-manager	$	$	2 times column 1
All other salaries and wages			3 times column 1
Rent			3 times column 1
Advertising			3 times column 1
Delivery expense			3 times column 1
Supplies			3 times column 1
Telephone and telegraph			3 times column 1
Other utilities			3 times column 1
Insurance			Payment required by insurance company
Taxes, including Social Security			4 times column 1
Interest			3 times column 1
Maintenance			3 times column 1
Legal and other professional fees			3 times column 1
Miscellaneous			3 times column 1
STARTING COSTS YOU ONLY HAVE TO PAY ONCE			Leave column 2 blank
Fixtures and equipment			Fill in worksheet 3 and put the total here
Decorating and remodeling			Talk it over with a contractor
Installation of fixtures and equipment			Talk to suppliers from whom you buy these
Starting inventory			Suppliers will probably help you estimate this
Deposits with public utilities			Find out from utilities companies
Legal and other professional fees			Lawyer, accountant, and so on
Licenses and permits			Find out from city offices what you have to have
Advertising and promotion for opening			Estimate what you'll use
Accounts receiveble			What you need to buy more stock until credit customers pay
Cash			For unexpected expenses or losses, special purchases, etc.
Other			Make a separate list and enter total
TOTAL ESTIMATED CASH YOU NEED TO START WITH	$		Add up all the numbers in column 2

Source: "Checklist for Going into Business," *Management Aid 2.016* (Washington, DC: U.S. Small Business Administration, 1975) 6–7.

MY PLANNING WORKBOOK (Continued)

2. The Total Estimated Cash I need to start this business is:

3. My start-up capital will come from these sources:

4. The money I have borrowed for my business operation will be paid back according to the following schedule:

D. Break-even point

I have calculated my break-even point to be _____ , using the following formula:

$$\text{Break-even Point (in dollars)} = \frac{\text{Total Fixed Costs}}{1 - \dfrac{\text{Total Variable Costs}}{\text{Sales Volume}}}$$

E. My two major accounting statements

1. I have completed my pro forma profit and loss statement (expected for my first year of operation) on the form in Exhibit 2–3.

2. I expect my first year's balance sheet to look like the filled-in form in Exhibit 2–4.

3. I have outlined my projected sales forecast for my first full year of operation in Exhibit 2–5.

EXHIBIT 2-3 Pro forma profit and loss statement

(Firm's Name)

PROFIT AND LOSS STATEMENT

For: Year Ended December 19XX

Net Sales. . . . . ____
Less cost of goods sold:
    Opening inventory   ____
    Purchases during year   ____
    Freight charges   ____
        Total goods handled. . . . . ____
        Less ending inventory, December 31   ____
            Total cost of goods sold. . . . . ____

Gross Margin   ____
Less Operating Expenses:
    Salaries and wages   ____
    Payroll taxes   ____
    Utilities   ____
    Telephone   ____
    Rent   ____
    Office supplies   ____
    Postage   ____
    Maintenance expense   ____
    Insurance   ____
    Interest expense   ____
    Depreciation   ____
    Delivery expense   ____
    Advertising   ____
    Dues and contributions   ____
    Miscellaneous expenses   ____
Total Operating Expenses. . . . . ____

Operating Profit. . . . . ____
Other income:
        Dividends on stock   ____
        Interest on bank account   ____
        Other sources   ____
            Total other income . . . . ____

Total Income Before Income Taxes. . . . . ____
    Less provision for taxes. . . . . ____
    NET INCOME . . . . ====

EXHIBIT 2–4   Pro forma balance sheet

_____
(Firm's Name)

BALANCE SHEET

For: Year Ended December 19XX

ASSETS

Current Assets
    Cash on hand and in bank   _____
    Marketable securities   _____
    Accounts receivable (less allowance for
    bad debts)   _____
    Merchandise inventory   _____
    Inventory of supplies   _____
        Total current assets............................ _____

Fixed Assets
    Office machinery and equipment (less
    depreciation)   _____
    Furniture (less depreciation)   _____
    Leasehold improvements   _____
    Other fixed assets (list)   _____
        Total fixed assets............................. _____
        TOTAL ASSETS   =====

LIABILITIES AND NET WORTH

Current Liabilities
    Accounts payable   _____
    Accrued expenses   _____
    Accrued taxes   _____
    Other current liabilities (list)   _____
        Total current liabilities......................... _____

Long-term Liabilities
    Loan payable, 19__   _____
    Loan payable, 19__   _____
    Mortgage   _____
        Total long-term liabilities...................... _____
        TOTAL LIABILITIES   _____
Net Worth   _____
        TOTAL LIABILITIES AND NET WORTH   =====

EXHIBIT 2–5   Projected sales forecast form

ESTIMATED CASH FORECAST												
	Jan.	Feb.	Mar.	April	May	June	July	Aug.	Sept.	Oct.	Nov.	Dec.
(1) Cash in Bank (Start of Month)												
(2) Petty Cash (Start of Month)												
(3) Total Cash (add 1) and (2)												
(4) Expected Cash Sales												
(5) Expected Collections												
(6) Other Money Expected												
(7) Total Receipts (add 4, 5 and 6)												
(8) Total Cash and Receipts (add 3 and 7)												
(9) All Disbursements (for month)												
(10) Cash Balance at End of Month. in Bank Account and Petty Cash (subtract (9) from (8)*												

*This balance is your starting cash balance for the next month.

Source: Office of Management Assistance, "Business Plan for Retailers," *Small Marketers Aid No. 150* (Washington, DC: U.S. Small Business Administration, 1972), 17.

MY PLANNING WORKBOOK (Continued)

F.   Tax obligations

    1.   Federal taxes

    2.   State taxes

    3.   Local taxes

V. MY MERCHANDISE OR SERVICE(S) PLAN

    A.   I plan to sell the following kinds of merchandise and/or service(s):

    B.   The customer needs my merchandise/service(s) will fulfill are:

    C.   Quality level(s) I expect to maintain:

    D.   Price ranges for my merchandise/service(s):

MY PLANNING WORKBOOK (Continued)

E. My pricing and mark-up approaches will be:

F. I plan to buy merchandise for resale. The pertinent information about my suppliers is:

ITEM   NAME/ADDRESS   TERMS/CONDITIONS

G. Additional sources I intend to check:

H. This year, I intend to visit the following trade shows:

I. I plan to read the following publications regularly in my search for items to sell:

J. I make some of the merchandise I sell. My sources for materials, components, supplies are:

MY PLANNING WORKBOOK (Continued)

K. A description of my inventory control system is:

VI. MY PROMOTION PLAN

A. My basic approaches to promotion are:

1. My firm's strong points are:

2. I'd like to project in my promotion and correspondence this kind of image:

3. My customers will find the following advantages in buying from me rather than from competitors:

4. I plan to handle customer credit by:

5. A statement of my return policy is:

6. My merchandise/service(s) will be backed by the following guarantee(s):

MY PLANNING WORKBOOK (Continued)

B. My advertising plans are:

1. I plan to spend this much on advertising:

    THIS YEAR

    NEXT YEAR

2. The media through which I can reach my customers most effectively are:

3. The specific appeals I intend to build into my advertisements are:

4. My advertising budget for this year is:

NAME OF MEDIUM	AUDIENCE SIZE	APPROXIMATE DATE TO APPEAR	SIZE OF AD	ESTIMATED COST

C. My direct mail plans for this year are:

1. Number of mailings I plan to make:

2. Quantities to be mailed each time:

3. Postal regulations to comply with:

4. Timetables for having mailing pieces printed:

5. Additional mailing list names to be rented/bought:

SOURCE	QUANTITY

MY PLANNING WORKBOOK (Continued)

VII. MY PERSONNEL PLAN

  A. Recruitment and selection

    1. (Check one of the following):

      _____ I need to hire people to fill one or more positions right away.

      _____ I don't need anyone now, but I anticipate some job openings will develop in the near future (six months to one year).

      _____ I have no need for any employees for the first year of operation.

    2. Titles and brief job descriptions of the openings I foresee:

    3. The job specifications I have outlined for these positions are:

    4. The methods and techniques I intend to use in selecting personnel are:

  B. Employee compensation and training

    1. I plan to pay these employees on the following basis:

    2. The fringe benefits my employees may expect to receive are:

    3. I plan to train my employees by:

SOURCES OF ADDITIONAL INFORMATION

Bacon, Mark S., *Do-It-Yourself Direct Marketing: Secrets for Small Business.* New York: Wiley, 1992.

Berle, Gustav, *The Small Business Information Handbook.* New York: Wiley, 1990.

Burstiner, Irving, *The Small Business Handbook: A Comprehensive Guide to Starting and Running Your Own Business,* (rev. ed.). New York: Simon & Schuster, 1994.

Cohen, William A., *Building a Mail Order Business: A Complete Manual for Success,* (3rd ed.). New York: Wiley, 1991.

Eyler, David R., *Starting and Operating Your Home-Based Business.* New York: Wiley, 1989.

Kremer, John, *The Complete Mail-Order Sourcebook.* New York: Wiley, 1992.

Lewis, Herschell Gordon, *Direct Marketing Strategies and Tactics.* Chicago: Dartnell, 1993.

Longenecker, Justin G. and Carlos W. Moore, *Small Business Management,* (9th ed.). Cincinnati: South-Western, 1994.

McLaughlin, Harold J., *The Entrepreneur's Guide to Building a Better Business Plan: A Step-by-Step Approach.* New York: Wiley, 1992.

O'Hara, Patrick D., *The Total Business Plan.* New York: Wiley, 1990.

Pickle, Hal B. and Royce L. Abrahamson, *Small Business Management,* (5th ed.). New York: Wiley, 1990.

Simon, Julian L. and Julian Simon Associates, *How to Start and Operate a Mail Order Business,* (5th ed.). New York: McGraw-Hill, 1993.

Stoner, Charles R. and Fred L. Fry, *Strategic Planning in Small Business.* Cincinnati: South-Western, 1987.

Touchie, Rodger, *Preparing a Successful Business Plan: A Practical Guide for Small Business.* Bellingham, WA: Self-Counsel Press, 1989.

Wilbur, L. Perry, *How to Make Money in Mail Order.* New York: Wiley, 1990.

GETTING STARTED
IN MAIL ORDER

Targeting Prospective Buyers

A favorite, centuries-old adage among owners of businesses of all types is "Know your customer." This applies just as strongly to mail order selling and, indeed, to the entire direct marketing arena.

To succeed in this business, you must know exactly *who* your customer is. This means that you first need to target selected groups of prospects, consumers, or organizations, and then study those potential buyers in depth. Learn all you can about them; get to understand them fully; find out their needs and wants. Only after you have done considerable homework should you set out to prepare the right combinations of merchandise, pricing strategy, offers, advertisements, and the like to sell them with comparative ease.

WITHOUT CUSTOMERS THERE *IS* NO BUSINESS!

You need to know the people you plan to sell to both as individuals and as members of groups. To accomplish the first objective, you'll need a thorough grounding in human psychology; for the second, a firm grasp of the fundamentals of social psychology is essential. That's because many factors influence the ways we behave. We're affected by both inborn traits and acquired characteristics, by our environment as well as by what we have inherited. Some of our needs and wants are innate; others we acquire as we go through life. We form attitudes toward both animate and inanimate objects. We develop value systems that support us.

We acquire personalities that we project to others. In many ways, we're much the same, yet we differ markedly from one another because each of us is the individual sum of our particular heredity and background.

To market goods and/or services successfully, you must know why—and how—people come to buy what they buy. You need to become familiar with those factors that influence purchasing behavior. Since the 1950s, many hundreds of investigations into the buying behavior of the American public have led to the accumulation of a sizable body of useful knowledge known as *consumer behavior*. (For greater understanding, read several of the books on this subject listed at the end of this chapter.)

UNDERSTANDING THE CONSUMER

Today, we know a good deal about why people buy, the motives behind their purchasing. We know what attracts them more readily to certain stores or suppliers than to others or to specific brands of goods. We know that our buying behavior is affected by such "outside" forces as family influences, the different groups we belong to, social class membership, lifestyle, and so on. Other more personal influences include sex, age, income level, occupation, and the like. Still other determinants of behavior include our perceptions, beliefs, attitudes, and values.

Some Common Motives

Throughout our lives, most of our actions (including our shopping behavior) are direct outcomes of the motives at work within us. Motives are inner forces that push us toward—or away from—people, things, and concepts.

Here are some of the things most people want:

Affection	Love
Beauty	Money
Comfort	Peace of mind
Companionship	Pleasure
Convenience	Praise
Ego satisfaction	Recognition
Enjoyment	Security
Entertainment	Self-actualization
Friends	Self-confidence
Good health	Self-esteem
Happiness	Self-improvement
Knowledge	Spiritual well-being

Most people also want to:

Accomplish	Enjoy a good standard of living
Achieve	Express their creativity
Acquire possessions	Express their individuality
Be accepted	Get ahead
Be appreciated	Have fun
Be attractive	Laugh
Be fashionable	Play
Be liked	Relax
Be successful	Save money
Belong	Save time

Most people also try to avoid:

Confusion	Hurt
Danger	Illness
Deprivation	Loss
Embarrassment	Pain
Failure	Sorrow
Fear	Tension
Grief	Thirst
Hunger	Worry

Culture

Our culture is a reflection of the society in which we live. It embraces everything—all that is material, intellectual, artistic. It represents the sum total of our society: its values, attitudes, philosophy, language, ideas, goods, publications, tools, and artifacts. Included, too, are the laws and regulations; the ethics, morals, and scruples; and the ways of living.

Given a fair amount of innate characteristics and traits, we're born into our culture and are then acculturated or socialized by it throughout our lifetimes, because we're constantly surrounded by all of its trappings—literally immersed in them. And it's perpetuated throughout generations by our schools and institutions.

Our culture influences the way we think and perceive.

Social Classes

As members of our American culture, we tend to form and hold attitudes toward ourselves and others. Society is stratified into different levels. We're able to discern differences among people. We recognize that some have higher status than we do. These we may look up to; others we may look down on; still others we feel are right on our level. Differences *do* exist, although many of us would like to ignore this fact of life. That's because we believe in and practice democracy, where everyone's supposed to be equal.

Social scientists identify a person's social class by studying such factors as occupation, type and place of residence, income, educational level, and the like. But most of us have an instinctive capacity for judging another's social class, albeit in a very rough fashion. In the way others live, we're able to perceive differences among at least three major classes: upper, middle, and lower. If we attended a college course in either social psychology or consumer behavior, we would learn more—that each of the three classes can be subdivided into two, resulting in six social classes. The two upper classes, the upper-upper and the lower-upper, together make up only a small fraction of our total population. Far bigger in size are the two middle and the two lower classes.

The class you belong to affects your buying behavior: what you buy, the brands you prefer, and the very stores at which you shop.

Subcultures

We can discern a number of subcultures within our society. These are comprised of substantial numbers of people who share traits and attitudes peculiar to these segments and in addition to the characteristics of the greater society. Subcultures may be segmented along racial, religious, geographic, age, and other lines.

For example, black Americans (who make up 12 percent of our population) constitute a major subculture. They have a younger median age, a higher birth rate, and a far lower median family income than do whites. Differences exist between black and white shoppers in both product and media usage. Senior citizens are our fastest-growing subculture; by the year 2000, Americans over the age of 65 are expected to surpass the 32-million mark and represent more than 13 percent of our population. Some of this group's more pressing needs readily differentiate it from other age subcultures; prescription drugs, dentures, health care, and transportation services are among the products and services that come readily to mind. Similarly, belonging to the Hispanic, Jewish, teenage, midwestern, southern, or other subcultures will be reflected in purchasing behavior.[1]

---

[1] For useful insights into several of these American subcultures, see Danny N. Bellenger and Humberto Valencia, "Understanding the Hispanic Market," *Business Horizons* 25 (May–June 1982), 47–50; Madhav N. Segal and Lionel Sosa, "Marketing to the Hispanic Community," *California Management Review* 26 (Fall 1983), 120–34; William Lazer, "Inside the Mature Market," *American Demographics* 7 (March 1985), 22–25*ff;* William Lazer, "Dimensions of the Mature Market," *Journal of Consumer Marketing* 3 (Summer 1986), 23–34; Warren A. French and Richard Fox, "Segmenting the Senior Citizen Market," *Journal of Consumer Marketing* 2 (Winter 1985), 61–74.

TARGET MARKETING AND SEGMENTATION

Today's marketers use the term *market segmentation* to denote various useful approaches to solving a specific problem: how to locate and separate potentially profitable segments, or groups, from among the total consumer population. Or, if the selling efforts are to be directed at business, industry, and/or other kinds of organizations, from among their entire populations.

Modern marketing theory underscores the futility of trying to sell to every person or organization, of trying to be all things to all customers. Some will never, never be interested in what you may have to offer. You would have problems attempting to sell room air-conditioners to Eskimos, twin-engined speedboats to people who earn less than $30,000 a year, toupees to healthy young women, or hair dryers to bald septuagenarians.

Instead, you must look for specific types of people or organizations toward whom or which to aim your sales efforts. Because they share one or more characteristics in common, ones that may indicate an interest in or the ability to pay for the kinds of products/services you'll be selling, they may be likely prospects for you. By concentrating on such segments of the population, you won't be scattering your advertising dollars like buckshot to the wind.

Among the more popular methods of market segmentation are those of geographic, demographic, value, psychographic, lifestyle, and usage segmentation. Each of these approaches is briefly treated in the next few paragraphs.

Geographic Segmentation

Geographic segmentation is the earliest segmentation approach of them all. Depending on the products or services being sold, a useful approach would be to target prospective buyers in the warmer or cooler sections of the country. Snowmobiles would be of little use to people residing in the southeast—and of much more interest to the mountain states. Obviously, if you plan to sell deep-sea fishing equipment, you would probably shy away from locating your shop in the Midwest.

Bear in mind, too, that there may be considerable differences in personal preferences and product usage from one region of the United States to the next.

Demographic Segmentation

Still the most useful approach to "carving up the pie," demographic segmentation is often referred to as *demographics*—from the word *demography*—the statistical study of populations with attention to specific characteristics. Marketing professionals look for those aspects that affect people's purchasing behavior, such as their sex, age, income, level of education, race, nationality, and so on.

Women, for example, clearly represent the major market for perfumes, cosmetics, and feminine hygiene products. And, obviously, teenagers haven't the slightest interest in many of the products and services that senior citizens use regularly.

As a mail order hopeful, you'll need to bone up on what we consumers really are like. Reading a book or two on consumer behavior, such as those listed at the end of this chapter, will provide many insights into the psychological and sociological foundations. An hour or two in consultation with the latest copy of the *Statistical Abstract,* in the quiet of the reference section at your local library, will yield lots of worthwhile data.

Meanwhile, here are some broad generalities about American consumers to mull over. They may help in your thinking about the market segments you may choose to pursue in your new business.

- *Our population continues to increase.* Before the century ends, we'll most likely reach the 270 million mark. Naturally, we'll need more goods and services than we now use—and more manufacturers and distributors to provide them. Ample room exists for thousands of new firms and for expansion on the part of established businesses.

- *Our population is growing older.* Our median age is inching up, year by year. By the late 1990s, half the population will be older than 35 or 36. Moreover, the age bracket between 35 and 55 appears to be increasing more rapidly than most other age groups, making it a desirable target at which to aim selling efforts. The number of senior citizens is also increasing.

- *Family incomes are still rising.* Fewer than one-third of all households had annual incomes of over $15,000 in 1970. Only ten years before that, no more than one person in ten earned over $25,000 a year. With the passage of time, bouts of inflation, and the growth of two- and three-income families, the median family income may soon surpass $40,000 annually.

- *People are more educated.* With more education, American consumers can be more knowledgeable and more efficient buyers. Close to 80 percent of all adults over the age of 25 have graduated from high school; of these, one out of four completed a college education.

- *More women are entering the workforce.* Nearly 60 percent of all married women are now in the workforce, indicating a need for time- and energy-saving products and services for quicker shopping.

OTHER WAYS TO SEGMENT THE CONSUMER MARKET

Other approaches to market segmentation are useful, including benefit, psychographic, lifestyle, and usage segmentation.

- *Benefit Segmentation.* Companies using benefit segmentation seek to carve out viable consumer groups to market to on the basis of the *benefits* people look for in a particular product or service. An example of this method's use comes from the toothpaste industry where they found large numbers of consumers who bought toothpaste largely to prevent cavities, others who coveted white teeth, still others who wanted their breath to smell fresh, and so on.[2]

- *Psychographic and Lifestyle Approaches.* In psychographic segmentation, the marketer attempts to group consumers according to personality, value systems, attitudes, interests, and the like. The lifestyle approach calls for pinpointing population segments whose ways of living are quite similar, or homogeneous. (Both psychographic and lifestyle segmentation methods have, in the main, been used by the larger corporations. They require more intricate study and analysis, including the use of psychological instruments. Usually, they're well outside the grasp of the smaller firm.)

- *Usage Segmentation.* Usage segmentation is simpler to employ than the psychographic and lifestyle segmentation approaches. People are first dichotomized into two groups: *users* and *nonusers* of a particular product or brand. Typically, nonusers are thereafter ignored; the only consumers of interest to the company are the users, who are then separated into three subgroups: *heavy, moderate,* and *light* users. Heavy users of a product—for example, beer, paper toweling, or mayonnaise—may, over a year, purchase up to ten times (or more) the amount than the light user will buy.

  By way of illustration, consider bingo, a common American diversion. Some people never play; they detest the game, think it's utterly devoid of challenge, and so on. These are the nonusers. Others play occasionally; still others play as often as three to five times or more each and every week of the year (barring holidays, of course!). These latter people are the heavy users—and of far more importance to the bingo hall than all the rest.

Often, a simple questionnaire is enough to categorize consumers according to their use of the product or services.

OPPORTUNITIES ABOUND IN THE ORGANIZATIONAL MARKETPLACE

You may elect not to sell to the final consumer, and aim instead at selling to organizations. You can count these in the millions, rather than in the hundreds of millions that make up the consumer markets, making it easier for you to target specific types and groups. Moreover, individual orders stemming from organizational customers are generally much larger than those that emanate from the consumer sector.

---

[2] See Russell I. Haley, "Benefit Segmentation—20 Years Later," *Journal of Consumer Marketing* 1 (2), 5–13; Paul E. Green, Abba M. Krieger, and Catherine M. Schaffer, "Quick and Simple Benefit Segmentation," *Journal of Advertising Research* 25 (June–July 1985), 9–17.

Types of Organizations in the Marketplace

Organizations in the marketplace may be industrial or business organizations such as manufacturing companies and other producers, wholesalers, retailers, and service enterprises. Or, they may be government organizations at all levels: federal, state, county, or local. Indeed, government is the biggest buyer of all. Massive purchasing of goods and services goes on continuously to support military forces, public works, schools and hospitals, police and fire departments, and so on. Markets also need to be serviced in other areas of economic activity, such as agriculture, fishing, mining, transportation, and so on.

These organizational markets require raw and semiprocessed materials, components, equipment, machinery, installations, and supplies of every conceivable kind. You can reach them through placing advertisements in trade publications and by direct mail. In fact, thousands of different mailing lists are readily available; they're organized not only by Standard Industrial Classification (SIC) number, but also by organizational size, annual sales volume, number of employees, location, and other factors. Directories of industrial and commercial firms, of government agencies and offices, and of other types of organizations are also available.

If you plan to sell to organizations, you'll need to learn a great deal about them beforehand—about their ways, their needs, and their preferences. You'll discover that their purchasing agents are far more qualified and knowledgeable than is the typical consumer buyer. They're skilled in the intricacies of negotiating prices and terms, in contract dealings, and in their awareness of the quality and prices of competitive products.

The rewards, however, may well make it worth your while to investigate this area.

SOURCES OF ADDITIONAL INFORMATION

Bonoma, Thomas V. and Benson P. Shapiro, *Segmenting the Industrial Market.* Lexington, MA: D.C. Heath, 1983.

Davidson, Jeffrey P., *Marketing to Home-Based Businesses.* Homewood, IL: Business One Irwin, 1991.

Emerick, Tracy and Bernie Goldberg, *Business-to-Business Direct Marketing,* (2d ed.). New York: AMACOM, 1988.

Engel, James F. et al. *Consumer Behavior,* (7th ed.). Fort Worth, TX: Dryden, 1993.

Mowen, John C., *Consumer Behavior,* (3rd ed.). New York: Macmillan, 1992.

Peter, J. Paul and Jerry C. Olson, *Consumer Behavior and Marketing Strategy,* (3rd ed.). Homewood, IL: Irwin, 1992.

Schiffman, Leon G. and Leslie Lazar Kanuk, *Consumer Behavior,* (4th ed.). Englewood Cliffs, NJ: Prentice-Hall, 1991.

Settle, Robert B. and Pamela L. Abreck, *Niche Marketing: How to Pinpoint Target Markets.* New York: Wiley, 1989.

Walters, C. Glenn and Blaise J. Bergiel, *Consumer Behavior: A Decision-Making Approach.* Cincinnati: South-Western, 1989.

Wilkie, William L., *Consumer Behavior,* (2d ed.). New York: Wiley, 1990.

4

What Can You Sell by Mail?

Chapter 2 introduced you to the exciting potential of mail order selling, a business you could start at home in your spare time. In Chapter 3, you learned about people and about organizations—prospective buyers for your wares. Now, you need to know about the merchandise or service(s) you may wish to sell in your new enterprise. Decisions must be made. Many direct marketers maintain that the single most important ingredient contributing to success is *what you sell*. It's thought of as the one vital component of your *direct marketing mix*. Indeed, you can't hope to start the business without one or two products (or services) in which you have utter confidence.

So, you now have a problem: What shall I choose to sell, at least at the start?

WHAT CAN YOU SELL?

Just about anything that can be sold at all can be sold by mail: products, services, even knowledge. You would do well to first explore your skills, talents, special knowledge, and hobbies for ideas for your new business. Learn how to put these things to work, earning money for you. As one example, consider the vast field of handicrafts. If you have expertise in any one of the crafts listed below, be assured that there are ways to develop that expertise into a thriving mail order operation (with some creative thinking on your part, of course):

Basket weaving	Macramé
Ceramics	Metal enameling
Crocheting	Metalwork
Drawing	Mosaics
Flower arranging	Needlepoint
Glassmaking	Painting
Graphic arts	Rug making
Jewelry making	Sculpture
Knitting	Sewing
Lamp making	Weaving
Leatherwork	Woodcarving

Some of you may already be operating a business at home. If so, you'll find you can expand it quite readily by selling your products or services via the mails. Here are a few examples of home enterprises that can benefit from this avenue of distribution:

Antiques	Jewelry repair
Art instruction	Music instruction
Bookkeeping service	Pet care information
Clock and watch repair	Rubber stamps
Coins for collectors	Shopping service
Craft instruction	Small appliance repair
Dressmaking	Stamps for collectors
Handbag repair	Typing service

HOW TO DECIDE WHAT TO OFFER

To get on the right track, ask yourself: "What would my customers be interested in?"

If you're targeting your efforts at consumers, as do the majority of direct marketers, you might begin by exploring your own attitudes, interests, needs, and wants. After all, you're a consumer yourself—and aren't you somewhat (at least) representative of the rest of us?

Try to come up with a short list of the things you hold most dear. Chances are that, with a bit of soul-searching, you'll devise one that more or less resembles the following:

- Health (physical, mental, emotional).
- Personal appearance.
- Family.
- Friends.

- Home.
- Work.
- Play.
- Saving money.

Granted, these areas of concern might paint you as somewhat self-centered. But, really, aren't we all?

Now, tackle each area in turn, devoting time and thought to spark literally dozens of product/service ideas for your mail order business. Consider, for example, the first item on the list, health. This area has to be prime for possibilities, for good health is something all of us earnestly desire. With several minutes of thinking, you might come up with such ideas as health foods, jogging or running shoes, vitamins, gym equipment, diets of all kinds, skin care products, health care information, books or seminars on self-control (or some other aspect of psychology); and so forth. An hour spent on this task might yield another one or two dozen useful thoughts. Moreover, each idea can in turn be broken down into more dozens of specific items, so that you'll never lack for product/service possibilities.

Then you can progress down the list to the next item, personal appearance, and repeat the process once more.

Characteristics of "Ideal" Mail Order Items

You'll be able to generate many suggestions as to the kinds of products, knowledge, or service(s) you may be able to market. Whatever you do decide to offer, try to match your selection(s) against this idealized picture of the "good" mail order item:

- It should satisfy a real customer need.
- It should be novel, unusual, interesting.
- It must not be readily available in stores.
- It must offer good value for the price.
- It should provide—as the very minimum—a gross margin percentage of between 60 and 75 percent of the selling price.
- It should be easy to mail or ship.
- The mailing/shipping cost should be modest.
- A potential for repeat orders should exist.

WHERE TO FIND SUITABLE ITEMS FOR RESALE

Where do you begin? What sources can you turn to in your hunt for products/services with sales potential for your new business?

The buying committees at the central headquarters of large supermarket chains have a continuous problem: they must screen several thousands of new products every year for their shelves. The manufacturers and wholesalers who present this merchandise to them are anxious to benefit from the tremendous purchasing power behind these retailers. They'll not be visiting your premises, of course, but you can read about these and other new items in the various trade publications. Nearly every product field is represented by some trade paper.

Perhaps your most fertile field for gathering merchandise or service ideas is the advertising of other direct marketing companies. You can find their ads in both men's and women's magazines, in general interest and shelter publications, in the large numbers of special interest periodicals, and in some newspapers. (See Chapters 15 and 16 for details on the print media.)

You'll see new items promoted on television, too, and hear about them over radio. Other sources include trade shows, trade directories, and directories of importers.

WHAT KINDS OF PRODUCTS OR SERVICES WILL CONSUMERS BUY?

Some mail order companies are general merchandisers, much like our traditional department stores. They offer an extensive assortment of merchandise lines from furniture, curtains and draperies, lamps, and other home furnishings through both large and small appliances and sporting goods to clothing for the entire family. The giants among them carry thousands of different products. Their big catalogs, running hundreds of pages, contain some items of interest to just about everyone.

Most mail order firms, though, are content to specialize in one or a few major merchandise lines. It may be that they realize full well their inability to compete on equal terms with the large distributors, and so prefer to carve out niches for themselves among particular consumer segments. Within each product line, they carry a broader variety of merchandise than the general house finds it profitable to do, and they maintain more depth as well. Some specialize in scientific instruments or musical instruments; others, in sporting goods, giftwares and novelties, educational games and toys, woodworking kits, country music (on records or tapes), women's sportswear, ceramic ware, coins for collectors, T-shirts, or hundreds of other lines.

Generally, companies that offer services by mail are specialists. An example is International Correspondence Schools (ICS), noted for its home study courses.

What should you offer by mail? Rarely can a direct marketing firm succeed over the long term with only one product, no matter how popular the item may prove to be. You need to think in terms of a number of products.

Pause and reflect for a few minutes. Most likely, you'll spend a considerable sum of money advertising your first item or two in the print media, or perhaps through direct mail efforts, to add a goodly number of names to your customer list. Wouldn't it seem a terrible waste of your investment if you failed to follow up by seeking additional sales from those buyers, either through circulars or folders (*bouncebacks*) that you enclose with every order you send out or through your own catalog? Think ahead to that point where you'll have accumulated an extensive list of people who have bought from you, and to the line of products that you intend to keep selling to them.

There are always new products to be found or to be developed. For many years, the simple hand magnifying glass has been sold by mail without much difficulty because it fulfills a need for people who have trouble reading fine print. And this is true despite the availability of the hand magnifying glass in many variety stores. Some years back, a mail order ad featured a new variation of an old theme: a plastic product that magnifies an entire page at one time, yet is so thin that you can use it as a bookmark to hold your place when you put the book down.

When you scan the sampling of merchandise possibilities in Exhibit 4–1, keep your imagination flowing freely. With a little twist or adjustment, an old-line, longtime seller may become an exciting novelty with brisk sales potential. Remember, too, that each listing represents an entire category within which you may be able to find five, ten, or perhaps twenty-five or more distinct product possibilities.

Knowledge: An Area of Vast Sales Potential

Opportunities abound in the knowledge area for the mail order marketer, for buyers must surely exist somewhere for every conceivable kind and type of information. We all thirst for knowledge often during our lifetimes, all 260 million of us. So do some 13 or 14 million business firms and countless other organizations of all descriptions.

You can't hope to reach every person or every organization. Nor should you think about trying to do so. You'll accomplish far more by searching out specific segments of the population, groups of people who share common ideas, interests, aspirations, attitudes, and lifestyles. Your challenge is to locate those types of individuals or organizations whose profiles indicate that they would be prime prospects for the knowledge you intend to sell. You then study these selected target groups to find out more about their needs and wants and then prepare the material that would satisfy them.

If you have had worthwhile and broad experience in a particular trade, occupation, or profession, or you claim expertise in any subject area, you should be able to find interested parties who will pay for your knowledge. Provided, of course, that you "package" it in a leaflet, booklet, pamphlet, or other type of printed work, or perhaps record it on a cassette. If you aren't well versed by virtue of your own hands-on experience, you can still tackle whatever subjects attract you by doing some thorough research. You can even seek to purchase information from others, then write it up yourself, or have someone who is a more accomplished writer prepare it for you. And make sure you hold the copyright!

Such "products" reflect many of the characteristics of the successful mail order item. They can't be obtained in stores or from other mail order

EXHIBIT 4-1   A sampling of merchandise possibilities

Apparel	Electronic games	Nursery stock
Aquarium supplies	Fabrics	Office supplies
Arts and crafts supplies	Farm supplies	Paintings
Astrological charts and	Figurines	Paperweights
medallions	Films	Perfumes
Beauty supplies	Fire alarms	Photographic equipment and
Binoculars	Fire extinguishers	supplies
Books	Fireplace accessories	Piece goods
Brassware	Fishing equipment and supplies	Porcelain items
Bridal items	Flashlights	Postage stamps (for collectors)
Build-it-yourself kits	Flower arrangements	Power tools
Burglar alarms	Footwear	Rainwear
Calculators	Formulas	Recipes
Cameras	Garden items	Records and tapes
Car care products	Giftware	Religious items
Ceramic items	Gymnastic equipment	Scientific equipment
Chairs	Handbags	Scissors
Cheeses	Handicrafts	Sculptures
Chemicals	Health foods	Seafood
Chinaware	Health-related products	Searchlights
Cleaning compounds	Hobby supplies	Seeds
and supplies	Home furnishings	Sewing supplies
Clocks	Home gardening supplies	Shoes
Coins	Home healthcare	Skates
Computers	Hunting equipment	Skin care items
Confectionery	Jewelry	Souvenirs
Construction sets	Knitting supplies	Sporting goods and equipment
Cookies	Lawn care products	Stationery
Cookware	Leather goods	Telescopes
Cosmetics	Luggage	Toiletries
Cutlery	Magic tricks	Tools and utensils
Decorative accessories	Magnifying glasses	Towels
Diet aids	Medallions	Toys
Diet foods	Medical appliances	Vitamins
Do-it-yourself manuals	Medical supplies	Wagons
Doll houses	Metalwork	Watches
Dolls	Microscopes	Weight-reducing aids
Educational toys	Mirrors	Woodenware
Electrical appliances	Models and kits	Work clothing

dealers (unless you sell them to these retailers); you can set the kind of selling price that will provide the big markup you need; there are no problems with breakage or perishability in mailing the item; handling is extremely easy; and the postage cost is minimal.

To whet your appetite, here's just a sprinkling of possibilities for *consumer group targets*. (In a similar fashion, business firms and other organizations may be broken down into innumerable classifications.)

Arthritis sufferers	Investors
Bicyclists	Jobseekers
Car owners	Joggers
Card players	Mechanics
College students	Parents
Dieters	Pet owners
Executives	Seafood lovers
Hobbyists	Sports fans
Home gardeners	Teenagers
Housewives	Veterans

The abbreviated list of topic areas offered in Exhibit 4–2 may really spark your thinking.

SELLING SERVICES

The most interesting aspect of selling a service by mail is the assurance of repeat sales. A satisfied customer will continue to use your service

EXHIBIT 4–2   Potentially profitable knowledge areas

Appliance repair	Glassmaking	Physical development
Arts and crafts (how to draw, paint, sculpt, etc.)	Health improvement	Pottery
Attracting the opposite sex	History	Raising animals, fish, pets
Beauty suggestions	Hobbies	Real estate
Blueprints	Home gardening	Resume preparation
Boating	Home protection	Sailing
Build-it-yourself plans	Homeowners' hints	Self-defense
Business opportunities	Horoscopes	Self-improvement
Car care	Hunting	Self-protection
Collecting (stamps, gemstones, many other collectibles)	Inventing	Self-publishing
Correspondence courses	Investments	Seminars and workshops
Dancing	Jewelry making	Sewing
Decorating (home, office)	Jewelry repair	Skiing
Designing clothes	Joke telling	Solving puzzles
Diets	Knitting	Sports
Doll making	Leisure activities	Stock market
Employment information	Making clothes	Toymaking
Entertaining	Making money	Travel
Entrepreneurship	Medical facts	Treasure hunting
Exploring	Metalwork	Vacationing
Fashions	Musical instruments	Weaving
Finances	Needlepoint	Weight reduction
Flower arranging	Party suggestions	Winning (at bingo, cards, dice, horse racing, etc.)
Formulas	Patternmaking	Woodworking
	Personal care	Writing
	Photography	

and may be induced to recommend other prospective clients to you. With this kind of "product," your annual sales volume will continue to increase along with the passage of time, so long as you deliver what you promise and people continue to have confidence in your service.

If you have had considerable experience in a particular line or trade, or if you have published articles or books in some field and thereby built a reputation, you may be able to transfer your background and expertise to a useful service business.

Here are some of the many services being marketed successfully by mail:

Accounting services	Personalizing products
Advertising agency	Photography (prints, enlargements,
Appliance repair	miniatures, photo stamps, etc.)
Bookkeeping services	Printing
Clipping bureau	Public relations agency
Commercial art supply	Publicity firm
Computer services	Reminder service
Consulting services	Research bureau
Equipment leasing	Resume preparation
Jewelry repair	Shopping service
Legal services	Stationery
Letter remailing	Tax form preparation
Machinery repair	Toy repair
Musical instrument repair	Translation bureau
Newsletter	Typing service

SOURCES OF ADDITIONAL INFORMATION

Connor, Dick and Jeffrey P. Davidson, *Marketing Your Consulting and Professional Services,* (3rd ed.). New York: Wiley, 1994.

Davidson, Jeff, *Marketing on a Shoestring.* New York: Wiley, 1994.

Dilworth, James B., *Production and Operations Management,* (5th ed.). New York: McGraw-Hill, 1992.

Hiam, Alexander and Charles Schewe, *The Portable MBA in Marketing.* New York: Wiley, 1992.

Lamb, Charles W., Jr., Joseph F. Hair, Jr., and Carl McDaniel, *Principles of Marketing.* Cincinnati: South-Western, 1992.

Lumley, James E.A., *Sell It by Mail: Making Your Product the One They Buy.* New York: Wiley, 1986.

McCarthy, E. Jerome and William D. Perreault, *Essentials of Marketing,* (5th ed.). Homewood, IL: Irwin, 1990.

Settle, Robert B. and Pamela L. Abreck, *Niche Marketing: How to Pinpoint Target Markets.* New York: Wiley, 1989.

Von Hoelscher, Russ, *How You Can Make a Fortune Selling Information by Mail.* Goessel, KS: Profit Ideas, 1991.

Webster, Frederick E., Jr., *Industrial Marketing Strategy,* (4th ed.). New York: Wiley, 1994.

Zikmund, William and Michael D'Amico, *Marketing,* (3rd ed.). New York: Wiley, 1989.

5

Basic Insights into the Financial Side

You have heard it before: to make money, you need money. Sure, it's an old axiom, but it's so true! Enthusiasm, hard work, and perseverance won't do the job! If you have no funds of your own that you can afford to gamble with, it would be prudent to remain at your present job until you have saved up several thousand dollars. Or, find yourself a better job and postpone your dream of owning your own business for another year or two.

Any business must run on money. Even to launch a modest, part-time, run-from-your-home venture requires some financial support. This is just as true of a new mail order business as it is of any other type of enterprise. Luckily, the mail order field often doesn't call for so heavy an initial outlay of capital as do most other business types.

WHERE TO FIND THE FUNDS YOU'LL NEED

You'll need only a modest amount of money to register your business name, pay for a partnership agreement, or file for a corporate form. You'll need much more in funds to purchase inventory and equipment, pay for media advertising and for stationery, buy postage stamps to affix to your letters and parcels, and so forth. If you start on a full-time basis, you'll need back-up capital to live on until your business begins to generate profit.

Essentially, there are only three avenues you can pursue in attempting to raise the money you need to start a business:

- You can provide your own money.
- You can borrow funds.
- You can sell part of your business to others, thus trading equity for ready capital.

Use Your Own Funds

Using your own money is usually best. Certainly, it's the one approach most recommended by bankers and other financial advisors and by many business owners. If you use your own capital, you won't have to worry about paying back loans directly or even by installments or about struggling to pay high interest rates. Nor will you have to give away any piece, large or small, of your business.

Bear in mind, too, that most small-scale enterprises cannot afford to pay their owners even a minimum salary for the first six or eight months after starting up.

Borrow Funds

You might consider borrowing *some* money to add to your own nest egg, from a close relative or two, or from one or two good friends. If this is your decision, be sure to proceed in a businesslike manner. Give them promissory notes to make things official. And make sure you pay those notes when they come due. You might also pay them interest at a fair rate on what they have loaned to you. After all, they'll be losing potential interest all along.

Take a Passbook Loan

Passbook loans are a relatively inexpensive way of borrowing. If you maintain a savings account, you might consider taking out a passbook loan. Your account continues to earn interest at the regular rate while you pay the bank back, usually in monthly payments. Of course, this does tie up the money you have in your account, at least to the extent of the current balance owed.

Other Bank Loans

If you have been steadily employed all along, earn a fair income, and have little outstanding debt, chances are that many banks will be willing to extend a personal loan on your signed application. Depending on your earnings and credit evaluation, you may be able to borrow anywhere from a few hundred to several thousand dollars without having to put up collateral. It helps, too, if you own an automobile, boat, home, or other property such as stocks or bonds. If you do have worthwhile assets, you can put up some of these as collateral for larger loans.

Borrow against Your Life Insurance

If you carry life insurance policies on which you have been paying premiums for years (except, of course, for term insurance), you may have accumulated substantial cash equity in those policies. Although you probably wouldn't want to surrender them for their cash value, you can borrow against the cash accumulation, generally at a low rate of interest. Whether or not you eventually pay back the loan is your decision. If you should die before repaying the loan, the outstanding indebtedness will be deducted from the face value of the policy when payment is made to your beneficiary.

Mortgage or Refinance Your Property

If you own your own home or apartment, or a summer place, look into the possibilities of getting a mortgage on your property, or on any business property you may own. If you already have a mortgage, you may be able to refinance it or secure a second mortgage. The same thinking can apply to other items of substantial value, such as a truck, car, or boat.

Check with the U.S. Small Business Administration

This federal agency may be a valuable source of additional funds, especially if you have already approached several banks and have been turned down for a loan. The Small Business Administration (SBA) offers a variety of arrangements to help small companies with capital for construction, expansion, purchasing of equipment and supplies, working capital, and so on. Also available are economic opportunity loans (designed for minority group members and the disadvantaged) and loans to small firms run by handicapped individuals. Visit your nearest SBA office to discuss the various programs and secure an application form.

Contact a Small Business Investment Corporation (SBIC)

SBICs are companies licensed and regulated by the U.S. Small Business Administration. They can provide the small firm with either equity capital or long-term loan financing; often, management assistance is offered as well. There are also MESBICs, similar institutions devoted to helping small companies that are run by members of minority groups. (The prefix ME stands for Minority Enterprise.)

Approach a Venture Capital Group

Some institutions, corporations, and groups of private investors conduct business by financing the expansion and growth of other organizations. They may invest substantial sums in firms that show promise and otherwise meet their criteria; in return, they become part owners. Their major interest is in making capital gains. They usually prefer to recoup their investment, plus perhaps some 300 or 400 percent profit on that investment, within a few years.

Venture capitalists are generally not interested in furnishing initial capital to a firm that is just starting up. They prefer to come in after the company is well established, shows a good financial picture, and is ready to move ahead at a more rapid pace.

Make Use of Trade Credit

If your credit rating is good, many of your suppliers will extend credit on the merchandise or supplies you buy. Usual trade terms are 1 or 2 percent, 10 days, net 30 days. This means that you'll have up to 30 days after the invoice date to pay for the merchandise you buy. Or, should you pay your bills early (within 10 days of the invoice date), you can deduct 1 or 2 percent from the amount indicated on the bill when you send out your checks. Effectively, then, you'll have the loan of your vendors' money for anywhere from a few days up to an entire month.

Along somewhat similar lines, an occasional vendor may offer you merchandise *on consignment,* which means you need not pay for the merchandise until you have sold it. Usually, return privileges go along with sales on consignment. If you haven't succeeded in disposing of all goods within a certain period of time, you can return the balance to your supplier.

Lease, Rather than Buy

A somewhat indirect way of "financing" your operation, leasing can free money that you would ordinarily have to allocate to equipment, fixtures, or machinery. (Of course, this aspect would be much more important if you have a manufacturing, wholesale, or retail business along with your mail order operation.) Instead of purchasing such goods outright, you rent them from willing suppliers.

Sell Part of Your Company

If you have incorporated your new business, there's always the possibility of selling shares of stock in your firm to friends, relatives, acquaintances, and even employees. (This doesn't refer to a public offering. It would be in your best interest to consult both your attorney and your accountant about this approach.)

THE BASIC ACCOUNTING STATEMENTS

The operator of any type of business should become thoroughly familiar with the two major accounting statements: the *balance sheet* and the *income statement.* A working knowledge of both forms is essential to executive decision making and to the success of the business itself. It's needed, too, even before you plan to launch your new business, so that you can work out just how much capital you'll need to begin your operation.

Later in this chapter, you'll have ample opportunity to work up these two reports for your first year of operation, well in advance of starting up. From the two pro forma statements, you'll be able to compute not only your expected sales, expenses, and profit, but also the amount of money needed to get started and to ensure the building of a successful enterprise.

Get Acquainted with the Balance Sheet

Like other business owners, you need to prepare (or have your accountant prepare) a balance sheet at least once a year—after the close of business on December 31 if you operate on a calendar year basis, or perhaps after June 30, if yours is a fiscal year operation. In accounting terms, you'll be *closing the books.*

The balance sheet is a summary of the assets, liabilities, and net worth of your business at a point in time. It's called a balance sheet because of its format: Typically, it's a single sheet of paper divided down the middle so that the two halves are shown side-by-side. In the left-hand section are the firm's assets; in the right-hand section, the firm's liabilities and net worth. Bottom-line figures in both halves are identical, or in balance.

Exhibit 5–1 shows a rather simplified balance sheet for a small direct marketing firm. You'll see that the last entry on the right side shows a figure for Total Assets of $82,580 and that this sum equals Total Liabilities plus Net Worth shown in the second section.

Terms that appear in the balance sheet are explained below:

- *Assets.* On the first half of your balance sheet, you indicate the value of all assets, or resources, owned by your company: money, merchandise, machinery, equipment, and other items of capital. These resources are grouped into *current* and *fixed* assets.

- *Current assets.* Current assets are the firm's resources that are actively employed in conducting business operations over the year. Cash, merchandise, and supplies (stationery, packaging materials, etc.) are examples.

- *Cash on hand and in bank.* Actually, this label is somewhat of a misnomer, for you'll also include in this category all checks and money orders not yet deposited in the bank; so, too, with any sum in your petty cash fund. Moreover, if you run a retail store operation in conjunction with your mail order business, you must add the total amount in your store bank; that is, the coins (loose and in rolls) and small bills you keep on the premises so that you can make change for customers each day.

- *Marketable securities.* Enter in the marketable securities category the current market value of all business-owned stocks, debentures, and other securities that can be readily converted into cash if necessary.

- *Accounts receivable.* If you encourage purchases on credit, you need to set up an individual record, called an *account,* for each customer. In these accounts, you carefully record all sales and all payments subsequently made. The balance sheet entry indicates the

EXHIBIT 5–1   A simple balance sheet

DINKY'S TOYS & GADGETS
Balance Sheet
for Year End December 31, 19XX

ASSETS

CURRENT ASSETS		
Cash on hand and in banks	$27,540	
Marketable securities	2,545	
Accounts receivable (less allowance for bad debts)	1,880	
Merchandise inventory	23,210	
Supplies inventory	3,715	
Total Current Assets		$58,890
FIXED ASSETS		
Office machinery and equipment (less depreciation)	11,830	
Furniture (less depreciation)	7,760	
Leasehold improvements	4,100	
Total Fixed Assets		23,690
TOTAL ASSETS		$82,580

LIABILITIES AND NET WORTH

CURRENT LIABILITIES		
Accounts payable	$13,530	
Notes payable within year	3,585	
Accrued taxes	2,410	
Total Current Liabilities		$19,525
LONG-TERM LIABILITIES		
Note payable, 1995	3,300	
Note payable, 1997	3,300	
Total long-term liabilities		6,600
Total Liabilities		$26,125
Net Worth (Owner's Equity)		$56,455
TOTAL LIABILITIES AND NET WORTH		$82,580

sum total of all outstanding balances owed. This term is often shortened to *receivables*.

- *Allowance for bad debts.* Some of your accounts receivable may never be fully paid. Not every person is ethical or trustworthy. In recognition of this sorry fact, you should deduct a small percentage of the outstanding balance (say, 1 percent) from the total receivables figure and enter only the net result on your balance sheet. In this way, the accounting statement reflects a more accurate appraisal of your financial status.

- *Inventories.* Like wholesale distributors and other retail businesses, the typical mail order company maintains a merchandise inventory. It stocks articles of merchandise so that incoming orders may be filled without delay. The overall figure that appears here is calculated at your cost or at the current market value of the goods, whichever is lower. Indeed, some mail order firms may resemble the manufacturer even more than the retailer. Such companies may manufacture the products they sell; others assemble or package merchandise on their premises. Consequently, they may maintain several different types of inventories: (1) raw materials, (2) semiprocessed goods (*work-in-progress*), and (3) finished, or ready, merchandise. The balance sheet will, of course, show these inventories separately.

  Finally, all enterprises maintain supplies necessary to operations. Examples of such material in a mail order business include packing materials of all sorts: cartons, shipping tubes, wrapping paper, and the like; envelopes and letterheads; printer ribbons, paper clips, and index cards. The total value of your supply inventory is also entered on your balance sheet.

- *Fixed assets.* Among those assets of a more permanent (or fixed) nature owned by the company are office equipment, machinery, perhaps a delivery truck, furniture, and so on. If the firm owns the building in which it's located or the land on which the building has been erected, this is also a fixed asset.

- *Depreciation.* With the exception of land, the value of a company's fixed assets declines with the passage of time. This is readily grasped by visualizing the effects of normal wear and tear alone, over the years, on an office copier or a small panel truck. Generally, you'll need to set up a depreciation schedule for each group of your fixed assets according to Internal Revenue Service regulations. (Request a copy of their Publication 534, "Depreciation.")

- *Leasehold improvements.* Leasehold improvements applies to the cost of any and all improvements made by a lessee on property leased for use in the business.

- *Liabilities.* Liabilities is a collective term for all your outstanding business debts: what you owe your suppliers, your employees, the advertising media (or agency), the banks from which you borrowed, various levels of government (for taxes due), and the like.

- *Net worth.* Subtract the sum total of your liabilities from that of your assets; what's left is the net worth of your business. For owners of sole proprietorships and partnerships, this term is also known as Owner's, or Owners', Equity. If you run your business as a corporation, this section of the balance sheet will show the amount of common stock held by your shareholders, plus any retained (not distributed) earnings.

- *Current liabilities.* Under current liabilities list all obligations you'll need to pay back within the next twelve months.

- *Accounts payable.* As with all of your accounts receivable, you need to keep records of all companies and individuals from which you buy on credit. Enter here the total amount owed to these suppliers.

- *Notes payable.* A note is simply a written acknowledgment of a debt and a promise to repay that debt. These are obligations you have contracted with banks and other lenders to pay back during the next twelve months (as against notes or loans shown under Long-term Liabilities).

- *Accrued taxes.* The verb *to accrue* means to collect, gather, or add to in an orderly fashion. Here you need to indicate the sum you have set aside to pay upcoming tax obligations.

- *Long-term liabilities.* These are debts your business is obligated to repay in the future, beyond the next twelve months.

UNDERSTANDING THE INCOME STATEMENT

The income statement is also commonly referred to as the operating statement, the profit and loss statement, or simply the P&L. It summarizes the outcome or results of operating the business for a period of time. Like the balance sheet, it's typically prepared once each year. However, many firms will make up an income statement quarterly, even monthly, so that management can keep on top of just what is happening in the business and so that decisions may be made promptly and with full knowledge of results along the way. Frequently, it's far too late to do much about a business operation after an entire year has gone by.

The major parts of an income statement are:

- Net sales for the period.
- Cost of goods sold.
- Gross margin.
- Operating expenses.
- Operating profit.
- Total income before income taxes.
- Net income (or net profit) after taxes.

More details are shown in the sample P&L in Exhibit 5-2. Income statement terms are:

- *Net sales.* The word *net* in this category should alert you to the fact that the term *gross sales* also exists. Your gross sales are the total amount of dollars taken in by selling merchandise during the period covered by the statement. From this amount, you must subtract debits, such as returns from customers, employee and

EXHIBIT 5–2   A profit and loss statement

HANDICRAFTS BY ROSLYN
Profit and Loss Statement
For: Year Ended December 31, 19XX

Net Sales		$204,655
Less cost of goods sold:		
Opening inventory, January 1	$ 4,830	
Purchases during year	83,890	
Freight charges	880	
Total goods handled	$89,600	
Less ending inventory, December 31	5,890	
Total cost of goods sold		83,710
Gross Margin		$120,945
Less operating expenses		
Salaries and wages	$37,740	
Payroll taxes	4,320	
Utilities	3,980	
Telephone	2,870	
Rent	12,000	
Office supplies	1,830	
Postage	11,270	
Maintenance expenses	3,385	
Insurance	2,200	
Interest expense	770	
Depreciation	3,220	
Advertising	22,250	
Dues and contributions	445	
Miscellaneous expenses	490	
Total operating expenses		106,770
Operating Profit		$ 14,175
Other income		
Dividends on stock	$ 410	
Interest on bank account	505	
Rental of mailing list	1,480	
Total other income		2,395
Total income before income tax		$ 16,570
Less provision for income tax		4,535
Net Profit		$ 12,035

customer discounts, and other allowances, to derive your net sales.

- *Cost of goods sold.* In this section, you enter those computations that enable you to arrive at your total cost of the merchandise sold during the period. To clarify the procedure, let's go through the steps for a single month, instead of trying to take the entire year into account:

  1. Compute the total cost of all merchandise you have in stock at the beginning of the month.
  2. Tally the costs of all stock you purchased during the month. (Generally, you ascertain the amounts from the invoices for the goods, less any returns you may have made to vendors. You also deduct any cash discounts earned.)
  3. If you had to pay freight charges on any of the shipments, these must also be counted.
  4. Add the amounts in 1 to 3 above. This gives you the complete cost of all merchandise handled.
  5. From 4 above, subtract end-of-the-month inventory value, at cost, of course. The resulting sum represents your cost of what you have actually "moved."

- *Gross margin.* Some people refer to this as *gross profit*. Either way, it represents the difference between net sales and cost of goods sold. For you to operate successfully, whether in the mail order field or in any other type of business, your gross margin must be large enough to pay all of your business expenses and still yield some net profit.

- *Operating expenses.* Operating expenses are the costs you need to cover while operating your business during the time period covered by the statement.

- *Operating profit.* Subtract your operating expenses total from the gross margin figure. The resulting amount is your operating profit—the amount of profit from the actual running of the business.

- *Other income.* You may find that extra dollars come into your business from sources other than your usual operation, for example, interest earned on your business savings account. (Naturally, excess cash should be put to work!) Other income might include dividends from stocks or bonds, money collected by selling an old piece of equipment, and so on.

- *Total income before income tax.* Both your operating profit and the other income entry are combined to form this category. It represents the business earnings before income tax is deducted.

- *Net profit.* This last figure is an exacting measurement of the performance of your business. It tells you how much after-tax profit your firm has earned. Its position on the income statement indicates why it's commonly referred to as the "bottom line."

HOW TO SET THE SELLING PRICES ON YOUR OFFERINGS

In pricing goods and/or services, most businesses rely on the *cost-plus method*. Under this approach, management takes into account both fixed and variable costs and then adds a profit margin to determine the selling price. Expenses that remain more or less constant, regardless of the amount of business you do, are considered fixed costs; rent, air-conditioning and heating costs, the salaries of company executives, property taxes, and insurance premiums are examples. Expenses that fluctuate in direct proportion to increasing or decreasing sales (or production) are labeled variable costs. Examples of such expenses are direct labor costs, commissions paid to telephone (or outside) salespeople, mailing or shipping expenses, and the cost of goods sold or materials used in manufacturing goods.

Bear in mind, though, that price setting under the cost-plus technique isn't all that automatic. Often, management will take into consideration several (and sometimes all) of the following factors:

- Level of customer demand.
- Value, as perceived by buyers.
- Competitors' prices.
- State of the economy.
- Newness of the product or service.
- Requirements of the distribution channels to be used.

In addition to the above factors, mail order companies in particular must devote close attention to two other aspects that are crucial to this form of distribution: gross margin and promotional costs.

Yes, you'll need to set selling prices on your offerings that will bring in enough total gross margin dollars to cover your cost of goods, all advertising expenditures, and all operating costs—and still leave you with a reasonable amount of profit.

An Illustration

Let's go through the price-setting procedure, by way of example. Assume that you're selling a relatively inexpensive gift item through mail order advertisements placed in magazines. You buy the merchandise by the dozen, at a cost of $3 per unit. You wish to place a small print ad in a forthcoming issue of one publication, at a cost of $1,000 for the space. (For the sake of simplicity, let's ignore the ad's production cost.) You discover that your cost to package and mail one item will come to approximately one dollar.

Basing your computations on projected sales of 200 pieces from the ad, you begin to calculate your overall costs, as shown below:

Cost of 200 pieces, at $3 each	=	$ 600
Cost of advertisement	=	1,000
Packaging/mailing 200 pieces, at $1 each	=	200
Total outlay	=	$1,800

Now, you calculate your break-even point by dividing your total outlay of $1,800 by the number of pieces (200) you expect to sell, yielding a suggested selling price of $9 per unit.

Of course, if you should sell no more than 100 pieces, you would take in only $900—and you will have advertised at a substantial loss.

Let's go back to our initial calculations and look at the situation from a slightly different perspective. Consider your costs per piece *without* the cost of advertising, as follows:

Cost of piece	=	$3.00
Packaging/Mailing	=	1.00
Total outlay	=	$4.00

You might then, for example, consider doubling your total outlay *per piece* to arrive at a selling price; this would, of course, be $8.00. If you subtract your cost ($4.00) from the selling price ($8.00), you'll see that you earn $4.00 in gross margin on each piece you sell. So, for you to break even on a print ad that would cost you $1,000, you'd have to sell 250 pieces (since 250 × $4.00 totals $1,000).

If your original estimate of 200 orders turns out to be accurate, you'd end up with a loss of $1,000 on your investment!

Here are the total gross margin dollars you might expect to take in, assuming 200 orders from the ad, at different selling prices:

Selling Price	Gross Margin per piece	Total Gross Margin Dollars
$10	$ 6	$1,200
11	7	1,400
12	8	1,600
13	9	1,800
14	10	2,000
15	11	2,200

As you can see, to make any profit at all under these conditions, you'll need to affix to that article of merchandise a unit selling price above the $13 mark!

You may sell more than 200 pieces from the one ad. Then again, you may sell less, even much less.

As you can readily discern, then, you need high markups to be successful in selling merchandise by mail directly through media advertising. Usually, you'll have to mark up your goods as much as 300 percent above cost, or even higher, to turn a profit.

It helps, too, to offer merchandise that can be packaged inexpensively and mailed at relatively low cost.

More often than not, you can expect to lose some portion of your initial investment in any mail order advertisements you place. Yes, you may occasionally be lucky enough to break even, or perhaps to earn a small profit. Bear in mind that in many cases, you can still come out on top. You may be able to pull additional sales dollars from the bouncebacks, brochures, and other enclosures you should send out with the item(s) purchased. There's value, too, in the names and addresses of customers that you're accumulating; you can be sure that this growing mailing list will bring you more sales from future direct mailings. Of course, the merchandise you advertise in your enclosures need not carry high markups for you to be successful. Indeed, if you're advertising expensive articles in the first place, you'd probably be better off using the so-called two-step approach to sales. In step one, you advertise the merchandise and call for inquiries in your ad, rather than seek immediate orders. Step two would then involve sending out to those who respond a direct mail package designed to sell the item.

You should be able to boost your usual weekly or monthly sales figures from time to time by utilizing one of the more popular promotional techniques. Among others, these include leader pricing (offering an article at a price that's well below the item's customary selling price), promoting a two-for-one sale, giving a free premium along with a purchase, and offering introductory or quantity discounts.

SOURCES OF ADDITIONAL INFORMATION

Alarid, William, *Money Sources for Small Business.* Santa Monica, CA: Puma, 1991.

Coltman, Michael M., *Understanding Financial Information: The Non-Financial Manager's Guide,* (2d ed.). Bellingham, WA: Self-Counsel Press, 1990.

Goldstein, Arnold S., *Starting on a Shoestring: Building a Business Without a Bankroll,* (2d ed.). New York: Wiley, 1991.

Hayes, Rick Stephan, *Business Loans: A Guide to Money Sources and How to Approach Them,* (rev. ed.). New York: Wiley, 1989.

Monroe, Kent B., *Pricing: Making Profitable Decisions.* New York: McGraw-Hill, 1990.

Nagle, Thomas T., *The Strategy and Tactics of Pricing: A Guide to Profitable Decision Making.* Englewood Cliffs, NJ: Prentice-Hall, 1987.

O'Hara, Patrick D., *SBA Loans: A Step-by-Step Guide,* (2d ed.). New York: Wiley, 1994.

Seglin, Jeffrey L., *Financing Your Small Business.* New York: McGraw-Hill, 1990.

Simini, Joseph P., *Budgeting Basics for Nonfinancial Managers.* New York: Wiley, 1989.

6

Organizing Your Mail Order Enterprise

Now that you have some knowledge of the financial end of running a business, you need to begin thinking about administrative management. This chapter will help you to understand and clarify several important areas, among them:

- Which legal form of business to choose.
- How to set up your operations center.
- What to do about your inventions and copyrights.
- What kinds of insurance coverage to seek.
- What business records to keep—and for how long.

DECIDE ON YOUR LEGAL FORM OF OPERATION

Before launching your new mail order business, you'll need to choose a legal form of operation for the enterprise. There are three common forms of business ownership: the sole proprietorship, the partnership, and the corporation. Each of these forms has its attractions and its drawbacks. Consider the following details with care; they can help to shape your decision.

The Sole Proprietorship

The sole proprietorship is the most popular ownership form of all. That's because the sole proprietorship is the easiest and least expensive way to initiate a business enterprise.

If you plan to do business under your own name, all you need to do in most locales is start your operation. In some places, you may have to place an announcement of your intent to carry on business in the local newspaper, or, perhaps, register that intent with the local or county authorities. Most new business owners, however, tend to operate under a company or trade name. If you do, you'll have to file a certificate of conducting business under an assumed, or fictitious, name. The form you need to file is often referred to as a D/B/A (doing business as) form. See Exhibit 6–1 for a sample of the type of form you must file, usually with the county or city clerk.

The sole proprietorship gives you the widest possible latitude of all legal forms of business for making decisions (as well as mistakes). Moreover, as the owner, you get to keep all the profit (less taxes, of course).

A major disadvantage, though is that you can be held personally liable for business debts, should your firm not be able to pay off its obligations, or for judgments against the business awarded to people who sue you. There's no distinction at all made between you as an individual and you as the owner of a business. (The same is true of the partnership form.)

Sole proprietorship will also affect your income tax liabilities. For example, any money you earn at a job while operating a part-time enterprise will be added to your firm's profits to ascertain your total taxable income. This may put you into a higher tax bracket.

There are some other disadvantages to the sole proprietorship. Since you're in business by yourself, you won't have the benefit of partners to supplement your talents or help you do some of the work. Furthermore, investors generally shy away from contributing equity capital to a one-person business since it's somewhat dangerous to do. After all, should you get sick or die, the business becomes defunct, and their investment goes down the drain.

The Partnership

If at all possible, you should try to avoid taking on a partner. Although this form of ownership does have a few attractive qualities, too many partnerships end up in disagreement, at times quite violent. In a partnership, you split not only the profits and losses, but the work and all the decisions as well. This means you're not entirely your own boss, and that, at times, your partner may make decisions you don't like. Yet, you have to live by them, legally!

Why, then, you may ask, are there partnerships at all? Most often, they exist because more capital is needed initially to get the new business off the ground, and the would-be entrepreneur doesn't have enough of it. Other reasons for taking on one or more partners include (1) getting

EXHIBIT 6–1   Certificate of conducting business under an assumed name

X 201—Certificate of Conducting Business under an Assumed Name
For Individual, 11-88

Blumbergs
Law Products

JULIUS BLUMBERG, INC.,
PUBLISHER, NYC 10013

Business Certificate

I HEREBY CERTIFY *that I am conducting or transacting business under the name or designation*

of

at

City or Town of   *County of*   *State of New York.*

My full name is*
and I reside at

I FURTHER CERTIFY *that I am the successor in interest to*

the person or persons heretofore using such name or names to carry on or conduct or transact business.

IN WITNESS WHEREOF, *I have this*   *day of*   *19*   , *made
and signed this certificate.*

....

* Print or type name.
* If under 21 years of age, state "I am................years of age".

STATE OF NEW YORK
COUNTY OF   } *ss.:*

On this   *day of*   *19*   , *before me personally appeared*

to me known and known to me to be the individual   *described in and who executed the foregoing
certificate, and   he   thereupon*   *duly acknowledged to me that   he   executed the same.*

....

Source: Forms may be purchased from Julius Blumberg, Inc., New York, NY 10013, or any of its dealers. Reproduction
prohibited.

EXHIBIT 6–1   *(Continued)*

INDEX No.

Certificate
of

_____

_____

_____

_____

CONDUCTING BUSINESS UNDER
THE NAME OF

_____

_____

someone with skills you don't have but need, (2) because the work load is expected to be too heavy for one person, and (3) because the new business owner doesn't have the courage to go it alone.

When you start up a partnership, you'll most likely want to use a company name. So, you'll need to file a Certificate of Partners planning to conduct business under an assumed name (see Exhibit 6–2). You should also find a good attorney to prepare a formal partnership agreement before you go any further.

The Corporation

Most small businesspersons would do best to form a corporation at the outset, for three good reasons:

- Barring any fraudulent acts on your part, your personal holdings are not placed in jeopardy. You can't be held personally liable for the corporation's debts.

- This is the only *permanent* legal form of business. A corporation exists independently of its owners (the stockholders). Business continues, even though the shareholders come and go. Moreover, stock ownership itself is readily transferred.

- The corporation enjoys a more favorable income tax rate than the individual or partner, when your new company really starts to earn money.

Other features of the corporate form of ownership include the fact that banks and other lenders, as well as investors, are far more attracted to the corporation than to sole proprietorships or partnerships. This attitude stems from a mix of reasons: the corporation has its own "life," more owners are involved than in the other two forms of ownership, more capital is usually invested in the business, and so on. Another feature is that the corporation can raise capital by selling shares of stock from its treasury.

What about the disadvantages? The biggest single drawback is the so-called double taxation aspect. In addition to your paying income tax on your earnings from working in the business (salary, bonuses, and the like), the corporation must pay a corporate income tax on profits earned. If you're the major stockholder in the company and you have set it up in the first place, you may feel especially put out because of being hit twice in the wallet. And in many states, you have to pay state income tax from both directions, too!

Another disadvantage is that, of the three forms of business ownership, the corporation is the most closely scrutinized and highly regulated by the government. And record keeping is quite complex.

To open a corporation, you must file a certificate of incorporation in the state in which you plan to do business (with the Secretary of State). You also need to pay a fee to the state for incorporating and, annually,

EXHIBIT 6–2 Certificate for partners conducting business

X 74—Certificate of Conducting Business as Partners
Individual — Corporation. 12-88

© 1973 BY JULIUS BLUMBERG, INC.,
PUBLISHER, NYC 10013

Blumbergs
Law Products

Business Certificate for Partners

The undersigned do hereby certify that they are conducting or transacting business as members
of a partnership under the name or designation of

at

in the County of _____, State of New York, and do further certify that the full
names of all the persons conducting or transacting such partnership including the full names of all the
partners with the residence address of each such person, and the age of any who may be infants, are as
follows:

NAME Specify which are infants and state ages.   RESIDENCE

-------------------------------   -------------------------------
-------------------------------   -------------------------------
-------------------------------   -------------------------------
-------------------------------   -------------------------------
-------------------------------   -------------------------------
-------------------------------   -------------------------------

WE DO FURTHER CERTIFY that we are the successors in interest to

the person or persons heretofore using such name or names to carry on or conduct or transact business.

In Witness Whereof, We have this _____ day of _____ 19____ made
and signed this certificate.

State of New York, County of _____   ss.:   INDIVIDUAL ACKNOWLEDGMENT

On this _____ day of _____ 19____, before me personally appeared

to me known and known to me to be the individual described in, and who executed the foregoing
certificate, and he thereupon duly acknowledged to me that he executed the same.

Source: Forms may be purchased from Julius Blumberg, Inc., New York, NY 10013, or any of its dealers. Reproduction prohibited.

EXHIBIT 6-2 *(Continued)*

State of New York, County of   ss.:   CORPORATE ACKNOWLEDGMENT

On this   day of   19   , before me personally appeared

to me known, who being by me duly sworn, did depose and say, that   he resides in

that   he is the   of

the corporation described in and which executed the foregoing certificate; that   he knows the seal of said corporation; that the seal affixed to said certificate is such corporate seal; that it was so affixed by order of the Board of   of said corporation, and that   he signed h   name thereto by like order.

INDEX No.

Certificate of Partners

CONDUCTING BUSINESS UNDER THE NAME OF

State of New York, County of   ss.:   INDIVIDUAL ACKNOWLEDGMENT

On this   day of   19   , before me personally appeared

to me known and known to me to be the individual   described in, and who executed the foregoing certificate, and   he   thereupon   duly acknowledged to me that   he   executed the same.

another fee for conducting business in this form. We suggest you don't try to start a corporation yourself, despite the books and manuals you may see advertised as "doing it yourself." Have an attorney set up the corporation for you. (See Exhibit 6–3 for a sample certificate of incorporation.)

SETTING UP YOUR OPERATIONS CENTER

The modern air-conditioned office, tastefully furnished and well equipped, is, indeed, a delight to behold and to work in. But you would be ill-advised to set your own sights so high at this time. Stifle the impulse to rent office space and furnish it with desk, swivel chair, electronic self-correcting typewriter, and copying machine; not to speak of filing cabinets, cabinets, carpeting, pictures on the walls, and other refinements you might be tempted to install.

All this and more lies, we hope, in your future. But for today, and for next year as well, don't tie up any of your working capital in this fashion. You'll probably need it for more important things.

One of the more attractive aspects of mail order selling is that it demands so very little in the way of capital investment at the outset. You need be concerned with little more than these basics:

- A modest amount of work space.
- A table to work on.
- A comfortable chair.
- A few shelves (an old bookcase will do).
- Any kind of typewriter in good working condition, and a stand or table for it to rest on, at the proper height for you.
- Inexpensive supplies.
- A simple order-handling system.
- A filing system.

For many new mail order entrepreneurs, their first office begins at home—in the basement or garage, spare room, foyer, or the kitchen. If you start this way, you're already way ahead of the game. Even a small office may cost you $600 or $700 a month; that kind of rental easily amounts to $7,200 or $8,400 annually. If you're lucky enough to wind up your first year in the business with an exceptional bottom-line profit figure of, say, 15 percent of sales, you would have to reach something like $48,000 to $56,000 in sales that year just to pay for your office!

Here are the kinds of supplies you'll need for now:

- Writing tools—pens, pencils, a few marking pens.
- Stationery—letterheads, envelopes, carbon paper, postcards (for quick messages), 3 × 5 index cards, ordinary paper clips, some rubber bands.

EXHIBIT 6–3   Certificate of incorporation

Blumbergs
Law Products

A 234—Certificate of Incorporation
Business Corporation Law §402: 1-89

© 1975 BY JULIUS BLUMBERG, INC.
PUBLISHER, NYC 10013

Certificate of Incorporation of

under Section 402 of the Business Corporation Law

IT IS HEREBY CERTIFIED THAT:

(1) The name of the proposed corporation is

(2) The purpose or purposes for which this corporation is formed, are as follows, to wit:
To engage in any lawful act or activity for which corporations may be organized under the Business Corporation Law. The corporation is not formed to engage in any act or activity requiring the consent or approval of any state official, department, board, agency or other body.*

The corporation, in furtherance of its corporate purposes above set forth, shall have all of the powers enumerated in Section 202 of the Business Corporation Law, subject to any limitations provided in the Business Corporation Law or any other statute of the State of New York.

*If specific consent or approval is required delete this paragraph, insert specific purposes and obtain consent or approval prior to filing.

Source: Forms may be purchased from Julius Blumberg, Inc., New York, NY 10013, or any of its dealers. Reproduction prohibited.

EXHIBIT 6-3 *(Continued)*

(3) The office of the corporation is to be located in the County of
State of New York.

(4) The aggregate number of shares which the corporation shall have the authority to issue is

EXHIBIT 6-3   *(Continued)*

(5) The Secretary of State is designated as agent of the corporation upon whom process against it may be served. The post office address to which the Secretary of State shall mail a copy of any process against the corporation served upon him is

(6) A director of the corporation shall not be liable to the corporation or its shareholders for damages for any breach of duty in such capacity except for

(i) liability if a judgment or other final adjudication adverse to a director establishes that his or her acts or omissions were in bad faith or involved intentional misconduct or a knowing violation of law or that the director personally gained in fact a financial profit or other advantage to which he or she was not legally entitled or that the director's acts violated BCL § 719, or

(ii) liability for any act or omission prior to the adoption of this provision.

The undersigned incorporator, or each of them if there are more than one, is of the age of eighteen years or over.

IN WITNESS WHEREOF, this certificate has been subscribed on   19   by the undersigned who affirm(s) that the statements made herein are true under the penalties of perjury.

.... Type name of incorporator	.... Signature
.... Address	
.... Type name of incorporator	.... Signature
.... Address	
.... Type name of incorporator	.... Signature
.... Address	

EXHIBIT 6-3 *(Continued)*

Certificate of Incorporation

of

under Section 402 of the Business Corporation Law

Filed By:

Office and Post Office Address

- Advertising materials, as you develop them—circulars, folders, order forms, business reply envelopes.
- Order-handling materials—shipping labels (you can use stock labels available at your business stationer's), parcel post tape, postage stamps, several rubber stamps (name and address, variable date) and a stamp pad, pad of standard purchase orders.
- Filing cabinet—either a used one you can pick up for little money or several heavy cardboard or corrugated cartons of the right sizes.

BE SURE TO PATENT YOUR INVENTIONS

One way to assure a steady supply of unique products to sell by mail is to create your own. In that way, you need not fear competition. If you have an active imagination and a creative bent, you may be able to invent useful gadgets, tools, toys, and thingamajigs that people will want to buy. Or, you may write up or tape information that will answer needs not now being met by anyone else.

When you patent your inventions, you can exclude others from making or selling them for a period of 17 years, long enough to make yourself a small fortune if the items prove popular. You should seek professional assistance since a patent search is usually needed. File your application with the Commissioner of Patents and Trademarks, Washington, DC 20231. Costs include a filing fee, some printing charges, and a final fee to be paid.

COPYRIGHTING YOUR WORKS

Most of us are not inventors, but many of us can write or put together a printed piece. Under the old Copyright Act of 1909, publication and registration were the keys to obtaining statutory copyright. No longer is this true. Unpublished as well as published works are automatically protected by copyright. So long as the work has been fixed in a tangible form of expression—written, typed, recorded on tape or phonograph record, and so on—the copyright becomes the property of the author. Publication, however, has its advantages; the main benefit is that it establishes a public record of the copyright claim, which can be useful in infringement suits.

Under the Copyright Act of 1976, your protection begins at the time the piece is created and extends for your lifetime plus fifty years thereafter. For complete information, write to the Register of Copyrights, Library of Congress, Washington, DC 20559. Ask also for Form TX, the application form for published and unpublished nondramatic literary works. To register a work, you must send them a completed application, a check to cover the modest fee, and two copies of the work.

PROTECT YOUR ASSETS WITH AN INSURANCE PROGRAM

Like politics, the topic of insurance sparks both favorable and unfavorable comments, especially life or fire insurance. Some people make statements such as "I don't believe in it," "It's a big ripoff," or "The insurance companies get richer and richer." They'll gladly tell you how they hate to pay premiums, year after year, on their automobile or fire insurance policies, and never collect a dime. Of course, the premiums are always far too high.

Other people are "insurance happy"; they try to take out insurance against almost any eventuality, perhaps because they fear all sorts of dire consequences if they're not protected. Or perhaps because they're gamblers who like to play the odds.

Still others are somewhere in between these two extremes. They carry insurance that's within their means; they protect themselves against the kinds of perils that can seriously affect their finances; and they shy away from covering unimportant or insignificant aspects.

You DO Need Protection

You plan to invest both money and time in your new business. Shouldn't you want to protect your investment? Every business needs some types of insurance coverages. Some are truly essential, like fire and liability insurances, because losses in these areas can totally ruin your business (see Exhibit 6–4). You may want to consider other types because they have special application to your business, or to your personal situation, or because it makes sense for some other reason. Additional coverages become even more attractive as you begin to earn profits from your operation.

For a complete review, talk over your needs with a good insurance representative. Select someone locally, so that he or she will be available when you need to ask questions. Look for someone who is knowledgeable and who, preferably, has had experience insuring other mail order companies.

Exhibit 6–5 offers an overview of how to go about setting up your insurance program. Exhibit 6–6 provides some valuable hints on how to save money with your program.

Check into the pros and cons of these other types, too. Your insurance representative can readily point out their benefits:

- Business interruption insurance.
- Key person insurance.
- Crime insurance.
- Health and disability insurances (group).
- Business life insurance.

EXHIBIT 6–4 Essential insurance coverages

Fire Insurance. A basic fire insurance policy protects you against loss due to fire and lightning. For a small additional premium, you can extend this coverage to insure against dangers such as damage from windstorm, smoke, explosion, and other sources. (*Note:* The standard fire insurance policy doesn't cover the loss of money or securities, or deeds to property and other papers. For that protection, you'll need additional coverage.)

Liability insurance. Should someone be injured on your premises, or off your premises as well, due to negligence on your part, you may be sued. Judgments today can easily run into the hundreds of thousands of dollars (and more). This kind of policy will pay any judgments against you, defend you in court, pay medical and surgical expenses for the injured party, and more. The size of your premium will depend on the limit of liability you choose, on where you're located, the size of your premises, and other possible bases.

Vehicle Insurance. Because you need your car or truck to take your mailings and packages to the post office, you'll be using it for business purposes. Consequently, you'll need two types of vehicle coverage: (1) physical damage insurance, in the form of a comprehensive policy to protect your car or truck against the perils of fire or collision, for example, and (2) liability insurance to cover you in the event of damage to other vehicles, property, or persons caused by your vehicle. You should also note that this second type is necessary to cover any vehicles used in or for your business, even if they're not owned by you (or your corporation, if you have incorporated your mail order business). As an example, your employee uses his or her car to go to the bank for you, to transport some packages to the post office, or to pick up some office supplies. On the way, there's an accident; your employee damages someone else's car or, perhaps, injures another person. You can be sued.

Workers Compensation Insurance. If you have one or more employees working for your firm, you need to think about workers compensation insurance. Discuss this insurance with your insurance agent. You may be able to cut premium costs in using safety and loss prevention methods.

POINTERS ON KEEPING RECORDS

Few owners of small-scale enterprises enjoy doing the tedious paperwork necessary to maintain the firm's records not only for supporting tax claims but also for providing needed information for management decision making. Such people are generally much more attuned to action than to desk work. Yet, the proper handling of the financial aspects of your business is essential to its successful operation. By setting up your records properly at the outset, you'll be able to spot trends, pinpoint problem situations, and arrive at sensible decisions more easily.

EXHIBIT 6–5   Organizing your insurance program

A sound insurance protection plan is just as important to the success of your business as good financing, marketing, personnel management, or any other business function. And like the other functions, good risk and insurance management is not achieved by accident, but by organization and planning. A lifetime of work and dreams can be lost in a few minutes if your insurance program does not include certain elements. To make sure that you are covered, you should take action in four distinct ways:

1. Recognize the various ways you can suffer loss.

2. Follow the guides for buying insurance economically.

3. Organize your insurance management program.

4. Get professional advice.

Recognize the risks. The first step toward protection is to recognize the risks you face and make up your mind to do something about them. Wishful thinking or an it-can't-happen-to-me attitude won't lessen or remove the possibility that a ruinous misfortune may strike your business.

Some businesses will need coverages not mentioned in the checklist. For example, if you use costly professional tools or equipment in your business, you may need special insurance covering loss or damage to the equipment and/or business interruption resulting from not being able to use the equipment.

Study insurance costs. Before you purchase insurance, investigate the methods by which you can reduce the costs of your coverage. Be sure to cover the following points:

1. Decide which perils to insure against and how much loss you might suffer from each.

2. Cover your largest loss exposure first.

3. Use as high a deductible as you can afford.

4. Avoid duplication in insurance.

5. Buy in as large a unit as possible. Many of the "package policies" are very suitable for the types of small businesses they are designed to serve, and often they are the only way a small business can get really adequate protection.

6. Review your insurance program periodically to make sure that your coverage is adequate and your premiums are as low as possible consistent with sound protection.

Have a plan. To manage your insurance program for good coverage at the lowest possible cost, you will need a definite plan that undergirds the objectives of your business. Here are some suggestions for good risk and insurance management:

1. Write down a clear statement of what you expect insurance to do for your firm.

2. Select only one agent to handle your insurance. Having more than one spreads and weakens responsibility.

EXHIBIT 6–5 *(Continued)*

3. If an employee or partner is going to be responsible for your insurance program, be sure he understand his responsibility.

4. Do everything possible to prevent losses and to keep those that do occur as low as possible.

5. Don't withhold from your insurance agent important information about your business and its exposure to loss. Treat your agent as a professional helper.

6. Don't try to save money by underinsuring or by not covering some perils that could cause loss, even though you think the probability of their occurring is very small. If the probability of loss is really small, the premium will also be small.

7. Keep complete records of your insurance policies, premiums paid, losses, and loss recoveries. This information will help you get better coverage at lower costs in the future.

8. Have your property appraised periodically by independent appraisers. This will keep you informed as to just what your exposures are, and you will be better able to prove what your actual losses are if any occur.

Get professional advice about your insurance. Insurance is a complex and detailed subject. A professionally qualified agent, broker, or consultant can earn his fees many times over.

Source: Mark R. Greene, "Insurance Checklist for Small Business," *Small Marketers Aids No. 148* (Washington, DC: U.S. Small Business Administration, 1971), 13–15.

EXHIBIT 6–6 Saving on insurance costs

Before purchasing insurance, you should investigate various ways by which you can reduce the costs of your coverage. Among these are the following:

1. Decide which of the different kinds of risk protection will work best and most economically for you. Commercial insurance is only one of the means available for handling risks. . . . Investigate the other methods—such as loss prevention, self-insurance, noninsurance, risk transfer, and so forth—to see if they offer better coverage for your specific needs. Frequently, you will find that various methods working together will serve you best.

2. Cover your largest loss exposure first, the less severe or more frequent as your budget permits. Use your premium dollar where the protection need is greatest. Some firms insure their automobiles against collision, loss, but neglect to purchase adequate limits on their liability coverage. Collision losses seldom bankrupt a firm, but liability judgments often have.

(continued)

Source: Mark R. Green, "Insurance and Risk Management for Small Business," *Small Business Management Series No. 30,* 2d ed. (Washington, DC: U.S. Small Business Administration, 1970), 63–64.

EXHIBIT 6-6 *(Continued)*

3. Make proper use of deductibles. In many lines of insurance, full coverage is uneconomical because of the high cost of covering the "first dollar" of loss. But if you cannot afford a $1,000 loss, do not select a deductible of this amount. Rather, reduce the deductible to the amount you can afford.

   In many cases, however, the rate reduction for accepting a larger deductible will be very small. For example, increasing the waiting period from three months to six months for income disability coverage in group health insurance saves very little in premiums.

4. Review your insurance periodically. Renewing your policies automatically greatly increases the likelihood that you will fail to increase limits of liability where indicated, or that you will deprive yourself of a rate reduction possible when you remove some risk factor previously charged for. Periodic review saves you from insuring property you have disposed of or have written off as valueless. And you also avoid overlaps and gaps in coverage.

5. Check the market occasionally to see if you are getting your insurance for a reasonable price. You should not switch insurers each time a lower price is quoted, but you should keep aware of average costs for the amount and types of coverage you require.

6. Analyze insurance terms and provisions. When a firm attempts to save money by purchasing a "cheaper" policy, it sometimes discovers that the specific hazard it wanted to insure is not covered after all because of a technicality; or it learns that the insurer is able to offer a cheaper policy only by reducing services or following a niggardly claims policy. You should always attempt to see *why* you are saving money before you change insurers or policies.

7. Insure the correct exposure. One firm purchased coverage against equipment breakdown, but later found that defective design was the real cause of the trouble. Correcting the design removed the exposure. Another business bonded its employees who handled cash, but did not bond those who handled materials. One of the latter stole large amounts of merchandise, and the firm suffered an extensive and unrecoverable loss.

8. Investigate whether you can assume certain administrative duties required by your policies, such as reporting changing inventories for a commercial property policy. Usually, the amount you will save in premiums will more than offset the expense you will have in performing the service.

9. Buy your insurance in as large a unit as possible. Thus you will be able to take advantage of the savings most insurers allow for large-unit policies. This is particularly true of life insurance and of many types of property insurance. Usually, the more property included in a single policy, the cheaper it is for the insurer to handle.

Essential Records You'll Need to Maintain

For purposes of taxation, you may be surprised to learn that the federal government mandates no specific bookkeeping approach. If your mail order business will be run as a sole proprietorship, record keeping can be quite simple. Your basic needs will include a checkbook, records of both cash receipts and cash disbursements (payouts), and a petty cash record. You must record all sales, and everything you pay out as well. If possible, cash disbursements should be made by check so that your checkbook can become your record of disbursements, especially if each check stub carries all the details: the firm to which it has been issued, the kind of expense (for merchandise, stationery, and so on), the number of the invoice paid, and the like.

Some items don't warrant making out a check. An example might be when you buy a roll of parcel post tape or a couple of typewriter ribbons at a local stationer's. These and other little items might be paid out of your petty cash fund. Each time you tap the petty cash box, be sure to fill out a slip on which you note the reason for the purchase as well as the amount taken out.

You should find a competent accountant at the outset, preferably one who has had some experience with mail order companies. This professional will advise you on how your books should be set up, not only for tax reasons but also to help you keep on top of what's going on in your business. Your accountant can teach you how to make all entries on a daily basis and handle things yourself until your operation has grown in size to the point where you may want to consider hiring a part-time bookkeeper.

A discussion of the principles of bookkeeping is beyond the scope of this book. However, both simplified one-book systems and other double-entry bookkeeping approaches, complete with instructions, may be readily purchased at a business stationery store.

Other Records to Keep

Even under the simple bookkeeping approach mentioned earlier, you may need to maintain additional records, depending on the size and type of business you operate. Among these other records can be:

- Payroll records—if you have employees.
- Accounts receivable records, generally kept together in one ledger—if you sell goods or services on credit.
- Records of your firm's assets, depreciation schedules, and insurance coverages.
- Copies of previous years' tax returns.
- Legal documents.

EXHIBIT 6–7 Records retention

Accounting Records

Journals, Ledgers, Registers: As the basic accounting summary, the general ledger should be retained indefinitely. Books of original entry, such as the cash receipts book and the cash disbursements book, should be retained for at least six years. They would be essential, for example, to support challenged items on income tax returns.

Accounts Payable (canceled checks, vouchers): Canceled general checks should be kept for the number of years required by your state's Statute of Limitations. Such laws range from three to twenty years and average six years. Many companies keep payroll checks for only three years. Vouchers may be divided into plant vouchers (retain indefinitely) and petty cash vouchers (retain for one to two years).

Accounts Receivable (billing copies of invoices, credit-memo invoices, accounts receivable ledger): Your chief concern is the unpaid invoices. Paid invoices often may be disposed of within three to four years because few complaints are received after that time. Your accounts receivable ledger—as a basic summary of credit sales—need be kept only so long as it is a ready index to invoices or total daily sales.

Tax Records: These are important, since they may be audited by local, state, and federal taxing authorities. For sales and use taxes most states and local jurisdictions require that the tax return forms be retained three years. After that, these jurisdictions would ordinarily not conduct an audit of the return. State and federal income tax returns and the records which back up the figures on the tax returns should be kept at least six years. The Statute of Limitations which applies to normal tax returns may be extended if the taxing authorities can prove the tax returns to have been fraudulently prepared.

Legal Papers

A small business may have many other types of records which should be kept for legal reasons. Some of them are evidences of ownership and, for that reason, are assets that should be guarded zealously while they have value. Typically, a copyright, a letter of patent, and a trademark registration should be kept indefinitely even though they have a definite expiration date. The possibility of having to prove ownership of such assets in law suits may arise even after the ownership has expired. Similarly, deeds and right-of-way and easement records should be kept indefinitely. Contracts and leases, on the other hand, can be destroyed six years after they expire (unless renewed annually). Records on law suits should be retained from six to ten years after they are settled.

When a business is a corporation, its bylaws, minutes of stockholders' meetings, and annual reports are usually retained indefinitely. Canceled stock certificates, except for those corporations regulated by the Securities and Exchange Commission, may be destroyed at the discretion of the company as long as a record of such destruction is

EXHIBIT 6-7   *(Continued)*

kept (ten years as a general rule). Since corporations are governed by some state agency, it is a good idea to check with the appropriate agency to see that the records being kept are the proper ones.

Payroll and Personnel Records

Information on employee wages and hours must be retained for three years to comply with the Fair Labor Standards Act. The records do not have to be kept on any particular form. Supporting data, such as timecards and piecework tickets, need to be kept only two years. Microfilm copies of such documents are generally acceptable.

Payroll records, which include wage payments and deductions for federal income taxes and Social Security, must be retained for at least four years after the tax becomes due or is paid, whichever is later. You should check your state and local authorities because some of these jurisdictions require that payroll records be kept longer than four years.

Pension records should be retained at least a year after the death of the pensioner. *Personnel records*, such as employee applications, however, can be retained according to your needs.

Production Records

Production records, such as job tickets, production orders, maintenance records, and operating reports, have a short life as far as retention is concerned. Job tickets can be discarded after a job is completed; the production order may be retained one year or longer. If a company is audited, all production records should be kept until the audit is completed. *Maintenance records* are kept usually for the life of the equipment on which the data are compiled.

Purchasing (purchase orders, requisitions, and receiving reports): Major purchase records, particularly where specifications are included, should be kept for six years. Routine items may be cut to three years and still be within legal requirements for tax purposes on proof of cash and charge purchases of supplies and other items used in the business. Purchase requisitions are usually supporting documents for the accounts payable vouchers and are retained accordingly.

Traffic (bills of lading, freight bills, packing lists): The only legal requirement on these items is by the Department of Labor, Wage and Hour and Public Contracts Divisions, on "order, shipping and billing records" and calls for retention for two years.

Source: Robert A. Shiff, "Records Retention: Normal and Disaster," *Management Aids No. 210* (Washington, DC: U.S. Small Business Administration, September 1973 reprint).

Corporations are a special case. More paperwork is required; for example, you'll need to keep records of the minutes of stockholder meetings, among other things.

For further details on record keeping, refer to Exhibit 6–7. This deals with the important subject of records retention, or how long records of different types should be kept on file.

SOURCES OF ADDITIONAL INFORMATION

Barber, Hoyt L., *Copyrights, Patents, and Trademarks: Protect Your Rights Worldwide.* Blue Ridge Mountain, PA: TAB Books, 1989.

Brody, David Eliot, *Business and Its Legal Environment.* Lexington, MA: D.C. Heath, 1986.

Davidson, Robert L., *The Small Business Incorporation Kit.* New York: Wiley, 1992.

_____ , *The Small Business Partnership Kit.* New York: Wiley, 1992.

Foster, Frank H. and Robert L. Shook, *Everything You Need to Know about Patents, Copyrights, and Trademarks.* New York: Wiley, 1989.

Goldstein, Arnold S. and Robert L. Davidson III, *Starting Your Subchapter "S" Corporation,* (2d ed.). New York: Wiley, 1992.

Green, Mark R., James S. Trieschmann, and Sandra G. Gustavson, *Risk and Insurance,* (8th ed.). Cincinnati: South-Western, 1991.

Hancock, William A., *The Small Business Legal Advisor,* (2d ed.). New York: McGraw-Hill, 1992.

Kaliski, Burton S. and Peter F. Meggison, *Management of Administrative Office Systems,* (2d ed.). San Diego, CA: Harcourt Brace Jovanovich, 1988.

Krevolin, Nathan, *Records/Information Management and Filing.* Englewood Cliffs, NJ: Prentice-Hall, 1986.

Lieberman, Jethro K., *The Legal Environment of Business.* San Diego, CA: Harcourt Brace Jovanovich, 1989.

Mehr, Robert I., *Fundamentals of Insurance,* (2d ed.). Homewood, IL: Irwin, 1986.

Perline, Neil, *The Small Business Guide to Computers and Office Automation.* Chicago: Dearborn, 1990.

Roberson, Cliff, *The Businessperson's Legal Advisor,* (2d ed.). Blue Ridge Mountain, PA: TAB Books, 1990.

Automation Alert: Go on Computer as Soon as You Can!

Within months after launching your operation, you'll find yourself accumulating vast quantities of information. To make life easier for you, purchase a personal computer (PC), some useful software, a printer, and a box of computer paper.

USING OUTSIDE ELECTRONIC DATA PROCESSING SERVICES

Up to the 1980s, most small- and medium-sized firms of all kinds relied on data processing services to manage their bookkeeping, payroll, inventory, and other information. Before then, computers were extremely costly to purchase and install. In general, the firm had two choices: sign up with a computer service bureau or get into timesharing. Under the first choice, the firm would have to pay a one-time set-up charge and, thereafter, a monthly retainer. Under the second, a terminal would be installed on the firm's premises and hooked up via telephone with the computer at the data processing company. The firm would pay a terminal rental fee and, in addition, would be charged for the number of hours the computer would be in use.

Nowadays, the small firm has a third choice, an avenue that opened up with the appearance and subsequent evolution of the microcomputer. Today's microcomputers, also known as desk-top or personal computers (PCs), cost much less than those of the early 1980s. User-friendly, they're exceptionally easy to understand and operate. Moreover, they can handle thousands of times more information and work much faster than those early machines.

You can even buy a powerful laptop computer, weighing no more than a few pounds, to carry along with you on business trips or vacations, or take home with you from your workplace at night or over the weekend.

WHAT A PERSONAL COMPUTER (PC) CAN DO FOR YOU

You can benefit greatly by using your new PC for many important, and often tedious, chores. Here are some examples:

- Address envelopes and print mailing labels.
- Analyze customer records by kinds of merchandise (or services) ordered, dates of purchases, amounts spent, and other criteria.
- Announce special sales and other promotions.
- Bill customers.
- Conduct many types of useful analyses (cash flow, merchandise movement, advertising or direct mail results, and so on).
- Create and print whatever business forms you may need.
- Design and print sales letters, order forms, flyers, and other printed promotional material.
- Do your payroll and print up paychecks.
- Draft and print all your correspondence.
- File and maintain employee records.
- Generate sales, expense, promotion, and other types of budgets.
- Keep the firm's books.
- Merge mailing lists and purge duplicates from them.
- Organize, store, and continually update mailing lists.
- Plan and control all inventories: merchandise, supplies, components, and others.
- Prepare and print up purchase orders.
- Produce both pro forma and actual operating statements and balance sheets as you need them and uncover all deviations from budgeted figures.
- Sell your goods and/or services through a telemarketing program.[1]
- Turn out a series of collection letters.
- Work up schedules for your mail order advertising and direct mail campaigns.

---

[1] See Chapter 19 for an extended treatment of telemarketing.

HARDWARE AND SOFTWARE CHOICES ABOUND

Computers

Many brands and models of personal computers are available; those mentioned in this section represent no more than a sampling of the types you can find readily at department stores, discount houses, and computer superstores. Today's PCs come equipped with hard disks that carry from 80 to 620 megabytes or more of information. As of this printing, for a 486-processor, top-quality computer with monitor, you'll be paying between $1,000 and $3,000, depending on the "bells and whistles" you want to include. You'll also discover that many software programs are already installed on the hard disk. In addition to word processing software, a dictionary, and a spelling checker, you're likely to find complete accounting and other useful programs for the small business (such as Quicken or MYOB)—and perhaps even a complete 21-volume encyclopedia.

Here are some examples:

- ACERPower 486DX2.
- AMBRA S450DX; DP60PCI.
- APPLE Performa 460; 476; 600/CD.
- COMPAQ Prolinea 486DX.
- DELL Dimension XPSP60.
- IBM PS/1 Advisor 2133-M46.
- LEADING EDGE 486SX.
- PACKARD BELL Axcel 2018 Multi-Media.

Laptop/Notebook Computers

Also available are a growing number of smaller, though quite powerful, computers that weigh no more than a few pounds. Portable and battery-powered, these machines are helpful supplementary aids, especially for the traveler or vacationer. Among the more popular ones are the:

- ACERNote 760ci 486DX2.
- COMPAQ Concerto 4/25.
- GATEWAY 2000 ColorBook.
- IBM ThinkPad 500/85.
- PACKARD BELL Statesman Plus 200C.
- SHARP PC-8650 II.
- TOSHIBA T1960CS; T1960CT.
- WINBOOK XP.

Printers

The older, familiar daisy-wheel printers have been supplanted by newer technology. Nowadays, most printers fall into one of three categories, each operating on a different principle: dot-matrix, ink-jet, and laser printers.

Dot Matrix Printer

Least expensive of the three types is the dot-matrix printer. Prices range from slightly less than $200 to as much as $400 for a machine that prints between 250 and 350 cps (characters-per-second) in draft mode and from 60 to 200 or so cps for near-quality printing. In a printer of this type, tiny pins in the print head are made to strike a ribbon; their action creates dots that, in turn, forms letters and graphics on the paper positioned behind the ribbon. Examples of dot-matrix machines include:

- CITIZEN GSX 230; GSC 240.
- EPSON AP 500 PLUS; AP 2250.
- IBM PPS II 2391.
- PANASONIC KX P2624; KX P2123.

Ink-Jet Printers

These machines operate on a rather unusual modification of the dot-matrix printer. Replacing the tiny pins in the print head are minute nozzles through which ink (from a cartridge within the machine) is jetted directly against the paper, thus circumventing the need for a ribbon. Today's prices for these printers range from $200 to $600. Here are some examples:

- APPLE StyleWriter II.
- CANON Bubble Jet BJ-2000e.
- EPSON HP Deskjet 520.
- IBM 4070IJ; ExecJet 4072-001.

Laser Printers

The most sophisticated of all printers at this point and the one that offers the highest quality printing is the laser printer. These machines print information at the rate of some 4 to 6 pages a minute and in various typefaces. Be prepared, however, to spend between $500 and $900 for one of the printers indicated below:

- APPLE Personal Laserwriter 300.
- EPSON AL-1500.
- HEWLETT-PACKARD Laserjet 4L; Laserjet 111P.
- IBM 4019.
- OKIDATA Laser 400E.
- PANASONIC KX 4430; KX P4410.

Helpful Software

Software is a collective term for the programs that provide computers with operating instructions for performing tasks. Thousands of software programs of every type and description are available. Like most other enterprises, you'll need one or two basic programs to help you run your operation more efficiently. A mail order business, however, has some special, additional needs as well.

The main categories of software you may want to acquire for your new computer are listed below, along with specific examples in each category. (*Note:* Where not obvious, the software source is identified in parenthesis immediately following the name.)

- **Accounting, bookkeeping, payroll**
  DacEasy Accounting
  Mind Your Own Business (Teleware)
  One-Write Plus Accounting Works (MECA)
  Peachtree Accounting
  Quicken, QuickBooks (Intuit)
  Star Network Accounting

- **Inventory management**
  Inventory Management (Argos)
  MailOrderManager (Dydacomp)
  Response Ltd. (Colinear)
  WordStar (Hewlett-Packard)

- **Graphics**
  Adobe Photoshop
  ClipArt Gallery (Activision)
  Design Studio (Manhattan Graphics)
  Express Publisher (Power Up!)
  Freelance Graphics (Lotus)
  GraphicsWorks (Mindscape)
  Harvard Graphics (Software)
  Microsoft PowerPoint
  PageMaker (Aldus)
  PagePlus (Serif)
  Print Shop Deluxe (Broderbund)
  Publish It! (Timeworks)

- **List management/mailing systems**
  ArcList (Group I)
  Avery List and MailPlus

Business Mail (Arc Tangent)
FastPak Mail (Bloc)
FastTrack (SoftServe)
File Force (ACIUS)
MailList (Artworx)
MailMiser (Kestrel Enterprises)
Mass Mailer (Alternative)
MBM Mail Business Manager (Metagroup)
MyMailList (MySoftware)
OmniMailer (Jamac)
PACE Mailing List System
Post Save (Accurate)
Professional Mail (Art Tangent)

- **Database management**
  Easy Order (MicroTyme)
  FileMaker Pro
  MyDataBase (MySoftware)
  Paradox (Borland)
  Pushbutton Works for Windows
  Q&A (Symantec)
  Workswizard (Microsoft)

- **Fulfillment**
  Easy Order (MicroTyme)
  Mail Order Wizard (The Haven)
  Response Ltd. (Colinear)
  Target-Sales (Target)

- **Telemarketing**
  ACT! (Symantec)
  Action+Plus
  Contact Caller (Stok)
  Procomm Plus (Datastorm)
  Smartcom Executive (Hayes)
  TeleInsight (Customer Insight)
  TeleMagic (Appentec)
  Telephone Delivery System (Early, Cloud)
  TMS Telemktg System (National)
  Totall Manager (Automation)

HOW TO DEVISE AN EFFICIENT DATABASE

In time, your company's database will become your strongest operating asset. Be sure to organize it properly from the beginning. If you can, enter all appropriate information every day or at least as soon as practicable. Update your files continually; weed out duplicate data; make every change as it comes up. Keep detailed production records on each and every mailing—and on all your print and air media advertising.

For your consumer database, enter:

- Name, address, and telephone number.
- Date of purchase.
- Total amount of purchase.
- Items purchased.
- Quantities purchased.
- Styles, colors, sizes, and other variants.
- Complaints.
- Returned goods and dollar value.
- Cumulative amount of purchases made.
- Demographic information: sex, age, marital status, number of children, income level, educational level, and so on.
- Particular likes and dislikes.
- Other information as needed.

For organizations, enter:

- Name of organization.
- Address and main telephone number.
- Type of organization.
- Size of organization.
- Individual to contact.
- Title of that person.
- Department.
- Trade discount given.
- Date of purchase.
- Total amount of purchase.
- Items purchased.
- Quantities purchased.
- Styles, colors, sizes, and other variants.
- Credit information.
- Returned goods and dollar value.
- Frequency of purchases.

- Cumulative amount of purchases made.
- Company profile information.
- Specific customer needs.
- Other information as needed.

SOURCES OF ADDITIONAL INFORMATION

Anis, Nick, *PC User's Guide.* Berkeley, CA: Osborne-McGraw, 1991.

Burns, James R. and Darrel Eubanks, *Microcomputers: Business and Personal Applications.* San Francisco: Western, 1988.

Cassel, Don, *Computers Made Easy.* Englewood Cliffs, NJ: Prentice-Hall, 1984.

Desautel, Edouard J., *Understanding and Using Computers.* Dubuque, IA: Wm. C. Brown, 1989.

Dologite, Dorothy G. and R.J. Mockler, *Using Computers,* (3rd ed.). Englewood Cliffs, NJ: Prentice-Hall, 1991.

Elwood, Brian C., *Introduction to Personal Computers,* (2d ed.). Palmyra, NE: BCS, 1993.

Hoskins, Jim, *IBM Personal Systems: A Business Perspective,* (6th ed.). New York: Wiley, 1993.

Kraynak, Joe, *The Complete Idiot's Guide to PCs.* Carmel, IN: Alpha Books, 1993.

LeDoux, John C., *The Computer Tutor: A Manager's Guide to Using Personal Computers.* Amherst, MA: Human Resources Development, 1991.

Lewis, Colin, *Essence of Personal Computing.* Englewood Cliffs, NJ: Prentice-Hall, 1991.

McComb, Gordon, *Executive Guide to PCs.* New York: Bantam, 1988.

The Software Encyclopedia, 1993. New Providence, NJ: R.R. Bowker, 1993.

Wollman, J., *Computer Workplace.* New York: McGraw-Hill, 1985.

Promotion: Your Master Key to Sales Growth

You have just started a brand-new mail order operation. As you no doubt realize, a newly launched business of any kind represents an unknown cipher to the general public. To begin selling your products and/or services, you must reach your target market(s) just as quickly as you can. You'll need to communicate with prospective buyers to get them to know your company and what you have to offer, and to sample your wares. You can accomplish all this through *promotion*.

Promotion is communication, pure and simple: deliberate and purposive communication designed to attain specific objectives. In your new situation, your immediate goals will be to tell your story; to locate, interest, and persuade customers to buy from you; to consummate sales; and, thereby, to earn profit for yourself.

THE MARKETING MIX

Marketing professionals can work only with those elements of company operation over which they can exercise some control; when grouped, these elements constitute a company's *marketing mix*. The four key components of the marketing mix are:

- Products and/or services.
- Pricing.

101

- Promotion.
- Distribution.

The Promotion Mix

One of the four major areas of activity in the marketing of goods and services, promotion is purposeful, goal-oriented communication that aims at informing, persuading, and reminding potential buyers as well as present customers about your organization, your products and services, your pricing approaches, and your method(s) of distribution.

Promotion is a complex of four different sets of goal-oriented communication activity; hence the popular use by marketers of the term *promotion mix*. The four categories of promotional activity are personal selling, advertising, sales promotion, and publicity/public relations.

Promotional Objectives

An organization has a wide selection of promotional goals to choose from. Here are some of the more common objectives of a promotion:

- To announce upcoming promotions.
- To arouse interest in a company's products and/or services.
- To attract new buyers.
- To differentiate a firm from those of competitors.
- To expand distribution.
- To foster customer loyalty.
- To help build a favorable company image.
- To increase sales.
- To inform prospective buyers about a company's offerings.
- To introduce a new product or service.
- To persuade people to buy.
- To popularize the firm's name.
- To provide information.
- To retain present customers.
- To revive lost accounts.
- To sell a product or service.
- To sell more to customers.
- To smooth the way for a salesperson to make a sale.
- To stimulate interest in a company and its products and/or services.

Elements in the Promotion Mix

It might be helpful at this point to offer brief definitions of three of the four components of the promotion mix: personal selling, advertising, and sales promotion. Additional information regarding sales promotion as well as a more extensive treatment of the fourth component (public relations/publicity) immediately follow the definitions. Later on in the book, you'll find separate chapters devoted to personal selling and advertising.

Personal Selling. Promotional activity that seeks to consummate sales of goods or services through oral communication on a person-to-person basis.

Advertising. Promotional activities paid for by individuals or organizations that involve communicating with numbers of prospective buyers and/or present customers about products and/or services through one or more of the advertising media.

Sales Promotion. This complex promotional area embraces just about every type of communication with customers, present or potential, that an organization can bring into play to stimulate sales—other than those involved in personal selling, advertising, and public relations/publicity.

PROMOTOOLS: THE TOOLS OF SALES PROMOTION

Here are the more familiar sales promotion tools used by business organizations:

Advertising Specialties. Inexpensive promotional items that bear the firm's name and/or a brief message and that are distributed free of charge to prospective and present customers.

Contests and Games. Many varieties of these can be used to generate considerable excitement and stimulate purchasing. Prizes, in the form of cash, articles of merchandise, or services are awarded to winners.

Coupons. A printed certificate, generally used to induce a prospect to try a new item at a savings from the regular selling price.

Demonstrations. Showing a product in use generates considerable interest and creates excitement. Most often seen in retail stores, this technique can be used advantageously by direct marketing firms in television commercials and in videocassettes distributed to prospective buyers.

Displays. When reproduced in magazine advertisements or shown in television commercials, attractive displays readily capture the attention of readers or viewers, arouse their interest, and help persuade prospects to buy.

Early-Bird and Preseason Sales. Off-price promotions designed to stimulate business in advance of an upcoming season or when business is slow.

Endorsements. Testimonials that have been submitted by satisfied buyers, when included in print advertisements, radio and television commercials, and promotional mailings, attract more attention to the advertised offer and cause the reader or viewer to place more trust in the claims made by the advertiser.

Exhibits and Shows. Useful, though sometimes quite expensive, promotional activities that not only gain public attention and arouse considerable interest in products and/or services but also provide good publicity for the firm.

Informative Literature. Leaflets, pamphlets, booklets, and other printed matter that are distributed for a variety of reasons; for example: instructions for putting together knocked-down furniture; directions for the use of equipment (tools, VCRs, cameras, and so on); descriptions of specialty goods; and the like.

Premiums. Articles of merchandise given to shoppers either free of charge or at a reduced selling price for various purposes, for example: to encourage customers to purchase another item or to continue patronizing an establishment, to introduce a new product, to reward buyers for referring other customers to them, and so on.

PMs ("Push Money"). Also called "spiffs," PMs are modest sums awarded to salespeople for pushing particular products or brands, overstocked goods, or slow-moving items.

Refunds and Rebates. Small sums of money returned to customers that effectively reduce the regular selling prices of specified articles of merchandise.

Sampling. This involves the delivery of merchandise to prospective buyers, in person or by mail, to encourage them to try new and/or unusual products. Once an extremely popular promotional tool, sampling has largely been replaced over the past several decades by couponning.

Special Promotional Events. In this category are various types of sales (clearance, seasonal, manager's, preholiday, and so on), grand-opening and anniversary events, cooperative promotions with other organizations, and the like.

Trade Discounts. Allowances offered to wholesale and retail distributors to compensate them for the work they do in facilitating the movement of goods and services through marketing channels to the final customers.

Trade-In Promotions. Cash discounts off the regular retail prices of specified new articles of merchandise offered to buyers who turn in an old item of the same kind.

Trading Stamps. Stamps distributed to customers when they make purchases; these may be accumulated and eventually exchanged for goods or services.

PUBLIC RELATIONS AND PUBLICITY

In the final analysis, the success of any new business will hinge to a considerable extent on its management's ability to set up, and effectively maintain, clearcut lines of communication with the firm's "publics."

The fourth element of the promotional mix is *public relations* (or, more simply, PR). Some marketing professionals regard PR as falling within the sales promotion classification. Many more prefer to assign PR to the advertising category, for it seems to be more closely aligned with media advertising than with the other two major elements of the mix. Like advertising, PR aims at forwarding messages to large numbers of consumers. It differs from advertising, however, in that it is free and not paid for, as is advertising.

Public relations has been defined as:

A wide range of activities expressive of the firm's attitudes toward others. In the main, it consists of meaningful, two-way communication between the company and its many publics: internal (employees, stockholders) as well as external (customers and prospective customers, suppliers, competitors, government agencies, and so on).[1]

The principal purpose behind a company's PR efforts is to influence its publics favorably, to cultivate goodwill toward the firm. Thus, you'll need to develop an effective PR program for your new mail order enterprise—or, perhaps, several PR programs, one for each public. Of course, your public relations activities must be founded on such basic premises as:

- Selling merchandise or services that fulfill consumers' (or organizations') needs.
- Charging prices that are proper and commensurate with the quality of the merchandise or service you offer.
- Being scrupulously honest and fair at all times with your customers.
- Handling all complaints promptly and to the buyer's complete satisfaction.
- Offering a full money-back guarantee on every purchase.

Keeping Customers Informed

It's helpful to prepare PR programs for half a year at a time, and at least two months or so in advance. Detail what you plan to do on a month-by-month basis. As much as you can, tie the details into your overall promotional plans. You'll need to tell others about your firm: where you are and what you stand for, your regular line of merchandise/service(s), new goods or services you intend to add, warranties and guarantees, planned growth/expansion (if any), and other "stories" that may be of interest to others. You should also strive to be active within the community where

---

[1] *The Small Business Handbook,* (rev. ed.) © 1994 by Irving Burstiner. Reprinted by permission of Simon & Schuster, Inc.

your business is located. Join community organizations. Participate in community affairs, and encourage your employees to do the same.

News Releases

Whatever positive publicity you can garner can only help your business to grow. The cornerstone of every PR program is the news, or publicity, release. Newsworthy stories should be capably written and forwarded without delay to the media. Here are a few suggestions for preparing these releases:

- Use good quality, white bond company stationery (8½ × 11 inches) for all news releases.
- Type neatly on only one side of the page, with no misspelled words or erasures.
- Submit complete stories. Make sure that they answer the Five W's: Who? What? Where? When? Why?
- Begin by entering your name, title, and telephone number so that the editor who receives the release can call you if he or she has any questions or wishes to find out more details.
- If the story may be used at once, type the words "For Immediate Release" above the copy. Otherwise, substitute the phrase "Hold for Release on" and follow this with the date (and, perhaps, time).
- If the news release runs to more than one page, type the word "MORE" at the bottom of each page except the final page.
- Specify the end of the news release by typing the number "30" below the last line of the text.

BUDGETING FOR PROMOTION

When planning its annual promotion budget, company management can avail itself of a number of different approaches. Among the more popular procedures are:

- Various arbitrary approaches.
- The meet-the-competition method.
- The percentage-of-sales approach.
- The objective-and-task technique.

Arbitrary Approaches

The use of arbitrary and illogical methods of devising promotion budgets is common practice across much of industry and commerce. One popular version is the so-called *status-quo approach,* where management simply decides to limit next year's budget to what it plans to spend on promotional activity this year. A variation on this theme is to add or subtract some percentage of the status-quo budget according to management's thinking (or, more often, feelings!) about whether next year's revenues will be higher or lower than this year's sales. There's also the "let's spend only what we can afford" school; a company that subscribes to this view will budget only as much as management believes it can afford to allocate to its promotion mix. Generally, the final budget figure amounts to what remains available after all other projected business expenditures are totaled.

The Meet-the-Competition Method

When employing this technique management first tries to determine approximately how much its closest competitor spends during the year on all forms of promotional activity. It will then decide to spend as much, or perhaps more, in order to "meet and beat the competition."

The Percentage-of-Sales Approach

This method appears to be the most popular of all budget-setting techniques, probably because the principle behind it is easy to understand and the method itself so convenient. Never mind the fact that the percentage-of-sales approach doesn't seem to make much sense inasmuch as it puts the cart before the horse by tying the promotion budget to company revenues (a cause-and-effect relationship), rather than adopt the more logical thought that promotional activity should create sales.

To establish your promotion budget using this approach, follow this five-step procedure:

1. Total all of the prior year's promotional expenditures (for personal selling, advertising, sales promotion, and public relations/publicity). Be sure to include your expenses for telemarketing, if you operate this type of program.
2. Add up your sales figures for all of last year.
3. Calculate last year's promotion-to-sales ratio by dividing your total expenditures by your total sales.
4. Arrive at as close an estimate as you can for the upcoming year's sales volume.
5. Using the promotion-to-sales ratio you obtained in step 3, work out the total dollar amount of your new promotion budget.

The Objective-and-Task Technique

Known also as the "job estimation method," this is perhaps the only thoroughly logical approach to setting a promotion budget. In essence, it involves choosing specific goals to be met, determining what needs to be done to attain those objectives, and then budgeting sufficient funds to do the job.

Yes, there are problems in using this technique. For one thing, it's difficult enough to select suitable goals, let alone ascertain how to go about reaching them. A high level of planning expertise is required; often, this expertise is not available in many small- and medium-sized companies.

PREPARE A YEAR-LONG PROMOTION SCHEDULE

A helpful practice is to prepare, with the aid of a calendar, a promotion schedule for the coming year. To get started, set aside four blank sheets of paper; these will be your planning worksheets. At the top of each page, write the name of one of the four components of the promotion mix: "Personal Selling," "Advertising," "Sales Promotion," and "Public Relations/Publicity."

Begin your planning by deciding what percentage of next year's promotion budget you'll spend on all personal selling activities. (You'll need this information for control purposes.) Then, calculate the dollar value of that percentage and enter both figures on the page directly below the title. Continue the same procedure with the remaining pages.

Your next step is to subdivide further each of the four categories. When you do this, be sure to add more pages as needed. As an example, if you begin writing down your "Direct Mail" plans on the single Advertising worksheet you prepared, you may then require a minimum of four additional pages—for "Newspapers," "Magazines," "Radio," and "Television."

Work on each element one at a time. Always keeping in mind your budgetary limitations, prepare plans for each of the subcategories; include activities planned, timing of those activities (inclusive dates when they will be conducted), approximate costs, media involved, and the like. Conclude your planning with a detailed, month-by-month promotion schedule for the year.

SOURCES OF ADDITIONAL INFORMATION

Bacon, Mark S., *Do-It-Yourself Direct Marketing: Secrets for Small Business.* New York: Wiley, 1991.

Baker, Kim and Sunny Baker, *How to Promote, Publicize, and Advertise Your Growing Business.* New York: Wiley, 1991.

Bly, Robert W., *Targeted Public Relations.* New York: Henry Holt and Company, 1993.

Bovee, Courtland and William F. Arens, *Contemporary Advertising*, (3rd ed.). Homewood, IL: Irwin, 1989.

Coppett, John I. and William A. Staples, *Professional Selling: A Relationship Management Process.* Cincinnati: South-Western, 1990.

Cummings, Richard, *Contemporary Selling*. San Diego, CA: Harcourt Brace Jovanovich, 1987.

Davidson, Jeffrey P., *Marketing to Home-Based Businesses*. Homewood, IL: Business One Irwin, 1991.

Dennison, Dell and Linda Tobey, *The Advertising Handbook*. Bellingham, WA: Self-Counsel Press, 1991.

Fletcher, Tana and Julia Rockler, *Getting Publicity*. Bellingham, WA: Self-Counsel Press, 1990.

Futrell, Charles M., *ABC's of Selling*, (4th ed.). Homewood, IL: Irwin, 1993.

Hair, Joseph F., Francis L. Notturno, and Frederick A. Russ, *Effective Selling*, (8th ed.). Cincinnati: South-Western, 1991.

Hausman, Carl and Philip Benoit, *Positive Public Relations*, (2d ed.). Blue Ridge Mountain, PA: TAB Books, 1990.

Holtz, Herman, *The Direct Marketer's Workbook*. New York: Wiley, 1986.

Jugenheimer, Donald W. and Gordon E. White, *Basic Advertising*. Cincinnati: South-Western, 1991.

McIntyre, Catherine V., *Writing Effective News Releases*. Colorado Springs, CO: Piccadilly Books, 1992.

Norris, James, *Advertising*, (4th ed.). Englewood Cliffs, NJ: Prentice-Hall, 1990.

Rothschild, Michael, *Advertising: From Fundamentals to Strategies*. Lexington, MA: D.C. Heath, 1987.

Smith, Jeanette, *The Publicity Kit*. New York: Wiley, 1991.

Stanley, Richard E., *Promotion: Advertising, Publicity, Personal Selling, Sales Promotion*, (2d ed.). Englewood Cliffs, NJ: Prentice-Hall, 1982.

9

Absorb the Fundamentals of Selling

It's imperative that you try to learn all you can about the art of selling, for skill in this area can ensure success in direct marketing. Direct, person-to-person selling is the most effective way known to persuade people to buy. Happily, it's also something we have all had experience with, if only at the other end. We have shopped in many stores; by now, we can certainly distinguish between the capable salesclerk and the uninspired one. Many of us have also been exposed to the sales presentations of house-to-house canvassers, who sell everything from Avon and Amway products to vacuum cleaners, encyclopedias, and household utensils.

Like all advertising, mail order selling operates under a serious handicap—the lack of personal contact. With no sales representative present, there's no chance to project a positive personality, vary the pitch and tone of the voice, take cues from the prospect, and modify the sales presentation accordingly. If you sell by direct mail or through the print media (newspapers, magazines), the printed matter replaces the salesperson's visit; you must depend on it to do the entire selling job, which is all the more reason why you need to understand the selling process itself. You need to know what your advertising must accomplish to make that sale.

This chapter will help clarify the personal selling process for you.

A REVIEW OF THE PERSONAL SELLING PROCESS

Traditionally, sales representatives have needed to be familiar with the company's history, products, and prices, as well as those of the competition. In addition, they had to be effective communicators. Today, that isn't enough. Today's salesperson must be sincerely interested in, and acquainted with, the needs, wants, and problems of prospective customers; must be an effective problem-solver; and must have a practical, working knowledge of psychology.

Personal Selling and the AIDA Concept

For decades, college students in marketing and sales courses have been taught various approaches to personal selling. One popular method involves selling by formula to the tune of AIDA—not the opera, but a mnemonic designed to help the student remember what the salesperson must do in order to accomplish the sale. Or, for that matter, what a print advertisement, direct mail "package," radio announcement, or television commercial must do.

The letters in AIDA stand for:

A—Attention

I—Interest

D—Desire

A—Action

To make the sale, the sales representative needs to (1) get the prospect's attention, (2) arouse the prospect's interest in the product or service being presented, (3) build desire on the prospect's part to have what is being offered, and (4) get action in the form of an order.

In applying the AIDA concept to an actual selling situation, the salesperson follows certain steps. In effect, these steps describe the selling process:

Prospecting

Qualifying prospects

Making the presentation

Meeting objections

Closing the sale

Following up the sale.

Prospecting

Career sales representatives face an ongoing challenge; they need to locate—and keep on locating—likely candidates for the goods and services they sell. Without a continuous pool of these *prospects,* salespeople cannot put their selling expertise to the test. So, they must use their intuition, insight, know-how, and creative abilities to ferret out these individuals (or organizations).

Some of the sources they tap are:

- Advertising (in the media for leads).
- Business directories.
- Cold canvassing (door-to-door).
- Conventions.
- Customers.
- Direct mail efforts.
- Family, friends, and acquaintances.
- Government records of all kinds.
- Magazines.
- Mailing lists.
- Newspapers.
- Organization memberships.
- Other salespersons.
- Radio.
- Recommendations.
- Reference works.
- Telephone directories.
- Telephone solicitation.
- Television.
- Trade directories.
- Trade publications.
- Trade shows.

You can, first of all, locate prospective customers by determining who would be most likely to purchase your merchandise or service(s) and what these individuals are like. You can secure worthwhile *leads* (names, addresses) by reaching these target prospects through advertising in the specific media (print, air) that they habitually use. Consider offering your readers or listeners a free catalog or other literature. If you market industrial products or services, you can readily locate prospective buyers by leafing through the many business and trade directories that are available. Another useful approach is that of canvassing organizations by means of a well-planned telephone solicitation program.

If direct mail activity is an integral part of your operation, you can certainly benefit by renting mailing lists of people (or organizations) you believe are logical prospects for what you are selling.

Qualifying Prospects

You might think that, having developed a lengthy list of prospects, the sales representative's next logical move would be to contact them for appointments. In effect, however, this would cost the salesperson far too much in time and effort; and time and effort are what translate into income. A distinction first must be drawn between the real *prospects* on the list and the more numerous *suspects,* as they're often referred to by salespeople. In reality, prospects are prospective buyers; suspects are those who *may* be buyers but need first to be converted into prospects. This is accomplished by *qualifying* them, involving a procedure whereby each person (or organization) on the list is queried directly, and/or checked on indirectly, to ascertain two vital points: (1) that the suspect needs or could use the product or service and (2) that the suspect can both afford it and is in a position to buy it.

There's more to the qualifying process than this, though. The salesperson should also attempt to gain insights into what the prospect is like: background, likes and dislikes, interests, and so on. This is the time for researching; the better the sales representative understands the prospective buyer, the more effectively he or she can shape the sales presentation so that the interview will most likely culminate with a signed purchase order. If a firm is the targeted prospect, the salesperson needs to become thoroughly familiar with the kind of business it's in, what problems it may have and where they lie, the company's approximate sales volume, its credit history, the size of the organization, and so forth. Moreover, there's a need to know as much as possible about the firm's purchasing agent as well.

If your customers are organizations rather than consumers, spend some time researching those prospects that can make good use of the product(s) or service(s) you offer. Use the telephone to research their needs and preferences, their likes and dislikes, and to determine just who it is to contact within the organization.

If, instead, you have targeted select groups of consumers as your primary customers, you'll need to study them intently before attempting to communicate with them. Learn everything you can about them: what they are like, their habits and customs, where they live and where they work, how they spend their leisure time, which newspapers and magazines they tend to read, the kinds of TV programs and radio formats they seem to prefer, what they may need and be looking for in goods or services, and so forth.

Some textbooks on selling and on sales management label this the *preapproach* phase. They consider it a separate step in the selling process, following that of qualifying. I can't see separating one from the other; both are essential preparation for the sales visit.

Making the Presentation

Experienced sales representatives enter the prospect's office with determination, confident in the knowledge that they have prepared thoroughly for the interview. They're determined to gain the prospect's attention and confidence quickly, establish rapport immediately, then use their selling skills to interest, woo, and convince the individual to make the purchase. They know that objections will most likely be raised along the way, and they're prepared to meet and resolve them readily.

A good sales presentation usually starts with a hook or opening designed to enable the salesperson to capture the prospect's interest and, at the same time, make a smooth transition into the presentation itself. As an example, there's the question or benefit opening: "Good morning, Mr. Barr. Would you be interested in saving your company $2,200 a month?" Now, there's just no way that Mr. Barr will say "I'm not interested" to that kind of beginning.

In all your advertising, you should strive to create ads (or commercials) that are bound to hook the audience's interest immediately. At the same time, you must try to initiate a sound, working rapport between these people and you. You'll need to build believability into any offers you make and cultivate confidence in your mail order company.

In this phase of the selling process, be sure to describe the product or service thoroughly. Explain its major features; spell out all of its important benefits. Stress how the customer (or firm) will gain from having and using it. Support this information with facts, and perhaps testimonials.

Naturally, a claim of this sort must be both truthful and supportable by evidence.

Many other openings are possible. You'll discover some of those more commonly used in any of the books on selling. They have even been given descriptive names; here are four examples:

- The product approach.
- The referral approach.
- The premium approach.
- The introductory approach.

During the presentation, salespeople use everything at their command to lead their prospects to the final placement of an order. Sure to be covered are the major selling points about the product or service and the benefits the prospect may expect. Charts, photographs, and other visual aids may help the process. Involving the prospects in the presentation, through appealing to the various senses and/or emotions, makes for increased interest and more conviction. The use of testimonials may really tie things up nicely so that all claims made are believable. Finally, the sales representative's ability to meet and counter objections that are raised will make (or break) the sale.

Meeting Objections

Nearly everyone will harbor doubts or misgivings during a sales presentation. Perhaps we're a little too suspicious of strangers, especially those who seem intent on getting money from us. Perhaps it's only natural to expect that, if we aren't wary, we may be taken advantage of. But it also makes sense to ask questions, to seek further information before making the commitment to spend.

The experienced salesperson also knows these things and is prepared, indeed trained, to handle objections that may be raised during the interview. Because certain types of objections recur time and again, sales trainers usually teach their students how to forestall them or how to overcome them. Most common are those that have to do with either the price or the quality of the product or service. There may be other kinds of objections as well: to the company, to its service, or to the particular sales representative.

Long before you begin preparing your ads, you need to gain a clear understanding of the types of objections your readers or listeners are likely to have in mind with regard to your offers. Be creative when writing ad copy; anticipate—and resolve satisfactorily—those objections that are more commonly conceived. The claims of satisfied buyers, or statements by celebrities, may often help you here. Counter objections to price by demonstrating, in dollars and cents if necessary, the true value of the item/service to the buyer.

As is the case with the many kinds of openings to a presentation, there are a variety of techniques for handling objections and they, too, carry popular labels. (The reader can easily learn how to apply half a dozen or more of these by reading through the appropriate sections in several of the sales texts listed at the end of this chapter.) Some of the techniques are:

- Direct rebuttal (or direct denial method).
- Boomerang (or conversion) method.
- "Yes, but . . ." (or indirect denial) method.
- Compensation method.

Closing the Sale

After the salesperson has satisfactorily resolved all of the prospect's objections and questions, he or she will then strive to bring the sales interview to its hoped-for end, the writing of the order. This is the *close* or the *closing;* both terms are used in selling. It may involve as simple a technique as the *assumptive close,* where the sales representative starts to write up the order, confident that the prospect is ready to buy. Of all closes, this is the one most frequently used.

Often, however, things do not run so smoothly. Good salespeople learn how to use other kinds of closes; these may be brought into play to handle different situations. There are literally dozens of practical closing techniques available.

One or two examples should suffice at this point. In the *SRO close* (the initials are for "Standing Room Only"), the salesperson suggests to the prospect the urgency of ordering today, implying that demand for the product or service is so heavy that should there be any delay, "we may not be able to fill your order." In the *T-account close,* the sales representative will draw a line down the center of a blank sheet of paper, then write the word *Yes* at the top of one half and *No* at the top of the other. Reasons why the prospect should buy are listed in the affirmative column; points against the decision to buy are shown in the negative column. The prospect readily sees on this balance sheet the weight of the arguments in favor of making the purchase.

If you're utilizing direct mail, make sure you enclose an order form with your sales letter and brochure. Occasional use of either the T-account or the SRO close may help to increase your usual percentage of returns. So may offering purchasers something extra: a gift, a discount for buying now rather than later, and so on. Try to include clip-out response coupons in all your print advertising. In your radio or TV spots, be sure to show consumers how to order, and repeat these instructions so that they may be thoroughly understood.

Following Up the Sale

The *follow up* is a term commonly applied to what takes place after the sale has been concluded and the salesperson holds a signed copy of the buyer's order. In the retail store, the salesclerk follows up by (1) thanking the customer, (2) assuring the customer that he or she has made a wise decision, and (3) suggesting that the customer "come back to visit us soon."

Selling to organizations and individuals outside the store environment isn't much different. The same things are done, but the sales representative goes even further. There's a need to check back with the buyer later on, after the order has been delivered, to make sure that the customer is thoroughly satisfied with both the goods and the service. Any complaints are taken care of at once, for the salesperson looks to establish a sound, lasting relationship, one that will ensure additional future orders.

Strictly follow a policy of "We guarantee your complete satisfaction with all purchases, or your money will be cheerfully refunded." In your sales literature, tell your customers to write to you directly at any time with any suggestions and/or complaints. Make them feel that you want a close relationship with them. Be sure you answer their correspondence promptly and in a friendly manner and that you handle all complaints expeditiously.

LEGAL ASPECTS FOR THE MAIL ORDER ADVERTISER

As is true of any other type of business enterprise, mail order firms must comply with all legislation and regulations that affect the business sector. Every company must operate within the confines of both *common law* and *statutory law*. American common law, also known as unwritten law, has its roots in both old Roman and British law and custom adopted by early colonists. What we refer to as statutory law is that huge, ever-expanding body of written laws enacted not only by the federal government but also by individual state and local governments.

We apply the general term *business law* to those laws that deal with the setting up (and dissolution) of partnerships and corporations; the handling, rental, and disposition of property; the representation of an individual or an organization by another person or organization ("agency"); contracts of all kinds; torts; bankruptcy, and so on. Such aspects of business operation as checks and drafts, collateral, product liability, and the like are collectively referred to as *commercial law*.

For your information, here are brief descriptions of three of the more significant categories of law within the business law classification:

The law of property. This designation embraces all laws that pertain to the buying and selling of all kinds of personal as well as business property, tenant-owner relationships, trademarks and copyrights (both are forms of property), personal wills and estates, bankruptcy, and so on.

The law of contracts. Contracts are voluntary agreements by two or more people or organizations. If contracts are *legal,* they can be enforced in court. When is a contract legal? It is legal when: (1) it contains an offer, the purpose of which must be legal, (2) the parties involved have agreed to its terms voluntarily, (3) each party to the contract gives the other(s) something of value, and (4) all parties involved are sound of mind and of legal age.

The law of torts. Laws that fall into this category cover civil, or private, wrongs, those wrongful acts aimed at individuals rather than at society itself. Examples of torts are assault, defamation of character, fraud, negligence, and nuisance.

SPECIAL RULES GOVERN MAIL ORDER SELLING

Mail order entrepreneurs need to be aware of the role of the Federal Trade Commission (FTC) both with regard to advertising and to business conducted by mail. In addition to other duties, the FTC watches for—and may take appropriate action against—such violations as untruthful or fraudulent advertising, bait-and-switch tactics, deceptive guarantees, the misuse of testimonials, and so on. Over the years, the Commission has issued a number of special regulations that govern mail order activity. One in particular applies to the goods you mail out in response to customers' orders. You should ship merchandise no later than thirty days after you received the order. If you can't, then you're obliged to notify the customer of the delay and furnish a new shipping date. At that time, the customer has the right to accept your offer or cancel the order.

It would be useful to contact the FTC in Washington and request their list of publications. If you sell food, you should also contact the Food and Drug Administration (FDA).

As a final suggestion, keep in mind the fact that the United States Postal Service takes a dim view of anything that goes through the mails and smacks of fraud.

Depending on the kinds of goods you sell, and also on your approaches to buying, merchandising, and the extension of credit, several of the following federal laws may apply to your business activity. Acquaint yourself with the more significant aspects of these legislative acts by reading through one or more of the pertinent titles listed in the Sources of Additional Information section at the end of this chapter. You might also consult your legal advisor.

Product-related legislation

Pure Food and Drug Act (1906)

Food, Drug, and Cosmetics Act (1938)

Wheeler-Lea Act (1938)

Flammable Fabrics Act (1953)

Hazardous Substances Labeling Act (1960)

Fair Packaging and Labeling Act (1966)

Child Protection and Toy Safety Act (1969)

Consumer Products Safety Act (1972)

Magnuson-Moss Warranty Act (1975)

Legislation related to consumer credit

Consumer Credit Protection Act (1968)

Equal Credit Opportunity Act (1975)

Fair Credit Billing Act (1975)

Fair Debt Collection Practices Act (1977)

Legislation related to competitive behavior

Sherman Anti-Trust Act (1890)

Clayton Act (1914)

Federal Trade Commission Act (1914)

Robinson-Patman Act (1936)

SOURCES OF ADDITIONAL INFORMATION

Anderson, Ronald A., Ivan Fox, and David T. Twomey, *Business Law and the Legal Environment,* (14th ed.). Cincinnati: South-Western, 1989.

Baker, Kim and Sunny Baker, *How to Promote, Publicize, and Advertise Your Growing Business.* New York: Wiley, 1991.

Cummings, Richard, *Contemporary Selling.* San Diego, CA: Harcourt Brace Jovanovich, 1987.

DuBoff, Leonard D., *The Law (in Plain English) for Small Businesses,* (2d ed.). New York: Wiley, 1991.

Futrell, Charles M., *ABC's of Selling,* (4th ed.). Homewood, IL: Irwin, 1993.

Hahn, Fred, *Do-It-Yourself Advertising: How to Produce Great Ads, Catalogs, Direct Mail, and Much More.* New York: Wiley, 1993.

Hair, Joseph F., Francis L. Notturno, and Frederick A. Russ, *Effective Selling,* (8th ed.). Cincinnati: South-Western, 1991.

Hausman, Carl and Philip Benoit, *Positive Public Relations,* (2d ed.). Blue Ridge Mountain, PA: TAB Books, 1990.

Hiam, Alexander, *The Vest-Pocket Marketer.* Englewood Cliffs, NJ: Prentice-Hall, 1991.

Jugenheimer, Donald W. and Gordon E. White, *Basic Advertising.* Cincinnati: South-Western, 1991.

Lane, Marc J., *Legal Handbook for Small Business,* (rev. ed.). New York: AMACOM, 1989.

Lieberman, Jethro K., *The Legal Environment of Business.* San Diego: Harcourt Brace Jovanovich, 1989.

Moran, John Jude, *Practical Business Law,* (2d ed.). Englewood Cliffs, NJ: Prentice-Hall, 1989.

Pesce, Vince, *A Complete Manual of Professional Selling.* Englewood Cliffs, NJ: Prentice-Hall, 1989.

Putman, Anthony O., *Marketing Your Services: A Step-by-Step Guide for Small Businesses and Professionals.* New York: Wiley, 1990.

Smith, Jeanette, *The Publicity Kit.* New York: Wiley, 1991.

PRINTING, PRINT ADVERTISING, AND THE PRINT MEDIA

10

The Basics of Print Production

So much promotional activity in a mail order business revolves around printed pieces that you'll need to learn a good deal about printing itself. You should also learn the necessity for scheduling all your print jobs well in advance and how to solicit quotations and compare prices before placing your orders for such material.

You should expect to acquire expertise in the more technical aspects of printing as you go along. You'll come to understand how and why to select different types of paper for each situation, according to weight, texture, color, and other characteristics. You'll be introduced to composition and to how typographers choose the type best suited to your presentation and your purposes. You'll learn more and more about how illustrations and photographs are reproduced in finished mailing pieces, and you'll become familiar with such terms as *serif, sans-serif, halftones,* and *mechanicals.*

PRINTING AND COPYING

A printer is skilled in reproducing images of words, artwork, photographs, and the like, usually through a transfer of ink onto paper. Such images can be imprinted on the surfaces of other materials: glass, plastics, metals, and silk are some examples. It's also possible to print without using ink at all. A studio photographer may print, or make prints from, a film negative; these prints are also called *positives.*

For the most part, printing in mail order applies to inked images reproduced on paper stock. Whatever the method, some type of printing mechanism is needed. Paper is fed to or through the machine; printing plates make contact with the paper (either directly or through an intermediate roller); printing ink is transferred to the paper; and impressions are deposited on the paper's surface.

Office Copiers

It's important to distinguish between ordinary office copying machines and professional printing methods. Many offices have one or more photocopiers; Xerox, Canon, and Sharp are the most popular brands. For the most part, these machines are used for reproducing memoranda, documents, correspondence, and internal forms needed in small quantities. Most do not require trained operators. There are modern and efficient desk-top copiers and larger, freestanding floor types that can produce as many as 60 copies per minute. Often, too, copies can readily be reduced or enlarged.

Some firms rent the equipment instead of purchasing it outright. Office copiers are mainly used to make small numbers of copies at one time; if larger amounts are needed, there are cheaper ways of duplicating.

Mimeographs

These machines use an original master sheet called a *stencil;* you "cut" the stencil by typing matter directly onto it, or by using a hand tool known as a *stylus.* The letters of your typewriter or the point of the stylus, when pressed against the thin but somewhat tough material of the stencil, cut into it. The backing—paper with smooth hard finish that makes for good, clear impressions—is removed from the stencil, which is then hooked onto the drum of the machine. The drum is then made to revolve; as it does, ink is forced through the openings cut into the stencil and pressed against the sheets of paper being carried through the machine. As many as 8,000 or 10,000 copies can be made from a single stencil.

True Printing Processes

Three different printing methods are used today: letterpress, lithography, and rotogravure. Basically, the three approaches differ according to the surface from which the printing is done—whether that surface is raised, level or flat, or depressed.

Letterpress

Letterpress is the oldest of the three printing processes. Images are transferred to paper from a raised, or relief, surface. The printer sets metal type into a printing plate, fastens the plate to the press, and then inks the plate. As the press operates, only the raised surfaces on the plate contact the paper; the result is printing of generally excellent quality.

Metal plates may also be prepared from drawings and photographs through an etching of the metal by chemical means.

Letterpress is still used to print wedding invitations, stationery, and other jobs where not much typesetting is involved. Some magazines are still printed by this method.

Lithography

Lithography is now the most popular printing method. While letterpress involves the reproduction of images from raised surfaces, lithography works from a completely flat surface. (Hence the equivalent term *planography;* the prefix *plano-* means "having a flat surface.")

There are two lithographic processes, direct and indirect. In the direct form, both printing plate and paper come in direct contact with each other. But the indirect form, popularly known as *offset,* or *offset lithography,* is by far the more commonly used. There's no direct contact between plate and paper. Instead, the printing plate deposits the image to be reproduced onto a *blanket* (a cylinder covered with thin rubber), and the image is transferred to the paper from the blanket.

This method of printing works on a simple principle: grease doesn't mix with water. The area of the printing plate that is *not* to be printed is so treated as to repel printing ink, and the image scheduled for reproduction will take the ink.

An offset press turns out many thousands of copies at exceptional speeds and at relatively low cost.

Rotogravure

Rotogravure is a fairly uncommon printing process today, except, perhaps, for its use by some newspapers in publishing Sunday supplements. Rotogravure printing is done on a rotary press, the word *rotary* carrying connotations of something that's wheellike and turns on an axis. And "gravure" comes from the same root as the word *engraving.* Indeed, the printing plate that is used is engraved (impressions being carved into it) through a chemical etching process.

This method is also known as *intaglio printing,* a term derived from the Italian verb *intagliare,* meaning "to carve" or "to engrave."

COMPOSITION: WHAT IT'S ALL ABOUT

Copy to be reproduced by any of the printing methods must be properly prepared so that it can be transferred to printing plates. Words and sentences must be broken down into individual characters: letters, numbers, and punctuation marks. These need to be prepared with an eye to legibility, appropriate style, size, spacing, and other considerations. Thus, composition becomes an area of substantial expertise in print production.

A compositor is a person who "composes" type; that is to say, he or she sorts, assembles, and readies the type according to instructions for use in printing. A compositor is also referred to as a typesetter.

An even more skilled craftsperson is the typographer. This technician analyzes the requirements of the print job, creates a mental picture of what the finished work ought to look like, then selects the ideal type (shape, style, size, and so on) for accomplishing the communication objectives.

Methods of Composition

Type can be composed by hand (using ready-made foundry type), by machine, or by photographic methods.

Typesetting by Hand

Printers stock different styles and sizes of type. These are generally of metal and purchased from foundries that specialize in casting type. When a print order comes in to be worked on, the printer selects the type to be used from stock (or orders it, if he or she doesn't stock it), then sets it by hand into the printing plate for letterpress printing.

Machine Composition

Machines such as the Linotype and the Monotype are used to fabricate type for printing. Hot, molten metal is poured into forms; as the metal cools, it hardens, forming letters and other type characters, and even words, as in the case of the Linotype (formed as slugs of metal).

Machines like the Varityper, the standard office typewriter, and the word processor are also used to "set type." Actually, they produce finished copy on sheets of paper, which are then used to produce the printing plates.

Setting Type Photographically

Keeping pace all along with the rapid growth in popularity of offset lithography, typesetting for print production is often arranged these days by a process known as photocomposition. Letters and words are filmed; the film is then linked to a phototypesetting machine, which can manufacture the type itself at tremendous speed. A computer may even be linked to this system.

More About Type

Most of us are familiar with those little rubber stamps, or stampers, you can order through your local stationery store—the name-and-address stamp, the first-class-mail stamp, the paid stamp, the variable date stamp, and many other varieties. With the aid of an inked stamp pad, you can "print" whatever is carried on the stamp literally thousands of times. You will, of course, recognize this as a "letterpress" process, pure and simple, for the characters on the stamp (usually of rubber) are raised.

In printing, the word *type* refers to a little block of metal that bears a character on its face, set off in relief. Here are some other common printing terms:

- Blueprint (or vandyke)—a print or proof from an offset negative, to be checked for possible errors.
- Boldface—typefaces that produce heavier and darker impressions than usual type.
- Copyfitting—fitting the copy to the required space.
- Font (of type)—a complete assortment of letters, numbers, and punctuation marks in one size of a typeface.
- Leading—the space between lines of type (pronounced "ledding").
- Points—this has to do with the size of type; there are seventy-two points to the inch.
- Sans serif—see serifs below. (*Sans* is French for "without.")
- Serifs—little lines, bars, or flourishes that extend from the ends of strokes in letters.
- Typeface—the shape and design of the type; the printing surface of type.
- Type family—a complete set of typefaces (all with the same design) in various sizes and widths.
- Type style—regular (copy), italics, script, light face, and boldface are examples.

Many hundreds of type families are available, although never all from one printer. Here are a few of the more common typefaces:

Baskerville	Franklin Gothic	Old English
Bodoni	Futura	Optima
Caledonia	Garamond	Serif Gothic
Caslon	Helvetica	Times Roman
Cheltenham	Korinna	
Cloister	News Gothic	

HOW ARTWORK AND PHOTOGRAPHS ARE REPRODUCED

The technical aspects involved in preparing both artwork and photographs for print production depend to an extent on the printing method chosen. You'll recall that the surfaces of the printing plates may be flat, depressed, or raised (for lithography, rotogravure, or letterpress printing).

Drawings are photographed or scanned and the film negative is then used to reproduce the image on the printing plate through a chemical process. In letterpress, a line cut is produced. With photographs, reproduction generally involves converting the original print into a halftone first.

USING COLOR TO ENHANCE PRINT ADVERTISING

Mail order firms frequently resort to color in their direct mail and occasionally in their print media advertising. Color provides more attention-getting capability for the advertisement or printed piece and serves several other purposes: to create a desired mood or atmosphere, to take advantage of the psychological associations people carry with certain colors, to contrast, or to highlight, certain aspects of the advertisement.

On the average, a two-color circular or brochure, for example, will generate more responses than a monotone piece. A full, four-color process job will be even more successful.

Printing an additional color can, however, add considerably to your costs. Often, you can accomplish much the same effect at modest cost by printing your mailing piece in one color, such as black, on paper of a second color (instead of on white paper). Naturally, you must watch the legibility factor.

In a true, two-color print job, where, for example, the copy is to appear in black and the headline and illustration in green, two separate impressions usually must be made on the printing press. First, the black plate is printed. The press is then stopped and washed, the second color (green) is added along with the second plate, and the partially printed paper, in sheets or rolls, is then run through the press again. Because of the two impressions needed, this process is costly. A two-color press, one that can do both parts of the job simultaneously, can save money for you. However, such presses are usually used only for long runs.

To reproduce material in full color, the printer must use a special four-color printing process. Four separate printing plates must be prepared, and, in the actual printing, the impressions made on the paper by each of the plates must register in perfect accordance with those of the other plates. In addition to the one plate necessary for reproducing black, three others are needed—one for each of the three primary colors, red, yellow, and blue. When these colored inks are mixed in the right proportions, they can yield all possible desired colors.

Negatives, called *color separations,* are made by photographing the original (the artwork or photograph) four different times. Each time a special filter is used, which permits only the one color to pass through. From the separations, halftones are then made. In turn, these are used for preparing the printing plates.

SELECTING THE RIGHT PAPER FOR PRINT JOBS

An exceptionally wide range of paper stocks is available to the direct mail advertiser for print production. Papers range in weight from ultralight, tissuelike paper to newsprint, parchment, and kraft (used for wrapping packages) to cardboards and book-cover stocks. Most of the paper used by the mail order company falls into the book stock classification, although writing papers constitute an important secondary genre. The latter group is used for such purposes as sales letters, company stationery, business forms, records, and other purposes that require paper to be typed or written on. Bond paper is a prime example. It's available in varying finishes and with varying contents of wood pulp and rag.

Papers in the book paper family run from the soft, somewhat rough, and uncoated antique paper to the English finish and machine-finished papers. Indeed, paper can be coated on one or both sides, with either a dull or a glossy finish, or can be left uncoated. It can also be textured or have a variety of different finishes, such as cockle, coral, leather, and so on.

In selecting the right paper for each print job, a printer will think in terms of cost, the size of the standard sheet (and its weight), the impression it will receive at the hands of the reader, and how well it will "take" the ink used in printing.

TIPS FOR CUTTING YOUR PRINTING COSTS

In your new mail order operation, you'll quickly discover what a vital asset a good print shop can be to your business. Early in the game, search for a local printer who isn't too big or too busy to devote full attention to servicing your initial needs, and one who's willing, even anxious, to work closely with you as your activity begins to expand. Seek to cultivate a friendly, mutually satisfying, long-term relationship with this important supplier.

The printer is a prime source of good advice and a good friend. Printers know where to go for the kinds of assistance you may need along the way: artists, layout people, compositors, mailing houses, and the like. They're familiar with the many different types, weights, and finishes of paper. They know the proper inks to use on papers that are selected; they're able to convert your copy, illustrations, and photographs into finished printing that's attractive and will do the job. They can show you how to save money on your mailings. For example, they may suggest using a lighter weight paper (and envelope) so that you can avoid paying for additional postage on each piece you mail, or running two print jobs of yours at the same time, instead of two single jobs to cut printing costs. This saves money for you by halving the number of impressions required by the press, and it avoids paper waste. Sometimes, the printer can offer you the chance to have your circular or brochure "ride along" with another company's printing, thus saving you money.

Often, the key to a profitable advertiser-printer relationship is early, thorough planning and giving the printer lots of lead time.

SOURCES OF ADDITIONAL INFORMATION

Books

Beach, Mark, *Getting It Printed,* (rev. ed.). Cincinnati: North Light Books, 1993.

Benton, Randi and Mary S. Balcer, *The Official Print Shop Handbook: Ideas, Tips and Designs for Home, School and Professional Use.* New York: Bantam, 1987.

Demoney, Jerry and Susan E. Meyer, *Pasteups and Mechanicals: A Step-by-Step Guide to Preparing Art for Reproduction.* New York: Watson-Guptill, 1982.

Holtz, Herman, *The Direct Marketer's Workbook.* New York: Wiley, 1986.

Levine, Mindy N. and Susan Frank, *In Print: A Concise Guide to Graphic Arts and Printing for Small Business and Nonprofit Organizations.* Englewood Cliffs, NJ: Prentice-Hall, 1984.

Nash, Edward L., *The Direct Marketing Handbook,* (2d ed.). New York: McGraw-Hill, 1992.

Pickens, Judy E., *The Copy-to-Press Handbook: Preparing Words and Art for Print.* New York: Wiley, 1985.

Ward, Dick, *Creative Ad Design and Illustration.* Cincinnati: North Light Books, 1988.

Woods, Bob and Herbert Holtie, *Printing and Production for Promotional Materials.* New York: Van Nostrand Reinhold, 1986.

11

How to Create Effective Print Advertisements

With the sole exception of personal selling, direct mail marketing is your most effective and most personal means of persuading people to buy. The mainstay of most mail order companies' sales efforts, direct mail is used in two ways: (1) to sell merchandise and/or services directly, and (2) to accomplish precisely the same aim *after* having advertised in some other medium to generate names and addresses of prospective buyers.

The most likely candidates among the various media for reaching that second objective, at least so far as the smaller mail order merchant is concerned, are magazines and newspapers. (The whys and wherefores for this are treated in later chapters.) Not that the print media cannot profitably be used to sell goods and services directly. Of course, they can! Both can be worthwhile vehicles for you.

DEVELOPING PRODUCTIVE ADVERTISEMENTS: A CONTINUOUS CHALLENGE

The preparation of newspaper and magazine advertisements has much in common with the creation of folders, broadsides, brochures, or other direct mail formats. Either approach calls for careful planning, ideation, the organization of elements, and execution in print. Both require writing persuasive copy, selecting headlines that stimulate reader interest and accent the highlights of your proposition, and introducing the kinds of illustrations that will help sell the item. Yet the challenge of preparing a print advertisement is more difficult than the problem of devising a typical mail order piece. Why? Basically because of space constraints.

In writing and laying out a circular or brochure, you can be as expansive as you wish to be. If you decide you need more space, you can tack on a second, or even a third, page to your first one. Or, perhaps, use a larger sheet, and make another flap or fold. Usually, your only added cost is for the additional paper.

On the other hand, the newspapers and magazines you use will charge you for every column inch and for every agate line of space you purchase. And space costs can be substantial! Smaller mail order firms, for instance, seldom will contract for full-page advertisements. More likely, they think in terms of small-space advertisements, perhaps ten or twelve inches in size (five or six inches by two columns across), or, perhaps, one-twelfth of a page in the mail order section of a magazine. (More on space costs and other details are found in Chapters 15 and 16.) You'll have to tell the whole story, effectively, within a relatively small area. And this is where your "expertise" will come in handy.

Start to Develop Your Skills

Even before starting up in your new business, you owe it to yourself to spend some time studying your new field. You need to do lots of homework to familiarize yourself with typical print advertising in mail order.

Visit the local branch of your public library. In the reading room, you'll find displayed current issues of several dozen magazines. Leaf through each one, checking for any advertisements that may call for immediate reader response by mail. Some magazines (for example, *Good Housekeeping, House Beautiful,* and other "shelter" publications) contain mail order sections toward the back of the publication. Most magazines, of course, do not. Still, in many of these magazines, you'll occasionally come across one or more mail order advertisements.

You might also consider adding to your studies the magazine section (and, possibly, the comics) of your own Sunday newspaper each week. These editions often carry some order-by-mail advertising.

Only part way into your preparation, you may conclude that most such advertising, whether designed to elicit inquiries, distribute catalogs or other literature, or sell merchandise directly, has these components in common:

- A headline and maybe one or two subheadlines.
- An illustration.
- Words and sentences that tell the story (*copy*).
- The advertiser's name and address.
- A coupon (in many cases) to be filled out, clipped, and mailed by the interested reader.

You'll also become sensitive to other attributes of mail order advertising: the frequent use of borders of different kinds around the ad; how the major elements (headlines, illustrations, copy blocks, and so forth) are arranged within the confines of the space; the interesting (or perhaps uninteresting) choice of objects or subjects used as illustrations; and how white space can be cleverly used to make an ad stand out from other surrounding ads.

Be sure to photostat some of the ads that seem to attract your attention smartly and make you want to read all of the finer print. Keep these for further study and analysis.

Finally, follow the procedure for creating your own print ads outlined in Exhibit 11–1.

EXHIBIT 11–1   Creating print advertisements

1. Clarify your perception of people with whom you'll be communicating. What are they like? (Think in terms of sex, age, income level, education, and other demographics.)

2. Describe the product (or service) you want to sell in writing. Be as detailed as you can. Ask yourself questions such as: Of what value is this item? What satisfactions would it bring to the purchaser? Why would people buy it? How can it be used? How does it differ from what's now available in stores?

3. Study what you have jotted down. Then try to compose one paragraph, however lengthy, that summarizes your thinking to this point about the product or service. Write as if you're speaking directly to one of your prospective customers. Keep your mental picture of that person in front of you; you must first try to pique his or her interest, then spark the desire to buy.

4. Make a list of *all* the customer benefits one can expect from the product/service. Then select the two or three that you judge most important to the potential customer. Describe each in one or two sentences, and integrate the results with the paragraph you wrote in step 3.

5. Conceive of an apt illustration. Ask yourself what kind of artwork would be most likely to grab the reader's attention, best convey the meaning of the story you would like to tell, or best complement the copy you plan to use. Should you use a line cut, a wash drawing, a photograph? (Don't attempt this step and those that follow until you have read—and thoroughly digested—the material in the rest of this chapter.)

6. Sketch a rough, but pleasing, layout for your advertisement.

7. Build in a "mail-back" coupon for your reader. (Study all the print mail order ads you can; clip samples of coupons that seem interesting to use as models, using your own creativity to make changes.)

8. Go back to the rough copy you created in steps 3 and 4. Start to cut and polish it in accordance with the copywriting suggestions outlined in Exhibit 11–3.

9. Select an appropriate headline (or headlines) to use with your advertisement.

10. Put everything aside. Two or three days from now, look at what you have done. Does it seem to accomplish what you want? Can you make any improvements in the advertisement? If you can, do so.

Source: Compiled by the author.

THE ELEMENTS OF ADVERTISING LAYOUT

The store designer who begins laying out the interior of a new store first draws a diagram of the space and then proceeds to sketch in all the elements: ceiling, walls, flooring, fixtures, aisles, bins, shelves, and so on. He or she anticipates the shopper traffic that will be flowing in and out and the need for behind-the-counter space so that salesclerks may pass back and forth freely. All of the details must be so arranged that the resulting total "package" will be as attractive as it will be serviceable; that is to say, it will accomplish the store's objectives.

In direct mail advertising, you follow essentially the same sort of process in laying out a print advertisement, a circular, or a brochure. All the necessary elements must be incorporated into it in proper position and arranged to accomplish the desired effect. The advertisement or printed piece must be functional (get the reader to act) and attractive.

Rough Layouts: Thinking on Paper

The process calls for getting one's thoughts down on paper, in what generally turns out to be a series of little drawings, one after the other, called *thumbnail sketches*. The professional layout artist draws them rapidly with charcoal or soft pencil, indicating the position of the artwork by a blob or mass of black, copy by straight or wavy lines, a coupon by a dotted horizontal line and scribbling below, and so forth.

When you're making your own layouts, you may discard quite a few of these thumbnails, just as the artist does, as you wrestle with the problem of coordination. You need to coordinate headlines and subheads, photograph or art, body copy, and other elements, all according to the basic principles of design, into an attractive unit. The result must be a total package that will stop readers and cause them to look and read on.

Once you have decided that you prefer a particular thumbnail, your next step is to outline the advertisement (or printed piece) on your paper, preferably drawing it to the exact size the finished piece is to be. Sketch in all elements, following up on what you did in the thumbnail. This new rough layout, however, will be more finished. For example, you put in the actual headline drawn to scale. You write (or type in) the actual body copy. Thus, it will contain enough information for your printer or the newspaper to follow easily in setting up the circular or advertisement.

Design Principles

The layout artist, in addition to worrying about incorporating the parts of an advertisement (headlines and so on), must think in terms of good design. An attractive ad, for example, reflects proper balance, unity, interesting contrast, and other characteristics. These are briefly described below. (For further information, be sure to read appropriate sections of the relevant books listed at the end of this chapter.)

Balance. An advertisement can be mentally split down the center into two halves as you look at it. Using *formal* balance, there's an equal distribution of sizes and shapes (and deep to light tones of black as well) on both sides. With *informal* balance the distribution is unequal. (The former is more conservative; the latter, perhaps, somewhat more interesting.)

Contrast. Contrast applies to varying the shapes and sizes of the ad elements: copy, artwork, and so on. Contrasting elements induce more reader interest.

Movement. Movement is a sense of rhythm or flow to the advertisement where the eye will follow a route intended by the layout artist.

Proportion. An advertisement is pleasing when no element is out of proportion to the others and only one dominates. Again, shapes and sizes are important here.

Unity. The layout artist seeks a unified effect—a complete package of the advertisement that blends all elements into one presentation.

ENERGIZE YOUR ADS WITH EYE-CATCHING ILLUSTRATIONS

In checking through magazines and newspapers, you may come across mail order advertisements that rely entirely on the printed word to sell products or services, especially in small-scale display (and, of course, classified) advertising because of cost constraints. In fact, to reduce the monotony of having to read through large blocks of copy, as well as to gain the attention of more readers, different techniques are often used. Some examples are the introduction of a catchy headline, the use of sub-headings on occasion, or the use of white space to set off paragraphs or special phrases.

Such approaches do help, of course. But reader interest level can drop rapidly if there's just too much copy in the ad, no matter how tastefully it has been arranged.

An illustration will break up the mass of "cold copy." More importantly, it can call the reader's attention to the advertisement in the first place. And, at the same time, it can inform the reader as to what the ad is all about. You can also use an illustration to set a mood, act as a hook to get the reader to read the copy, highlight a product benefit or show an item being used, demonstrate how a product is made, and for many other purposes.

People like to see what they're being offered. They want to understand what a product or service is all about, what it can do for them, how it's to be used, and the like. Artwork, if not worth a thousand words, is certainly the equivalent of at least several hundred—*if* it's appropriate artwork!

A look through current issues of publications produced a list of these illustrations:

Bicycles	Free catalogs	Rare coins
Binoculars	Games	Records and tapes
Books	Handbags	Self-defense courses
Bracelets	How-to reports	Shirts
Burglar alarms	Kites	Shoes
Calculators	Knives	Slacks
Calendars	Ladders	Small engine repair
Car covers	Lamps	Sporting goods
Cheeses	Magazines	Toys
Clocks	Mittens	T-shirts
Correspondence courses	Nameplates	Vases
Earrings	Necklaces	Vitamins
Exercise bikes	Nutmeats	Watches
Fishing equipment	Pendants	Weathervanes
Foreign stamps	Perfume bottles	

Kinds of Illustrations

Several different types of illustrations are used in printing. These include line and wash drawings and halftones. The *line drawing* consists of solid lines, drawn in black ink for best reproduction, or filled-in masses of black. It's a simple drawing that shows no shadings or tones, being characterized by the contrast of black on white. A *wash drawing,* on the other hand, does show variation. It's drawn in different color paints. Often, the most productive artwork you can use in mail order is an actual glossy photograph of the merchandise.

CREATE HEADLINES THAT GRAB THE READER'S ATTENTION

The headline in an advertisement is like a traffic signal, like a blinking red light or a stop sign. It signals the reader to stop, then look attentively. It also acts much like the title of a short story or a magazine article. Not only must it catch the reader's attention, but it must also act as a hook or cue that stimulates the reader to read on to find out more about what is "promised" in the headline.

This function is why the headline is typically set apart from the body copy and why it appears in larger (and often bolder) type.

But in mail order advertising, there's more to the headline of an advertisement than just being a signal device. It's probably far easier (and quicker) for the mind to grasp the significance of a headline than to understand an illustration or make out the intent behind a photograph. Often, the headline is used to instantly inform readers about the product or service, or about its benefits, or to arouse their curiosity and lead into the copy below it.

In the mail order game, if all other elements in the advertisement remain the same, a change of headline alone can make a drastic difference in the number of responses. One headline can draw three, four, five, or more times the number of returns that an alternate headline pulls—or one-fifth of the number.

For this reason, each time you prepare a print ad or direct mail piece, devote considerable energy and time to playing around with alternative headlines. It's wise to work up a list of ten or more appropriate headlines for each ad, then select the one you feel will best do the job. These must be completely relevant; keep both your objective and your customer clearly in mind while ideating. And it's a good idea to *limit* the number of words in the headlines. Most of the time, the shorter the better!

Types of Headlines

Headlines may be couched in simple declarative statements or in question form. They may also be positive or negative in tone, although the latter type is seldom used. Here are some examples from recent mail order advertising:

- Desk Organizer.
- Electric Television Antenna.
- Extra Income Can Be Yours.
- Hand-Engraved Jewelry.
- Income Tax Organizer.
- Original Mexican Paintings.
- Stops Leaks Instantly.
- Thousands in Profit through the Mail.

Here are questions used as headlines:

- Are You a Back Sufferer?
- Ever Wonder Where Your Money Goes?
- Need Energy?
- Overweight?
- Want to Earn Big Money?
- What Are Your Chances of Success?

Also used is the phrase or sentence that is a command, or imperative, such as:

- Be an Electrician!
- Be Your Own Boss!
- Borrow by Mail!

- Control Paperwork Expense!
- Learn Accounting at Home!
- Quit Smoking!
- Remove Unwanted Hair Forever!
- Win at Poker!

Headlines may also fall into a number of categories depending on their purpose or effect—the benefit headline, the how-to headline, the news or announcement headline, and so on. Some examples are offered in Exhibit 11–2.

EXHIBIT 11–2   Sample headlines

Benefit Headlines	"How to" Headlines
• Buy Direct and Save	• How to Build Your Own Gun Cabinet
• Cut Your Electric Bills in Half	• How to Cut Your Income Tax
• Get Your Promotion Fast	• How to Earn Big Money
• Reduce Without Dieting	• How to Write a Resume
• Save on Perfumes	• How to Prepare Your Own Will
• Spare Time Cash at Home	• How to Save on Grocery Bills
• Win on Slot Machines	• How to Start Your Own Part-Time Business
• You Can Look Prettier	• How to Survive During Inflation
	• How to Win at Blackjack

News or Announcement Headlines

- Amazing New Calculator
- Get This Free, Money-Saving Report
- Good News for Back Sufferers
- Here's the Fishing Rod You Always Wanted
- Just Out! Our New Spring Catalog
- New Treatment for Itchy Skin
- Now, Free Yourself of Debt
- Pre-Holiday Sale
- Special Introductory Offer

Source: Compiled by the author.

IDEAS FOR STRENGTHENING YOUR COPYWRITING SKILLS

Even if you have an excellent command of the language, bear in mind that copywriting is both a skill and an art that takes a great deal of time and practice to develop. Indeed, it's probably wise, especially if you plan to advertise frequently in the media or use direct mail regularly, to tie up with a small advertising agency, especially for the first year or two in the mail order business.

Nevertheless, you'll want to write your own copy sooner or later. Read all you can on the subject. Play with writing copy for your own needs as often as you can, even though you leave the "finalization" to the agency. Along the way, study and analyze advertisements that have been placed by other direct marketing firms, especially those that are repeated time and again.

Later in this section, you'll find a list of suggestions for writing effective advertising copy. But first, heed well the next two paragraphs; they'll help to set the boundaries and the guidelines more clearly for you.

Economize. When you first tackle the job of writing copy, be sure to think *economy*. Remember that you'll be paying the print medium for every agate line or column inch of space you decide to use. Therefore, each word you choose for an ad costs you money. Be frugal. Stretch your money: make every word and sentence count. Every word and sentence must contribute to the total purpose. This means you must write, rewrite, and rewrite again, always trying to convey your thoughts more concisely and in less and less space.

Think of Your Target Reader. Before you start to write a piece of ad copy, build a firm picture of your reader in your mind. Holding that vision before you, list all the important points you would want to get across if you had the opportunity to speak directly with that person on a one-to-one basis. Write them down, freely using the second person "you" form of address, with the very language you would use in conversation. Think in terms of *interesting, exciting, involving, motivating,* and *persuading* your reader. Appeal to emotions, capitalize on the news value of your offer (if it does contain newsworthiness), explain all benefits, add a testimonial or two if you feel these would help, and offer a guarantee.

Your print advertisement (or mailing piece) is as much a real-life sales presentation that you would make to a prospective customer as if you were there in person.

No one develops overnight into a capable copywriter. So, to repeat, read several of the books at the end of this chapter and others you may locate at the library. And then practice, for practice (eventually) makes perfect—or, at least, near perfect.

The copy suggestions outlined in Exhibit 11–3 will help to develop your skill.

EXHIBIT 11–3   Twenty hints for more effective copy

1. Don't write to impress your reader with your superior knowledge of English.

2. Present your information clearly. Good communication implies reader understanding.

3. Use short words. They do the job far better than long words, especially those of three and four syllables.

4. Make your sentences short and to the point.

5. Make every word contribute toward your objective and toward the kind of impression you want to make.

6. Be as brief (but clear) as possible. Don't write more, or less, than is necessary.

7. Be specific. Avoid generalities.

8. Bear in mind the reader's natural skepticism, especially when it comes to a sales pitch.

9. Be honest. Never look to stretch the truth.

10. Work on the reader's feelings and emotions.

11. Select words and phrases your reader will be familiar with.

12. Use active, fresh words and phrases.

13. Build reader interest and involvement.

14. Tie your copy to the reader's needs and wants. Show him or her how your product or service will satisfy.

15. Specify the benefits of what you're offering.

16. Write in an enthusiastic, personal style.

17. Strive to be convincing. Offer proof, if this is needed.

18. Make sure your proposition is clear.

19. State the price. Point out why your offer is a good value.

20. Show the reader how to order or respond to your advertisement.

Source: Compiled by the author.

A COUPON WILL BRING A GREATER RESPONSE

As you'll discover in the next chapter, most of the direct mail "packages" you'll plan to send out each year will contain separate order forms and return envelopes. These tools make it easy for interested recipients to respond to your offers. Should you, however, decide to distribute circulars or folders without accompanying order forms, be sure to print return coupons directly on these advertising materials.

Advertising in magazines and newspapers poses a different challenge. Adding a well-designed coupon in each ad (preferably at the bottom) can increase the number of replies by anywhere from 20 to 50 percent and frequently more. Make room on your coupon for the respondent's name and address, description of the item (catalog number, color, size, and so on), quantity, price, total amount of order (including charges for postage and handling), method of payment, and other important details. Also give your firm's name and address (including a department, box, or section number so that you can determine from which ad the responses have come).

Of course, not all ads you place will be large enough to include a coupon. With a really small ad of, say, 3 inches by 1 column (42 agate lines), consider framing your ad with a margin of dots or dashes all around so that the ad looks as though it's begging to be clipped out. In your copy, add a line or two suggesting that the reader cut out the entire ad and write in his or her name and address in the blank space at the bottom. This is an especially useful technique when offering a free brochure, catalog, or additional information.

GAIN READER TRUST WITH APPROPRIATE TESTIMONIALS

You can also look forward to a substantial jump in replies to your print ad if you include one or two testimonials from satisfied buyers. They will lend believability to whatever claims you make in your ad copy. Reader reaction to a decent testimonial can push your returns up as much as 30 to 40 percent.

Even better results can be expected if a well-known person has offered the testimonial. Moreover, if you can introduce a photo of that celebrity into your ad, you can expect to double or triple the numbers of people who read the ad.

A word of caution: You'll need to obtain permission, in writing, from these individuals to be able to include their comments or use their photographs in your advertising.

SOURCES OF ADDITIONAL INFORMATION

Book, Albert C., *Fundamentals of Copy and Layout: A Manual.* Lincolnwood, IL: National Textbook, 1990.

Crompton, A., *The Craft of Copywriting: How to Write Great Copy that Sells.* Englewood Cliffs, NJ: Prentice-Hall, 1982.

David, Bruce E., *The Profitable Advertising Manual: A Handbook for Small Business,* (2d ed.). Twinsburg, OH: Worthprinting, 1986.

Donahue, Bud, *The Language of Layout.* Englewood Cliffs, NJ: Prentice-Hall, 1978.

Hahn, Fred, *Do-It-Yourself Advertising: How to Produce Great Ads, Catalogs, Direct Mail, and Much More.* New York: Wiley, 1993.

Klein, Erica Levy, *Write Great Ads: A Step-by-Step Approach.* New York: Wiley, 1990.

Levine, Mindy N. and Susan Frank, *In Print: A Concise Guide to Graphic Arts and Printing for Small Business and Nonprofit Organizations.* Englewood Cliffs, NJ: Prentice-Hall, 1984.

Lewis, Herschell Gordon, *Direct Mail Copy that Sells.* Englewood Cliffs, NJ: Prentice-Hall, 1986.

_____ , *How to Make Your Advertising Twice as Effective at Half the Cost.* Chicago: Dartnell, 1993.

_____ , *How to Write Powerful Catalog Copy.* Chicago: Dartnell, 1993.

Pickens, Judy E., *The Copy-to-Press Handbook: Preparing Words and Art for Print.* New York: Wiley, 1985.

Rothschild, Michael, *Advertising: From Fundamentals to Strategies.* Lexington, MA: D.C. Heath, 1987.

12

Direct Mail: The Powerhouse of Direct Marketing Methods

Among the advertising media, direct mail occupies a unique position. It's in a class by itself, for through no other medium are you able to focus on specific types of prospects with such unerring accuracy. Furthermore, it's the most personal and most intimate of all media. It can deliver your messages directly into the home or workplace with the strict confidentiality of private correspondence, and without the clutter of surrounding advertisements competing with them.

DIRECT MAIL: WHAT IT IS AND HOW TO USE IT

Today, direct mail is big business. More and more companies that are not ordinarily involved in mail order marketing are getting into it every month. Direct mail advertising now occupies third place in total expenditures for all media, behind only newspapers and television. In 1992, some $243 billion went for media advertising; of that total, $112 billion went into direct response advertising and direct mail alone accounted for nearly $25.5 billion.[1]

Manufacturers use direct mail to secure leads for their sales representatives and to obtain orders directly. Retailers use it to generate traffic in their stores and to sell more merchandise to their charge account

---

[1] "Direct Marketing Flow Chart," *Direct Marketing* 56 (December 1993), 3. (*Direct Marketing* magazine, 224 Seventh Street, Garden City, New York 11530-5771.)

customers. But these are only a few of the ways organizations use direct mail. Other possibilities include:

- To aid the firm's personal selling efforts.
- To announce new products or services.
- To build a positive company image.
- To build customer loyalty.
- To help increase demand for a product or service.
- To inform prospective buyers about special sales or other events.
- To make new customers.
- To obtain inquiries.
- To open new territories.
- To solicit new accounts.
- To update mailing lists.
- To win back lost customers.

Direct mail usage has been growing rapidly despite the ever-increasing costs of postage, materials, and printing. Today, direct mailers segment the names and addresses of potential buyers not only by age group, sex, income level, and other customary demographics, but also by geographical location, personal lifestyle, range of interests, recency and/or frequency of purchase, and other factors.

Direct mail is a highly specialized field, calling for specific talents. If you plan to make money with it, you'll need professional counsel and lots of practice. Proper timing, for example, can be vital to success. Some months, like November and January, are excellent for mailings, at least for the majority of merchandise items. On the other hand, summers can produce poor results. Even the days of the week on which direct mail pieces arrive can affect the number of replies.

Of course, the list you work from is a significant factor. Lists of your own customers pull better than the names and addresses you may have collected from incoming inquiries. Rented lists generally pull even fewer returns than inquiries. Pieces you may mail out in cooperative venture with another firm will probably show still poorer results.

In the consumer goods field, some areas of the country are more productive of sales than others. A lot, of course, depends on what you're offering. You're not likely to sell too many winter blankets by mail to residents of southern California or Florida. Neither can you count on many sales of tractors or other farm equipment if you target people who reside in metropolitan areas.

Attractions of Direct Mail

Why is direct mail so attractive a medium? To the buyer, it offers an exceptionally convenient means of shopping from one's home or office.

There's no need to hop into a car, travel a few blocks or perhaps several miles, and spend time shopping around in stores, let alone the wear and tear on your car and the cost of fuel. And there's usually a wide variety of merchandise to choose from when ordering by mail, often far broader a selection than most stores carry, in addition to items that just can't be found in stores at all!

From your company's point of view, let's look at some of the major benefits of selling through this medium:

- *Selectivity.* You decide who is to receive your advertising. You send your advertising material only to people (or organizations) who presumably can use—and have the money to pay for—the merchandise or service you sell. You can confine your efforts to a small area anywhere in the country or expand them to cover the entire nation. You can tailor your messages deliberately to accountants, dentists, science or English teachers, people who earn upward of $100,000 a year, motorcyclists, numismatists, apparel or shoe retailers, manufacturers of health foods or electrical equipment, beauty salon operators, or any other group or segment of the population you choose to go after.

- *Flexibility.* Outstanding flexibility characterizes the direct mail medium. You may use the simplest kind of presentation or the most elaborate. You can mail an entire "package" or a single-sheet self-mailer. You're not required to fit into the constraints of a typical magazine mail order advertisement that might cost anywhere from several hundreds to several thousands of dollars. You can get your mailing out within a week or so after preparing it, rather than waiting for six to ten weeks before you see your advertising in print. With little expense and effort, you can test all sorts of minor changes in your mailing pieces that might result in increased sales.

- *Control.* Direct mail offers near-perfect control of your advertising effort. With newspapers and magazines, your ad generally appears where the publishers think best (except where you pay for a preferred position). And there's lots of competition from other ads in those publications, along with news, stories, and editorial matter. Your mailing piece arrives intact. You can schedule your mailings during optimum times of the year, so that you obtain the best results. Moreover, you have the space to tell the entire story and to back up your statements with illustrations, testimonials, and guarantees.

- *Knowledge of results.* It's easy to record every sale made from each mailing so that at all times you can appraise the success or failure of your advertising. You code each mailing in some manner so that when the orders arrive, you're able to identify their source and assign them to the proper mailing. To code, you may use mechanical methods such as notching or clipping the corners of order forms. Or add tiny distinguishing marks to the form, or to the return envelope, with pen or crayon. Many mail order firms place their codes directly on the mailing labels. Often, these codes are deliberately complex in format, so they yield far more information than simply the source.

Drawbacks to the Medium

As with all other things human, not all is happiness and bliss in direct mail. The medium has its disadvantages, too. The biggest drawback is its cost per thousand in relation to other media. It's by far the most expensive way to reach quantities of people. For example, you can place a classified ad in newspapers and some magazines for as little as $2 to $5 per word or insert a small display advertisement in such periodicals for several hundred dollars. With either, you may be able to reach many thousands of readers; this means your cost per thousand breaks down in actuality to only pennies per person. By contrast, direct mail, even at the lower third class rate, will run you much more for just the postage alone. Then there are the printing costs; the cost of the envelopes; the charges you pay for collating, folding, and inserting the enclosures; rental fees for outside mailing lists; and so on. Even at an inexpensive per unit cost of 40 cents, your cost per thousand would run to $400.

Though bothersome, the other drawbacks to using direct mail are not too disheartening. They include the "junk mail" attitude that leads many consumers to discard advertising mail without reading it, the fact that you may need professional help in preparing your mailings, and the dependency of results on the quality of your mailing list.

KNOW THE BASIC PROMOTOOLS OF MAIL ORDER SELLING

No medium is more challenging to the exercise of one's creativity than direct mail. You can draw upon an astounding variety of tools of the trade. These range from the simple postcard through self-mailing circulars or folders to the mail order catalog. Probably the most frequently used tool is the so-called classic mailing piece. This consists of a cover envelope and a number of enclosures: a sales letter, a main advertising piece, an order form, and a return envelope.

Advertising pieces themselves are available in every conceivable shape and size, printed in many different colors of ink on an almost infinite selection of papers. They may be miniatures or giant-size pieces. They may be diecut into round, square, oblong, triangular, diamond-shaped, or dozens of other geometric patterns. They may even be made to pop up when unfolded. They may also be designed to look like:

Banknotes	Checks
Book pages	Documents
Boxtops	Invitations

Invoices	Paper bags
Licenses	Photographs
Newspaper pages	Posters
Oversized coins	Sheets of music
Package labels	and a hundred other formats

They may carry messages written in invisible ink or revealed when you scratch off a special coating with a coin. They can be used as package inserts, as statement stuffers, in cooperative mailings with other mail order concerns, or even hand-delivered door-to-door.

Major Types of Direct Mail Advertising Enclosures

You'll have no problem whatsoever identifying those parts of a mailing known as the order form, sales letter, or return envelope. But there are a number of other, perhaps unfamiliar, terms commonly used to denote the different types of printed advertising pieces, such as booklets, broadsides, brochures, and the like. Brief descriptions of the more commonly used mailing pieces follow:

- *Booklets.* Booklet literally translates to "little book." A booklet is meant to be read; most of its contents consists of typed matter. Examples include booklets of instruction on how to play chess, build an outdoor barbecue, or repair clocks.

  The booklet is generally not bound like a regular book, may have a paper cover, or may lack a cover page entirely. Booklets are also called pamphlets.

- *Broadsides.* Broadsides are large, often impressive-looking printed pieces that contain artwork (halftones, drawings) and printed matter. Actually, they are extralarge circulars, printed on both sides of the paper, then folded for delivery to prospective buyers. When unfolded, some of the printing (or art) runs across the folds of the broadside. This is the characteristic that distinguishes it from other enclosure formats.

- *Brochures.* More select or fancier mailing pieces than the circular or folder, brochures carry a feeling of quality. Brochures are usually folded two or more times before use as enclosures in a mailing piece or being used directly as a self-mailer.

- *Catalogs.* Catalogs are the powerhouses of the mail order companies (and are discussed later in more detail). They carry a quantity of illustrations, or halftones, of different merchandise, along with descriptions, prices, details regarding special promotions, and other information. An order form, along with shipping instructions, may appear as one of the catalog pages or may be attached to the catalog. Often, a return envelope is also bound in. Catalogs come in various sizes; 6×9, $8\frac{1}{2} \times 11$, and 9×12 inches are quite common.

They may run from as few as six or eight pages to many hundreds of pages.

- *Circulars.* Circulars are often used by smaller mail order firms when first starting in business. They are inexpensive print jobs, consisting usually of a single sheet of paper carrying advertising matter in the form of one or two halftones and descriptive copy. Printing may be on one or on both sides of the paper. An order coupon may appear on the circular itself, or a separate order form may accompany the circular. Circulars are also useful as package inserts to be enclosed in each package you mail out, to bring in extra sales. They may also be profitably used as bill enclosures, if you extend credit to any of your customers. You mail them along with your monthly statements.

- *Folders.* Folders is a term often used by the public to denote printed pieces, like circulars, broadsides, and others, which need to be folded for insertion into mailing envelopes, or for use as self-mailers. Actually, this label is a catch-all.

- *Leaflets.* Leaflets are circulars, too. A leaflet, however, refers to a single sheet of paper (a circular can be, although ordinarily is not, composed of more than one sheet). In addition, a leaflet may not carry any illustration or other art at all, but simply typed matter.

THE STANDARD DIRECT MAIL PACKAGE

The so-called direct mail package consists of four items: the cover envelope, sales letter, order form, and return envelope.

The Cover Envelope

It's obvious to all that the main purpose of a cover envelope (also referred to as an *outside* or *mailing envelope*) is to see to it that the contents it holds get to their destination via the U.S. Postal Service. Yet, there's so much more purpose to it in direct mail than this mechanical aspect. Because many people dislike receiving junk mail, there's a good chance that an uninteresting-looking envelope will wind up in the trash can, unopened. For this reason, mail order companies will occasionally depart from using the standard #10 white envelope, even to the point of substituting brown paper bags, little cloth sacks, cardboard tubes, and other variations.

More often, they choose more acceptable varieties from the extraordinary selection of papers, sizes, shapes, and colors available. Cover envelopes come with both covered and uncovered *windows,* or are completely windowless. They can be diecut or cut out in a thousand ways, or made to command attention through what has been printed on them. There may be one or more lines of catchy copy, line drawings or bendays, even photo reproductions. The printing may be on the envelope face, on the reverse side, or on both sides.

Still, the most popular cover envelope seems to be the #10 size mentioned earlier, with the firm's corner card (name and address) neatly printed in the upper left-hand corner.

To get away from the unwanted advertising mail image, the names and addresses of your prospective customers may be typed, or even handwritten, directly on the envelopes, instead of appearing on labels or being imprinted by addressograph. Most often, mail order houses use printed indicia or metered stamps. You may prefer affixing postage stamps, especially new issues or commemoratives, for more attention-getting value.

The Sales Letter

Of all the tools available to the direct mailer, the sales letter is the most widely used. No other printed piece approaches its versatility or possesses its power to persuade and convince the reader to act. Its possibilities are endless; it can be adapted to almost every type of sales objective. Representing one-to-one contact, seller with buyer, it replaces both the personal visit and the sales presentation.

Although most often accompanied by other enclosures—folders, brochures, order forms—the sales letter is frequently used by itself. In its simplest form, you can even print your letter on a simple postcard or on a double or three-part card.

Actual letters, neatly clothed in quality envelopes, are preferable to postcards. Relegate the postcard to its proper place in the scheme of things, at least in the mail order business. It ought to be restricted, in the main, to these two "mechanical" areas: notifying people of delays in shipment or responding to brief queries. Once in a great while, you might use postcards effectively for something a bit more creative, like sending out an informal, friendly announcement about an upcoming promotion.

Letters are inexpensive to reproduce, too. Once you have prepared the original, thousands of offset copies can be run off at a very low cost.

A sales letter may run less than a page in length, or it may be as long as three, four, or more pages. It may be printed on only one side of the paper or on both. Often, it appears on both sides of a single sheet of paper, measuring 11×17 inches, then is folded into a four-page booklet.

How long should a sales letter be? As long, or as short, as is needed to do an effective job of selling the reader.

Contents

The format of most direct mail letters is much like that of an ordinary piece of business correspondence. They're printed on regular business stationery, usually with the firm's name, address, and telephone number appearing at the top and centered. Some companies have letterheads printed with this information running along one side or along the bottom of the sheet. Often, a line cut or some other form of artwork accompanies the name and address. The typing's neatly done; ample margins surround the typed matter on all sides; and the typical parts of a letter are readily seen: date, name and address of the prospect, greeting (salutation), body of the letter, closing and signature, and occasionally a postscript.

There are differences, however. In the direct mail sales letter, there are problems in inserting the prospect's name and address properly in the correct space and in the exact typeface and color that match the printed page (unless, of course, you do it all by computer). Frequently, a headline is employed instead of personalizing the sales letter, or a general greeting, such as "Dear Worried Home-Owner" or "Dear Stamp Collector."

Then, too, direct mailers often rely on the postscript to play a significant role in the sales letter. They may use it to hammer home one more time an important selling point already stressed in the body copy. Or to furnish additional support for the claim. Or to add a sense of urgency, so the reader responds more quickly.

But over and above these and other relatively minor details, there are two major keys to writing sales letters: the *copy* and the *offer*. We needn't discuss the former here, for the skill (and art) of copywriting are treated elsewhere in this book. But that second item, the offer, merits attention at this juncture.

It's *what you have to sell* that clinches the sale, not just how you describe the item or service. This includes, of course, the terms or conditions under which the offer is made, as well as the guarantee with which you back it up.

A sincere and unequivocal statement of your guarantee should appear in your letter. However it's worded, it must convey clearly your willingness to refund the customer's money fully and promptly if he or she isn't completely satisfied.

The Order Form

Experience strongly suggests that you send along a separate order form with every mailing piece. A separate order form is preferable to having your order coupon printed on the piece itself, one that the shopper-by-mail has to clip out with a pair of scissors. This is perfectly sensible in your newspaper or magazine advertisements; it does help increase the number of replies. But using a separate order blank in your direct mail generally results in a minimum 10 percent jump in orders, and often much more.

The form itself may be a single sheet of paper (5×8 or 6×9 inches) or it can be printed directly on the back of a business reply card if no payment is required with the order. Mailers often also resort to a combination order form and return envelope, printed in one piece.

You may have to leave space on the form for the following items:

- Customer's name and address.
- Account number (with *your* company).

- Credit card number and necessary data (for MasterCard, Visa, and others).
- Name and address the merchandise is to be shipped to, if not destined for the customer.
- Item number, name, color, size, quantity, unit price, total price.
- Page number (if items selected are from your catalog).
- Instructions regarding postage, shipping, and handling charges.
- Sales tax, where applicable.
- Names and addresses of friends and others who might be interested in receiving your cards or mailings. (Space for this item can be left to the back of your business reply envelope. Note that some firms affix peel-off labels to their mailing pieces and catalogs. The shopper is asked to peel these off and place them in the space allotted to the customer's name and address, to save time and trouble.)

The Return Envelope

You would be wise to include a return envelope with most of your mailings; or, if no money must be enclosed with the order, a return postcard. This tactic will increase the number of returns. Why permit the reader's interest to wane for three or four minutes while he or she searches for an envelope and then has to write your company's name and address on it? In fact, anything you can do to make the ordering process simpler for the by-mail shopper is bound to help your sales. (An exception might be where your budget absolutely precludes the use of any kind of mailing piece but a self-mailer. But even in this situation, you might use a folder with a detachable return envelope or card.)

It's even more pleasurable for the customer not to have to pay any postage when placing an order. This doesn't mean, of course, that you should affix postage stamps to all of these envelopes. That would be a criminal waste of your funds! Instead, consider using business reply envelopes. You order these from your printer or envelope house by the thousands at relatively low cost; there's no additional cost to you if they aren't used by your customer. When you do receive orders in these envelopes, you pay the appropriate first-class postage plus a small fee.

TEST BOTH COOPERATIVE MAILINGS AND SYNDICATION

Some mail order companies will permit your enclosures to be mailed along with theirs and those of other firms under an arrangement by which postage and handling costs are shared. The names and addresses of such companies can be found in the *SRDS Direct Marketing List Source*[2] and in occasional advertisements in *Direct Marketing* magazine. Information is

---

[2] For information, call 1-800-851-SRDS.

also available from some direct marketing concerns that offer cooperative approaches. You'll have to submit your proposed materials to these co-ops well in advance of their shipping dates, for their approval, and, of course, pay the required fee.

Syndicators invite mail order firms with sizable mailing lists to use their professionally prepared direct mail materials. These companies prepare complete mailing packages for you. You send them out to your house list; they supply the merchandise you're able to sell at a wholesale cost. You may decide to maintain some of their inventory on hand, or you can have the syndicator drop ship the merchandise for you to your customers.

It's also possible, with some mail order companies, to arrange for your catalogs or brochures to be inserted in the packages they ship out to their customers.

BOOST SALES WITH YOUR OWN CATALOG

Catalogs are heavily used by department store and specialty chain store organizations. The biggest catalogs are, of course, aimed at the fall-winter season, but today's spring-summer books aren't that much smaller. In addition to the catalogs of the big store retailers, you have most likely come across those put out by the major mail order houses, like Alden and Spiegel, or those of specialty mail order firms, such as Foster and Gallagher, Sunset House, Spencer Gifts, Hanover House, and the like.

Sooner or later, you'll want to try out your first catalog. It may not be much more ambitious than a small six- or eight-pager, printed in one color on white paper. However, if your first effort brings in any profit at all, you have arrived; you're probably well on your way to a healthy and successful mail order business. Eventually, you can expect your catalogs to generate the largest share of your sales, with most of the balance derived from your direct mail and the rest from media advertising.

However, you should avoid putting out a catalog until you have acquired an extensive list of customers to mail to. Although some direct marketing experts maintain that a list of at least 10,000 to 15,000 names and addresses is needed to tackle catalog selling, you can probably make a go of it with as few as 5,000 or 6,000, provided, of course, that these are all people who have already bought merchandise from you and that you have maintained your house list in top order. Given these conditions, you can anticipate close to a 10 percent return much of the time, and occasionally, you might reach as high as 20 percent. (Your percent of return depends, to a large extent, on your catalog merchandise, the quality of your list, your pricing approaches, and the time of year.) With even a 7 or 8 percent return, you can expect several hundred orders, and the profit margin on those orders may be more than enough to cover your printing and distribution costs, especially if you start out with an inexpensive catalog.

Getting Started on Your Catalog

Well in advance of trying your own hand at catalog mailing, you should send for and analyze as many catalogs as you can get your hands on. Write for a copy of every catalog offered free in the magazine ads. And it would be worth your while, several times over, if you have to part occasionally with a dollar bill, where the company has put a price tag on its catalog. The education will pay for itself. But even after that, you'll need a capable catalog consultant, or an advertising agency experienced in catalog sales, to develop your catalogs for you. Designing and producing these showrooms in print call for highly specialized skills.

A catalog is never a simple, haphazard collection of pictures and descriptions. All of the following elements, and more, need to be taken into consideration and handled with extreme care:

- Physical dimensions of the book.
- Format.
- Merchandise to be displayed.
- Positioning of merchandise items within the catalog.
- Artwork: drawings, illustrations, halftones, and the like.
- Typography.
- Headlines, subheadlines, and selling copy.
- Prices of the merchandise shown.
- Promotional information.
- Instructions for ordering from the book.
- Order form and return envelope.
- Printing method to be used.

Ready-Made Drop Ship Catalogs

A number of companies advertise their own professionally made catalogs for use by mail order operators. These firms offer to sell their catalogs on a per hundred or per thousand basis, usually at a price you couldn't duplicate yourself (unless you print a couple of hundred thousand at a time). For a nominal charge, they'll print your firm's name and address on the cover page, and they're prepared to *drop ship* most of the items in the catalog for you. This means that when you get orders, you send your own labels to the company with your customers' names and addresses properly typed out, and they'll mail the merchandise for you. You pay them the wholesale price for the goods. You *might* want to test this arrangement for yourself to see if it pays (experience says that it seldom does).

You might, however, want to try these catalogs out as "stuffers" along with the merchandise you ship. This way, you face no additional postage costs, and you might receive enough orders to make it worthwhile.

SOURCES OF ADDITIONAL INFORMATION

Crippen, John K., *Successful Direct-Mail Methods*. New York: Garland, 1985.

Govoni, N. et al., *Promotional Management*. Englewood Cliffs, NJ: Prentice-Hall, 1986.

Hahn, Fred, *Do-It-Yourself Advertising: How to Produce Great Ads, Catalogs, Direct Mail, and Much More*. New York: Wiley, 1993.

Harper, Rose, *Mailing List Strategies: A Guide to Direct Mail Success*. New York: McGraw-Hill, 1986.

Kremer, John, *The Complete Mail-Order Sourcebook*. New York: Wiley, 1992.

Lewis, Herschell G., *Direct Mail Copy That Sells*. Englewood Cliffs, NJ: Prentice-Hall, 1986.

_____ , *How to Write Powerful Catalog Copy*. Chicago: Dartnell, 1993.

Lumley, James E. A., *Sell It by Mail: Making Your Product the One They Buy*. New York: Wiley, 1986.

Maas, Jane, *Better Brochures, Catalogs and Mailing Pieces*. New York: St. Martin's Press, 1984.

Nash, Edward L., *The Direct Marketing Handbook,* (2d ed.). New York: McGraw-Hill, 1992.

Smith, Jeanette, *The Publicity Kit: A Complete Guide for Entrepreneurs, Small Businesses, and Nonprofit Organizations*. New York: Wiley, 1991.

Stone, Bob, *Successful Direct Marketing Methods,* (5th ed.). Lincolnwood, IL: National Textbook, 1993.

13

Managing Your Direct Mail Efforts

In the previous chapter, we explored that most personal and most powerful of all advertising methods: direct mail. After reviewing some of the objectives that business organizations seek to attain via this unique medium, we spelled out both the advantages and disadvantages that it offers advertisers. You were then introduced to the more popular formats for marketing by mail and given detailed descriptions of the major elements that make up the "standard" direct mail package. Finally, you were provided with information on cooperative mailings, syndication, and selling by catalog.

This chapter aims at furthering your knowledge of direct mail marketing. We begin by stressing the importance of proper scheduling for each direct mail campaign. You're shown how to construct a code to help you identify the source of every response you receive from all your advertising (all mass media, direct mail, and telemarketing). We then present useful tips for handling your incoming mail. You learn how to convert inquiries into orders and how to increase your sales volume by inserting package stuffers into the shipments you make. Suggestions are then offered for holding down mailing costs. A thorough treatment of postage and mailing information concludes the chapter.

SCHEDULING YOUR DIRECT MAIL CAMPAIGNS

In direct-mail marketing, a one-shot offer is a rarity. Most letters are part and parcel of ongoing campaigns. If you're going to sell merchandise or a service via direct mail, plan on sending as many as five (and sometimes more) letters about your proposition to every prospect on your list. Naturally, you'll need to prepare a detailed schedule for each campaign you design. After your first mailing goes out, send your follow-up letters at two-week intervals. Tally your responses from each batch and keep posting your letters just as long as you can still earn a bit of profit on each mailing.

Watch Your Calendar, Too!

Choosing the right time to distribute your direct mail can bring you sizable profits. Two identical mailings, dispatched at different times of the year, will not yield identical results; often, one brings in twice as many replies as the other.

What's the right time? Although some items may sell well at just about any time of year, direct mail offers distributed in January and February—and from September through December—seem to bring in a greater number of responses than letters sent out during other times of the year. For most types of merchandise, the least productive months for direct-mail offers are May, June, and July.

Seasonal items are exceptions; post your mailings for such goods two months in advance of the upcoming season. And be sure to make that three months for Christmas merchandise!

As a last comment, expect to accumulate 60 to 65 percent of all your replies within the two-week period immediately following a distribution by first-class mail. (Add another 7 to 10 days to this period if you affix third-class postage to your letters.)

HOW TO KEY YOUR MAILINGS AND TRACK RESULTS

If you have already advertised in other media, you may have already adopted a procedure designed to help you determine from which sources your orders and inquiries have come. If you have, you can rely on the same (or a similar) procedure to identify the source mailings that bring you your responses.

For those of you who haven't as yet originated a master key and identification code for your advertising, here's one simple approach to the problem:

Assume that you plan to run the same ad in four different magazines: A, B, C, and D. Begin developing your code key by listing on a sheet of paper the letters A through D. Leave space for at least twelve lines below each letter.

Write the name of each magazine after one of the letters. Since you may decide to advertise in several issues of the same publication, you'll need to add a number to your magazine identification letter. Under each letter, list the numbers 1 through 12; 1 will signify the January issue; 2, the February book—all the way through to 12, for December's issue.

This, then, will constitute your key to your code. To identify readily the source of an order or inquiry, encode your ad by placing the word "Department" (or, if you prefer, "Section" or "Box"), followed by the I.D. letter and number, directly before your firm's name and address.

Let's suppose, for example, that you've scheduled the same ad in Magazine C for four different months. For the October issue, then, your firm's signature would look something like this:

> Department C10
> Melissa's Giftware
> 16 State Street
> Horsham, PA 19044

The above procedure is just one suggestion; with a bit of time and some creativity, you can develop your own personal tracking code. Moreover, you should devise similar coding techniques for your newspaper ads, radio, and television advertising, and for each and every mailing you distribute.

One way of keeping track of each distribution is to print or stamp a code (letters and/or numbers) on your order forms. If you send out thousands of letters at a time, consider printing your order forms in different colors or, perhaps, addressed to different people in your organization. Another simple approach is to cut a notch somewhere on the side of your order forms, in different spots for different mailings.

Tracking Your Responses

Record the replies you receive from all your advertising and, if this is part of your operation, through telemarketing as well. Enter returns just as soon as they come in so that you can determine the effectiveness of every one of your promotional efforts. Among other details, be sure to record the following information:

- Date received.
- Source of the response.
- Name and address of the buyer or inquirer.
- Merchandise or service(s) ordered.
- Total amount of the order.
- Sales tax, if applicable.
- Telephone number and contact person (if an organization).
- Discount granted, if any.

Prepare a separate summary record for each and every source. If you have computerized your mail order operation, your information flow will proceed much faster and far more smoothly.

GUIDELINES FOR HANDLING INCOMING MAIL

Shortly after your first classified or small-space advertisement appears in print or your first direct mail pieces reach their destination, letters from respondents will begin to show up in your mailbox. Be sure to open and examine all incoming mail *daily*. The letters will fall into one of two categories: those that contain orders and those that ask questions. (Later on, you may expect an occasional letter of complaint, but you should be able to keep these to a minimum if you run your business properly.)

Read each letter carefully and staple its contents to the envelope. Prepare an index card; on it, enter the name and address of the sender, the date received, and all details pertinent to the order or query. Clip the index card to the letter. When you have finished your stack of mail, separate orders from queries. Strive to fill and mail out every order within 48 hours. If you expect a serious delay in filling the order because you're temporarily out of stock on an item, be certain to notify your customer by postcard or letter and explain why the shipment will be delayed. (Consider ten days from the date you received the letter as a serious delay.)

At the end of each day, file the letters together with carbon copies of your responses, duplicate shipping labels, and other notes attached. File them by last names and in alphabetical order.

Use your index cards to start your house mailing list. If you have not as yet computerized your operation, buy sheets of blank labels, gummed and perforated, and type the names and addresses from the cards on these sheets. (They come 33 labels to the sheet.) Type them in triplicate, using carbons. Later on, you can use the original set of labels for the first mailing of a new offer—and the duplicate and triplicate copies for follow-up mailings.

If and when you do purchase a computer, feed the information you've collected on your index cards to initiate your new database!

HOW TO CONVERT INQUIRIES INTO ORDERS

After you have processed all orders for the day, set to work answering your inquiries. Some may require an original letter on your business stationery; others can be answered with a form letter or, perhaps, a brief note on a postcard. The reason for answering promptly is simple: when the prospective customer wrote to you, he or she was very interested in what you were offering, but as each day goes by, that interest wanes more and more until it's too late to make a sale.

Send out your reply. Then, check the calendar, counting off 15 days from the time you posted your reply. Enter both dates on your record (index) card. If no order is forthcoming by the second date, mail the prospect a second letter that repeats the same offer. If you're disappointed, you may still get action by sending out two or three additional mailings, approximately at ten-day intervals.

EARN MORE WITH PACKAGE STUFFERS

A simple and truly inexpensive way of boosting your sales volume is to insert promotional material into every package you send to your customers. As the U.S. Small Business Administration advises:

> A regular catalog or a special offer rides "free" in outgoing orders. Since postage and packing costs already are being paid to ship the merchandise, package enclosures can bring in new sales and profits.[1]

Remember: when you insert a booklet, brochure, catalog, circular, folder, or leaflet into each order you fulfill, your only additional expense is that of the printed matter itself.

TIPS FOR SAVING ON MAILING COSTS

Planning, organizing, and directing your firm's direct mail efforts will consume a great deal of your time and energies, not to mention the considerable depletion of your financial reserves. A tight and secure system for handling internal operations is mandatory if you're to be successful in your mail order enterprise. At the outset, you'll most likely be doing all the related work by yourself, or with the help of your spouse and/or children. After your company has been firmly established and is in a growth track, you should delegate these responsibilities to one or more employees to free your time for other, more important tasks. By this time, your system should be firmly in place and your mailroom well managed under a trained executive.

To help you trim your direct mail costs, here are a few additional thoughts, courtesy of the U.S. Postal Service:[2]

- Mechanize repetitive chores—automated metering, opening, inserting, and wrapping equipment can speed business mail.
- Save postage costs by presorting and bundling first class mail.
- Get special bulk mail rates.
- Staff your mailroom properly.
- Check and recheck your scales.

---

[1] William A. Cohen, "Selling by Mail Order," *Management Aid 4.023* (Washington, DC: U.S. Small Business Administration, n.d.), 4.

[2] Excerpted from the U.S. Postal Service, "Modern Mailroom Practices," *Publication 62* (Washington, DC: U.S. Government Printing Office, August 1977).

- Save unused envelopes with meter tapes for refunds.
- Keep your house list up-to-date; be sure to clean your list every year.
- Consider making a "double postcard mailing" to ask recipients if they'd like to continue receiving your mailings.
- Switch to trays for modern mailing convenience.
- Consult your local postmaster or customer service representative for assistance.

POSTAGE AND MAILING DATA

The U.S. Postal Service classifies all mailable material into four categories. Pertinent details for each of these classifications follow.

First Class

Included as first-class mail are handwritten and typed letters, postcards, greeting cards, statements, bills, checks, and money orders. Business reply mail is also considered first class. If the item weighs more than 11 ounces, it is then called priority mail. Current postage for a priority mail item of up to two pounds in weight is $3.00; beyond that weight, postage is charged according to postal zones. The maximum allowable weight for priority mail is 70 pounds. Envelopes and packages must be clearly marked "Priority Mail" on all sides.

Heavy mailers may wish to presort their first class mail to save postage. (Consult your local post office for details.)

Express Mail

Available seven days a week, this overnight delivery service features noon delivery between major business markets, along with other services. Express mail letter rates are: $10.75, for up to 8 ounces and $15.00 for mail weighing between 8 ounces and 2 pounds. (See postmaster for rates for heavier mail, up to 70 pounds.)

Second Class

Second-class mail is available only to newspapers and periodicals that have been authorized second-class mail privileges.

Third Class

Mail sent under this classification costs less and moves more slowly than first-class mail. This classification is often referred to as advertising mail. It includes circulars, books, catalogs, and other printed matter, as well as merchandise, seeds, cuttings, bulbs, roots, scions, and plants weighing less than 16 ounces. Both regular and bulk rates are available only to authorized mailers (consult postmaster for details).

A bulk mailing fee of $85 must be paid annually, in advance. This payment enables you to mail at a single post office at the third-class bulk rates for 12 months. Certain conditions must be observed; for example, the letters must be properly ZIP-coded and presorted, and postage must be prepaid by meter stamp, permit imprint, or precanceled stamps. (See postmaster for further information on the handling of bulk-rate mail.)

Fourth Class

Also called parcel mail or parcel post, this category offers a service for parcels and packages that weigh from 1 to 70 pounds. Domestic fourth-class mail charges are based on both weight and distance factors. The country is divided into eight parcel post zones, each requiring a different rate scale.

Other Pertinent Facts

Other common postal service terms to know include:

Business reply mail. Mailers use business reply mail to encourage responses. Such mail is turned over to the sender from any post office in the country. When received, both the regular first-class rate and a small business reply fee are charged. An annual permit is required as well as a postage trust account.

Certified mail. Used for items of no intrinsic value and is handled in transit as ordinary mail. A return receipt is available for an additional fee (currently, $1.10); this provides proof of service.

C.O.D. service. May be used in connection with parcel post, or first- and third-class mail. When the recipient is to pay for the merchandise sent, the mail carrier collects the amount due plus a C.O.D. (collect on delivery) fee. This fee includes insurance protection.

Insurance. Available on third- and fourth-class domestic mail and on merchandise sent by first class. The value is limited to $600.

List correction. The post office provides a series of list correction services, as well as a list sequencing service (where the addresses on a mailing list are sorted into a carrier route sequence).

Plant load. When a very large mailing is prepared for one or several destination points, the postmaster may send a vehicle to your place of business to pick it up. The mail is then taken directly to its destination.

Precanceled stamps. May be used only at the post office that issued your permit for using such stamps. Their use reduces the time and costs of mail handling.

Presorting. For each advance in the degree of presorting by a mailer, more time is saved in processing the mail. Faster handling is also accomplished by traying the mail in trays furnished by the post office. Such mail may be bundled and labeled, or trayed and sacked, depending on your preference and the post office's recommendation. Presorting saves postage, when properly prepared according to requirements.

Registered mail. Offers security for valuable and irreplaceable items, with insurance protection and a return receipt (for an additional fee).

Special delivery. Applies to all classes of mail, at an extra fee. Such mail is also delivered on Sundays and holidays.

Special handling. Useful for items requiring special handling; available only for third- and fourth-class mail at an additional fee.

Size Standards for Domestic Mail[3]

Minimum Size

Pieces that do not meet the following requirements are prohibited from the mails:

1. All pieces must be at least .007 of an inch thick and
2. All pieces (except keys and identification devices) that are ¼ inch or less in thickness must be:

   (a) Rectangular in shape,
   (b) At least 3½ inches long, and
   (c) At least 5 inches deep.

Note: Pieces *greater than ¼ inch thick* can be mailed even if they measure less than 3½ by 5 inches.

Nonstandard Mail

All first-class mail (except presort first-class and carrier-route first-class) weighing 1 ounce or less and all single-piece rate third-class mail weighing 1 ounce or less is nonstandard (and subject to a surcharge in addition to the applicable postage and fees) if:

1. *Any* of the following dimensions are exceeded:

   Length—11½ inches
   Height—6 inches
   Thickness—¼ inch

2. The length divided by the height is not between 1.3 and 2.5 inclusive.

---

[3] This information has been excerpted from "Postage Rates, Fees, and Information," *Notice 59* (Washington, DC: U.S. Postal Service, April 1988).

Postage Rates

- First class: Letters, 32¢ the first ounce, 23¢ each additional ounce; postcards, 20¢.
- Third class (circulars, books, catalogs, and other printed matter; merchandise, seeds, cuttings, bulbs, roots, scions, and plants, weighing less than 16 ounces):

  Single-piece rates for piece not exceeding:

1 oz	$0.32
2 oz	0.55
3 oz	0.78
4 oz	1.01
5 oz	1.24
6 oz	1.47
7 oz	1.70
8 oz	1.93
9 oz	2.16
10 oz	2.39
11 oz	2.62
Over 11 oz. but not exceeding 13 oz.	2.90
Over 13 oz. but less than 16 oz.	2.95

- Fourth class: Parcel post, zone rates. (Consult postmaster for weight and size limits; see zone rate chart.)

Special Services—Domestic Mail Only

- Insurance (additional fee for covering against loss or damage, besides postage):

Liability	Fee
$0.01 to $50	$0.75
50.01 to $100	1.60
100.01 to $200	2.50
200.01 to $300	3.40
300.01 to $400	4.30
400.01 to $500	5.20
500.01 to $600	6.10

- Registry—for maximum protection and security: (Fees shown below are in addition to postage.)

Value	For articles covered by postal insurance	For articles not covered
$0.01 to $100	$4.90	$4.85
$100.01 to $500	5.40	5.20
$500.01 to $1,000	5.85	5.55

For higher values, consult postmaster.

- Certified mail: $1.10, in addition to postage.
- C.O.D.: Consult postmaster for fee and conditions of mailing.
- Special delivery (in addition to required postage): For first class and priority mail, up to 2 lbs., $9.95; over 2 but not more than 10 lbs., $10.35; more than 10 lbs., $11.15. All other classes, $10.45, $11.25, and $12.10, as above weight categories.

SOURCES OF ADDITIONAL INFORMATION

Crippen, John K., *Successful Direct-Mail Methods.* New York: Garland, 1985.

Gosden, Freeman F., Jr., *Direct Marketing Success: What Works and Why.* New York: Wiley, 1985.

Govoni, N. et al., *Promotional Management.* Englewood Cliffs, NJ: Prentice-Hall, 1986.

Harper, Rose, *Mailing List Strategies: A Guide to Direct Mail Success.* New York: McGraw-Hill, 1986.

Kremer, John, *The Complete Mail-Order Sourcebook.* New York: Wiley, 1992.

Stone, Bob, *Successful Direct Marketing Methods,* (5th ed.). Lincolnwood, IL: National Textbook, 1993.

14

Building and Maintaining Your Mailing List

If you're like the typical newcomer to the mail order business, you have most likely found a product (or a service) that you believe will sell well by mail. And you have had the courage to test its potential by investing a few hundred dollars, or perhaps as much as $1,000, in several small ads in the print media. Possibly, you have found that one or two of these earned a small profit and that the rest didn't pull enough in the way of orders to cover your advertising cost.

Disheartened? You shouldn't be. You have accomplished something very important. You now "own" the names and addresses of a number of persons who have bought from your new mail order firm. These are worth money to you. They constitute the nucleus of your own mailing list.

I found this out many years ago, when I launched a part-time mail order business to supplement my regular income. My plans were to sell inexpensive novelties through small space and classified magazine and newspaper advertising in order to develop a good customer list that I would be able to use to send gift catalogs later on. One tiny advertisement in particular brought in more than 100 orders for the novelty salt-and-pepper shaker set I had displayed. After deducting my cost of merchandise and my packaging and postage expenses, I found I had lost nearly one-half of my advertising investment (let alone the work and time involved)! But, each set that was mailed out carried a bounce-back in the form of a one-page circular containing photographs and descriptions of four other salt-and-pepper sets. This circular had cost me about $35 at the time to have printed, for about 500 copies. I received orders from more than 20 percent of my customers, and some ordered as many as six or twelve of the sets for holiday gifts. I hadn't realized before this happened that some people collect these items as a hobby.

So, I finally earned a bit of profit, after all. *And* I had the start of a valuable house mailing list for the future.

DEVELOPING THE HOUSE LIST: YOUR MOST PRECIOUS ASSET

Just how important your own list will become may be difficult to perceive at the beginning. Yet, you can't be successful in mail order selling without it—and without one that keeps growing and that you monitor zealously.

One direct marketer began in business by selling office supplies to commercial firms. Advertisements in trade publications brought in hundreds of orders initially. Some of the offers advertised were so powerful they brought in enough sales to cover the advertising costs; others did not. Yet, all the names the marketer obtained in this manner, customers and inquiries, went into building the company's house list. During the first year, three mailings followed the publication advertising: a self-mailing folder and two small catalogs. The business prospered and grew.

Replies to your own advertising are, of course, a major approach to developing a mailing list, but there are other ways to go. For example, you can ask your own customers to recommend friends and neighbors who might be interested in your product(s) or service(s). This is easily done by leaving room for one or more names and addresses on your mailing pieces and catalogs. You can also rent lists from mailing list houses and brokers (discussed later in this chapter).

Or, you can do some research and compile your own mailing lists. Here are some of the sources you can refer to:

Automobile registrations

Birth notices in newspapers

Business directories

Civic association memberships

College alumni groups

Contest entrants

Convention attendees

Fraternal order memberships

Industrial directories

Magazine advertisements

Marriage/engagement notices in newspapers

New business starts

Newspaper advertisements

Organization memberships

Professional group memberships

Social organizations and clubs

Tax rolls

Trade association memberships

Trade directories

Trade show attendees

Union memberships

Voter registrations

Who's Who, and similar reference works

Yellow Pages

A useful tactic is to separate your mailing list early in the game into three separate groups:

1. *Active customers,* people who have purchased merchandise through your advertising efforts
2. *Prospective buyers,* persons who have requested information from you as well as those whom your customers have recommended
3. *The catch-all list,* which should include all the names and addresses you're able to compile through your own research

Keep these three lists separated while your names begin to mount into the thousands. Remember: the key to mail order success is to keep building your lists and, all along, try to convert the names in lists 2 and 3 into Active Customers. Since you do prepare a master index card for every entry, make certain you update these masters regularly, so that at all times they contain all vital information for ready reference. When you send out mailings, type the names and addresses directly on your outside envelopes, or use perforated gummed labels. Don't invest in equipment, such as addressograph plates or a computer; you can't afford to automate until you're well established in your new business.

RENTING LISTS FROM LIST BROKERS AND COMPILERS

You can expand your own mailings by renting, or occasionally buying, names and addresses from companies that offer other mailing lists. These list houses may be classified into general-line and limited-line firms. The latter specialize in specific list types, for example: older people, medical personnel (doctors, psychiatrists, and so on), lawyers, engineers, and other professionals. The general-line list house offers a far broader range. Commonly, these firms issue catalogs that describe and indicate the rental costs for many hundreds, even thousands, of different lists. (See Exhibits 14–1 and 14–2 for sample catalog pages from two different mailing houses.)

EXHIBIT 14–1   Sample page from list catalog

QUANTITY		PRICE
18,500	Medical Malpractice	MIN.
31,200	Patent, Trademark, Copyright	$50/M
130,900	Probate, Trust & Estate	$50/M
33,500	Product Liability	$50/M
24,100	Public Utility, Communications	MIN.
135,400	Real Estate, Property	$50/M
106,000	Taxation	$50/M
23,800	Transportation	$50/M
112,000	Trial	$50/M
11,500	Auctioneers & Liquidators	$50/M
3,400	Audio-Visual Production	$50/M
1,300	Audio Visual Dealers	$50/M
9,500	Audio Visual Education Directors by Title	Inquire
1,800	Auditoriums, Arenas, Conv. Halls	$50/M
22,900	Auditors, Internal	$50/M

AUTOMOTIVE

QUANTITY		PRICE
25,100	Auto Dealers, New Cars	$50/M
73,000	Auto Dealers, Used Cars	$50/M
3,700	Auto Driving Schools	$50/M
17,200	Auto Muffler Shops	$50/M
5,200	Auto Parking Lots & Garages	$50/M
5,600	Auto Paint Shops	$50/M
550,000	Auto Parts & Supplies (Retail)	$50/M
351,000	Auto Parts & Supplies (Wholesale)	$50/M
300,000	Auto Repair Shops	$50/M
8,400	Auto Seat Cover, Top & Upholstery Shops	$50/M
88,000	Auto Service Stations	$50/M
1,300	Auto Supply Chains	Inquire
40,000	Auto Towing & Wrecking	$50/M
42,000	Auto Tire Dealers (Retail)	$50/M
5,200	Auto Tire Dealers (Wholesale)	$50/M
64,800	Auto Body Repair Shops	$50/M
19,000	Auto Transmission Shops	$50/M
14,700	Auto & Truck Dealers	$50/M
48,000	Auto Truck Renting & Leasing	$50/M
64,000,000	Automobile Owners, By Make, Year, Model (See Page 18)	$85/M
360,000	Automobile (Exotic) Owners	$85/M
7,000	Automobile Towing/Road Service	$50/M
25,900	Aviation Executives	$50/M
2,500	Aviation Parts Mfrs., Aircraft Equipment Mfrs.	$50/M
700	Aviation Tower Operators	MIN.
58,000	Awnings & Canopies Dealers	$50/M

CAN'T FIND THE LIST YOU WANT? WE HAVE IT. PLEASE CALL!

B

QUANTITY		PRICE
1,400	Bagel Shops	$50/M
29,000	Bakeries, Retail	$50/M
1,100	Ballet/Dance Companies	$50/M
12,255	Band Directors, High School	$50/M
10,000	Bankers, Mortgage, Executives	$50/M
47,200	Bankers, Mortgage, Firms	$50/M

BANKS

QUANTITY		PRICE
12,000	Banks, Main Offices	$50/M
400	Banks - Assets $1 Billion or more	MIN.
700	Banks - Assets $500 Million or more	MIN.
3,400	Banks - Assets $100 Million or more	$50/M
4,500	Banks - Assets $75 Million or more	$50/M
6,300	Banks - Assets $50 Million or more	$50/M
10,900	Banks - Assets $25 Million or more	$50/M
13,000	Banks - Assets $10 Million or more	$50/M
400	Banks - Assets less than $10 Million	MIN.
53,000	Banks, Branches	$50/M
21,400	Banks, Cashiers	$50/M

QUANTITY		PRICE
108,000	Banks, Executives	$50/M
36,000	Banks, Executives, Women	$50/M
3,300	Banks, Savings & Loan (HQ)	$50/M
14,600	Banks, Savings & Loan (Branches)	$50/M
4,800	Banks, Trust Officers	$50/M
14,300	Banks, Loan Officers	$50/M
10,000	Barber & Beauty Supplies	$50/M
60,000	Barber Shops	$50/M
70,300	Bars, Taverns, Cocktail Lounges	$50/M
2,500	Beauty Schools	$50/M
222,300	Beauty Shops	$50/M
340	Beekeepers	MIN.
9,100	Beer & Ale Retailers	$50/M
4,400	Beer & Ale Wholesalers	$50/M
37,000	Behavioral Scientists	$50/M
170	Better Business Bureaus	MIN.
1,800	Beverage Bottlers	$50/M
11,200	Bicycle Dealers & Repairs	$50/M
3,400	Billiard Parlors & Poolrooms	$50/M
3,100	Billion Dollar Companies	$5/M
5,673	Biological Chemists	$50/M
27,000	Biologists	$50/M
4,200	Birth Control Centers	$50/M
6,400,000	Black Families	Inquire
1,050	Blood Banks	$50/M
3,200,000	Blue Collar Workers	Inquire
15,686	Boards of Education	$50/M

BOATS

QUANTITY		PRICE
3,600	Boat Building & Repairing Yards	$50/M
23,000	Boat Dealers	$50/M
3,400	Boat & Marine Supplies	$50/M

BOAT OWNERS

4,000,000 boat owners may be selected by size, hull type, propulsion, pleasure, commercial, income, age and telephone. Please inquire.

QUANTITY		PRICE
65,000	Body Repair Shops, Automobile	$50/M
3,600	Boiler Contractors	$50/M
138	Book Clubs	MIN.
10,000	Book Publishers	$50/M
4,000	Book Publishers (Major)	$50/M
1,000	Book Wholesalers	MIN.
20,000	Bookkeeping Services	$50/M
24,000	Bookstores	$50/M
500	Bookstores, Chains	Inquire
3,400	Bookstores, College	$50/M
3,600	Bookstores, Religious	$50/M
1,200	Botanical Gardens and Specialists	MIN.
2,400	Botanists	$50/M
2,750	Bottlers, Soft Drink	$50/M
4,300	Boutiques	$50/M
7,000	Bowling Alleys	$50/M
2,200	Box & Container Mfrs	$50/M
920	Boy Scout Councils	MIN.
2,400	Bread, Baked Goods Mfrs	$50/M
14,100	Bricklayers, Masonry	$50/M
8,000	Bridal Shops	$50/M
186,000	BRIDES TO BE	Inquire
31,000	Broadcasting Executives	$50/M
3,540	Broadcasting Stations - Radio AM	$50/M
2,200	Broadcasting Stations - Radio FM	$50/M
1,300	Broadcasting Stations - TV	MIN.
1,500,000	Brokers & Agents, Insurance	Inquire
209,000	Brokers & Agents, Insurance (Offices)	$50/M
3,100	Brokers, Business	$50/M
200,000	Brokers, Agents, Real Estate (Individuals)	$50/M
160,000	Brokers & Agents, Real Estate (Offices)	$50/M
38,000	Brokers, Securities, High-Level Executives	$50/M
33,000	Brokers, Securities - Offices	$50/M
325,000	Brokers, Securities, Registered Representatives	Inquire
201,000	Building/General Contractors	$50/M
95,000	Building Materials & Supplies Retailers	$50/M
62,000	Building Materials & Supplies Wholesalers	$50/M

QUANTITY		PRICE
27,000	Building & Office Cleaners (Janitorial Services)	$50/M
13,500	Burglar Alarm Wholesalers	MIN.
11,300	Burners (Furnace) Wholesalers	$50/M
9,500	Bus Companies (All)	$50/M
5,000	Bus Companies (Charter & Retail)	$50/M
4,350	Bus Companies (Inter-City)	$50/M
8,050	Bus Company Executives	$50/M

BUSINESS EXECS./OWNERS

QUANTITY		PRICE
3,100	Business Brokers	$50/M
3,100	Business Economists	$50/M
1,600,000	Business Executives	$50/M
2,420,000	Business Executives, Top Salaried Home Address	$50/M
4,200	Business Forms Manufacturers	$50/M
10,000	Business Forms & Systems, Whol	$50/M
2,800,000	Business Owners (Small)	Inquire

BUSINESSES BY EMPLOYEE SIZE & SALES VOLUME
Telephone Verified

Number of Employees Range	Sales Volume $ (in thousands)
1 - 4	1 - 499
5 - 9	500 - 999
10 - 19	1,000 - 2,499
20 - 49	2,500 - 4,999
50 - 99	5,000 - 9,999
100 - 249	10,000 - 19,999
250 - 499	20,000 - 49,999
500 - 999	50,000 - 99,999
1,000 - 4,999	100,000 - 499,999
5,000 - 9,999	500,000 - 999,999
10,000+	1,000,000+

QUANTITY		PRICE
1,500	Business Schools (Collegiate)	MIN.
7,700	Business, Secretarial Schools	$50/M
3,600	Business & Trade Organizations	$50/M
8,500	Business & Trade Publications	$50/M
13,300	Butcher Shops	$50/M
7,300	Butchers, Wholesale	$50/M

C

QUANTITY		PRICE
17,400	Cabinet Makers	$50/M
20	Cable TV, Networks	MIN.
7,200	Cable TV Operators	$50/M
10,600,000	Cable TV Subscribers	Inquire
513,000	Cafes, Restaurants, Eating Places	$50/M
3,300	Calculators Wholesale	$50/M
168,000	Camcorder Owners	Inquire
3,100	Camera Equipment Wholesalers	$50/M
5,900	Camera & Photo Stores	$50/M
10,900	Campgrounds	$50/M
10,200	Camper & Trailer Dealers	$50/M
2,100	Camping Equipment Retailers	$50/M
6,250	Camps, All Types, Summer	$50/M
2,000	Camps, Children's Summer (Accredited)	$50/M
1,800,000	CANADIAN BUSINESSES	Inquire

Businesses, Professionals & Institutions selectable by SIC and all provinces.

Inquire for specific counts.

QUANTITY		PRICE
5,700	Candy, Confectionery Wholesalers	$50/M
1,320	Candy Manufacturers	MIN.
10,400	Candy Stores	$50/M
25,100	Car Dealers, New	$50/M
73,000	Car Dealers, Used	$50/M
24,000	Car Washes	$50/M
11,800	Cards (Greeting) Shops	$50/M
37,900	Career Women	$50/M
52,000	Carpenters (Individuals)	Inquire

ALVIN B. ZELLER   224 FIFTH AVE., NY, NY 10001   ORDERS - TOLL FREE (800) 223-0814   IN N.Y. (212) 689-4900   FAX (212) 481-4245

4

Source: Reproduced courtesy of Alvin B. Zeller, Inc., 224 Fifth Avenue, New York, NY 10001.

EXHIBIT 14-2   Sample page from list catalog

SIC Code	List Title	United States Total U.S. List Count	State Counts: See Page #	Canada Total Canadian List Count	SIC Code	List Title	United States Total U.S. List Count	State Counts: See Page #	Canada Total Canadian List Count
6141-02	Financing	15,422	44	1,139	8641-01	Fraternal Organizations	11,905	47	325
6282-04	Financing Consultants	3,800	‡	444		*** Available By Type/Name ***			
7231-02	Fingernail Salons	35,393	45	409	8641-07	Fraternities & Sororities	2,144	‡	26
5063-08	Fire Alarm Systems	6,511	‡	951		French Food (See Restaurants)			
1521-14	Fire Damage Restoration	8,895	‡	746	4731-02	Freight Consolidating	676	‡	5
5087-52	Fire Department Equipment & Supplies	591	‡	1	4731-04	Freight Forwarding	6,282	‡	1,061
9224-04	Fire Departments	27,147	47	2	4222-01	Frozen Food Locker Plants	726	‡	15
5099-03	Fire Extinguishers	3,968	‡	576	5421-03	Frozen Foods Retail	506	‡	297
6331-01	Fire Marine and Casualty Insurance	3,169	‡	3	5142-01	Frozen Foods Wholesale	1,463	‡	404
8748-32	Fire Protection Consultants	685	‡	156	5148-05	Fruit & Vegetable Growers & Shippers	3,271	‡	441
5063-15	Fire Protection Equipment & Supplies	2,949	‡	713	5947-13	Fruit Baskets Gift	9,246	44	1,259
5719-33	Fireplace Equipment Retail	2,380	‡	291	5431-01	Fruits & Vegetables Retail	8,368	‡	1,779
5719-32	Fireplaces	3,515	‡	1,393	5148-01	Fruits & Vegetables Wholesale	6,784	‡	898
7349-16	Fireplaces Cleaning	4,542	‡	593	7539-06	Fuel Injection Equipment (Repairing)	539	‡	126
1799-24	Fireproofing	583	‡	110	5172-06	Fuel Oils	15,313	42	1,880
5989-03	Firewood	3,171	‡	417	5812-23	Function Rooms	26,706	44	3,217
5092-02	Fireworks	727	‡	77	8399-07	Fund Raising Counselors & Organizations	2,735	‡	347
5912-03	First Aid Supplies	1,649	‡	386	5199-07	Fund Raising Merchandise	1,299	‡	1
5421-01	Fish & Seafood Retail	8,112	‡	1,032	7261-03	Funeral Directors	29,223	45	3,133
5146-01	Fish & Seafood Wholesale	4,868	‡	962	7261-01	Funeral Directors' Service	580	‡	1
0921-01	Fish Hatcheries	817	‡	282	7261-05	Funeral Plans Pre-Arranged	3,388	‡	726
5941-34	Fishermens Supplies	1,602	‡	227	7261-02	Funeral Service and Crematories	4,281	‡	185
5941-33	Fishing Bait	5,009	‡	381	5632-02	Fur Business Retail	1,372	‡	676
7999-28	Fishing Parties	2,373	‡	469	7219-03	Fur Cleaning & Dyeing Retail	607	‡	90
5941-31	Fishing Tackle Dealers	5,052	‡	771	7219-01	Fur Storage	1,138	‡	512
5091-07	Fishing Tackle Wholesale & Mfrs	926	‡	157	5075-07	Furnaces Heating	11,145	42	2,623
7991-01	Fitness Centers	11,620	46	1,247		*** Available By Brands Sold ***			
5941-36	Fitness Equipment & Supplies	3,577	‡	284	1711-10	Furnaces Repairing & Cleaning	2,948	‡	1,166
5331-01	Five Cents To One Dollar Stores	10,481	43	3,545	5712-02	Furniture Childrens	1,873	‡	165
5039-12	Flag Poles	799	‡	66	7217-01	Furniture Cleaning	8,281	‡	1,188
2399-05	Flags & Banners	3,146	‡	236	5712-16	Furniture Dealers Retail	38,100	43	4,803
5932-18	Flea Markets	2,487	‡	350	5021-07	Furniture Dealers Wholesale	2,662	‡	315
1752-03	Floor Laying Refinishing & Resurfacing	5,407	‡	1,231	5712-17	Furniture Designers & Custom Builders	6,361	‡	1,117
5087-12	Floor Machines	1,072	‡	111	2599-01	Furniture Manufacturers	5,153	‡	1,301
7359-29	Floor Machines Renting	538	‡	58	5712-01	Furniture Outdoor	2,654	‡	347
5713-06	Floor Materials	14,015	43	1,856	7359-30	Furniture Renting & Leasing	5,410	‡	138
5023-13	Floor Materials Wholesale & Mfrs	523	‡	37	7641-05	Furniture Repairing & Refinishing	8,821	‡	1,219
1752-05	Floor Refinishing & Resurfacing	728	‡	99	7641-04	Furniture Stripping	1,698	‡	2
7349-19	Floor Waxing Polishing & Cleaning	3,953	‡	115	5712-18	Furniture Unfinished	1,085	‡	78
5992-01	Florists Retail	49,800	44	5,491	5932-17	Furniture Used	8,828	‡	955
5193-05	Florists Supplies	1,043	‡	109	5712-23	Futons	683	‡	224
5193-04	Florists Wholesale	3,573	‡	581					
0181-01	Flower Growers & Shippers	6,335	‡	688		**G**			
5999-67	Flowers Artificial	4,403	‡	788					
5199-02	Foam & Sponge Rubber	1,309	‡	203	5945-09	Games & Game Supplies	1,995	‡	556
5141-02	Food Brokers	7,968	‡	587	1521-02	Garage Builders	1,494	‡	70
8748-31	Food Facilities Consultants	727	‡	120	5211-01	Garage Doors	1,464	‡	*
5411-01	Food Markets	10,257	43	33	7538-01	Garages (Auto Repair & Service)	182,292	46	22,529
5046-01	Food Processing Equipment & Supplies	744	‡	106	4953-02	Garbage Collection	9,697	42	995
5141-01	Food Products	6,997	‡	1,866	5722-04	Garbage Disposal Equipment Household	1,228	‡	142
5411-04	Food Products Retail	617	‡	1	7629-12	Garbage Disposal Equipment Service & Repair	763	‡	42
5963-05	Food Service Management	1,517	‡	200	5261-01	Garden & Lawn Equipment & Supls	9,274	42	1,139
5812-06	Foods Carry Out	37,926	43	2,501	7359-03	Garden & Lawn Equipment & Supls Renting	612	‡	63
6099-05	Foreign Exchange Brokers	585	‡	163	5261-04	Garden Centers	6,063	‡	1,490
0851-02	Foresters Consulting	1,318	‡	608	0782-06	Gardeners	22,693	41	2,227
5084-57	Fork Lifts	4,302	‡	635	5172-07	Gas (L P G) Bottled Bulk Equipment Supply	502	‡	10
	(See Trucks-Industrial)				5074-09	Gas Burners	547	‡	80
7299-08	Formal Wear Rental	9,108	45	1,357	4925-01	Gas Companies	5,748	‡	693
1794-05	Foundation Contractors	3,425	‡	909	5172-05	Gas Industrial & Medical Cylinder & Bulk	2,007	‡	20
8733-03	Foundation Educational Philanthropic Research	2,064	‡	261	5172-08	Gas Liquified Petroleum Bottled & Bulk	14,986	42	111
3325-03	Foundries	1,838	‡	249	4924-01	Gas Natural	684	‡	4
5261-03	Fountains Garden & Display & Etc	911	‡	84	5085-15	Gaskets	848	‡	82
5999-27	Frames Picture	16,700	44	2,776	5172-02	Gasoline Service Station Equipment	2,187	‡	321
6794-01	Franchising	579	‡	162	5541-01	Gasoline Service Stations	83,406	43	15,725
						(See Service Stations - Gas & Oil)			

Source: Reproduced courtesy of American Business Lists, 5711 South 86th Circle, Omaha, NE 68127.

Another useful approach for the mail order operator is to identify such suppliers as either *compilers* or *brokers.*

List Compilers

These firms do just what the name implies. They collect and put in order names and addresses from a great many sources: from every conceivable type of directory, government publications, magazine subscriber lists, organization memberships, and other sources. The compiler will study your requirements and recommend available lists that might produce good results for you. Lists may also be custom-compiled for special needs.

List Brokers

Like real estate brokers and their counterparts in other fields, list brokers act as go-betweens to bring together mail order companies with owners of lists. They're very knowledgeable people who are ready, willing, and usually able to give you their best thinking on the kinds of lists that will best match your needs. When you use these brokered lists, you're often required to submit your mailing package in advance to the list owner for approval.

Both compilers and brokers will counsel you on your list needs.

How List Suppliers Work

The mailing list supplier usually designates a minimum order size that will be accepted. It may be for $100, $200, or more, or for a minimum of anywhere from 2,000 to 10,000 names. The names and addresses are rented customarily for *one-time use.* You may not use them for a second mailing. Indeed, *dummy* or *decoy* names are usually introduced into a rented list so that the list owner or distributor can readily discover any violation of this agreement, since your second mailing piece will arrive at one of these decoy addresses.

Lists, or parts of lists, are typically rented on a per thousand basis. Going rates with compiled lists run from about $40 to as high as $70 per thousand and sometimes more. There are additional charges for other selection factors. For instance, if you select particular states rather than buy a national list, you may need to pay an additional charge. (See Exhibit 14–3 for a list of state abbreviations.) If telephone numbers are to be added, you may be charged another $15 or $25 per thousand.

Lists are made available according to your needs on labels, on 3×5 index cards, on your mailing envelopes, or on magnetic tape. Ungummed Cheshire labels (for automatic machine affixing) and pressure-sensitive labels command premiums of anywhere from $60 to $80 per thousand. Names and addresses supplied on 3×5 index cards may cost you as much as $100 additional per thousand.

Mailing list distributors usually guarantee a high percentage of deliverability of their names, anywhere from 90 to 95 percent, because they clean and update their lists regularly. They'll refund postage charges for pieces not delivered, if returned to them.

EXHIBIT 14–3   U.S. Postal Service approved state abbreviations

State	Abbr.	State	Abbr.	State	Abbr.
Alabama	AL	Louisiana	LA	Ohio	OH
Alaska	AK	Maine	ME	Oklahoma	OK
Arizona	AZ	Maryland	MD	Oregon	OR
Arkansas	AR	Massachusetts	MA	Pennsylvania	PA
California	CA	Michigan	MI	Rhode Island	RI
Colorado	CO	Minnesota	MN	South Carolina	SC
Connecticut	CT	Mississippi	MS	South Dakota	SD
Delaware	DE	Missouri	MO	Tennessee	TN
Florida	FL	Montana	MT	Texas	TX
Georgia	GA	Nebraska	NE	Utah	UT
Hawaii	HI	Nevada	NV	Vermont	VT
Idaho	ID	New Hampshire	NH	Virginia	VA
Illinois	IL	New Jersey	NJ	Washington	WA
Indiana	IN	New Mexico	NM	West Virginia	WV
Iowa	IA	New York	NY	Wisconsin	WI
Kansas	KS	North Carolina	NC	Wyoming	WY
Kentucky	KY	North Dakota	ND		

Source: U.S. Postal Service.

TESTING AND EVALUATING RENTED LISTS

You rent or buy additional names to supplement your own in-house mailing list so that you can find new customers for the products or services you offer through the mails. An outside list may run to tens or even hundreds of thousands of names, and there are many thousands of lists to choose from. It thus makes good sense to rent *segments* of a number of different lists, and test these for results, instead of renting an entire single list. For example, should you want to add 20,000 names for your next mailing, you would be better off choosing a 10,000-name segment from each of two lists instead of the entire lot from one. Or even better, smaller amounts from three or four different lists. Some direct mail people suggest that you should never test fewer than 3,000 names from a list; others feel more comfortable assessing the results from a test of at least 5,000. What you would be looking for, of course, are those list segments that bring enough responses to be able to break even, or earn some profit, on your mailing.

Make sure you're really testing the *lists,* not one or more of ten or twenty variables that have nothing to do with the lists themselves. This means you need to send the identical mailing piece (or "package") to all names and addresses on all list segments. It also means that you should drop all mail at the same time, to rule out possible effects of time variations. Further, since differences in geographical areas can produce varying results, you need to make sure the lists you're comparing go to the same parts of the country, same states, and so on.

Each list you sample will pull differently. Even three or four samples from the same list will show different results. (Probability theory tells us that samples of a large *universe,* such as a list of 200,000 names, will show different mean results, and that these means will themselves be distributed over a range. However, without getting in the area of statistics and the finer nuances of the so-called normal curve, you'll be able to observe which samples outpull the others rather readily.) Some may not pay off at all; others will. And you'll add the names and addresses of these new customers to your house list, for future mailings. Of course, you'll be most interested in buying more thousands of names from the better-producing lists you sampled.

Sampling of List Sources

In Exhibit 14–4, you'll find names, addresses, and telephone numbers of some mailing list organizations. Some are compilers; others are list brokers; still others combine both activities and can also act as *list managers* for you when your own house list has grown substantially. A few of these companies offer complete in-house printing services and have automated mail-processing equipment.

List Maintenance

One day, you'll discover that your mailing list has become your most valuable asset. You'll want to protect it, to keep it current. You'll also find that lists are dynamic, not static; about one out of every five consumers moves to another address each year. Some estimates range up to 25 percent of the population. What this means is that, out of a list of only 5,000 names, over 1,000 may well become worthless each year unless you're able to locate their new addresses.

Many mail order firms see to it that the statement "Address Correction Requested" is printed, along with their company names and addresses, in the corner cards of their mailing envelopes. The post office will inform you of the new address for each person that has moved in the interim—for a small charge, of course. It's also a good idea to "clean" your list at least once each year by sending out a first-class mailing, since such letters will be forwarded automatically to new addresses. Be sure you enclose a note somewhere in the mailing package, asking whether the addressee has moved and requesting that he or she write down the new address and return the information (perhaps on a postage-free return card or on the order form enclosed).

Despite your every precaution, however, some pieces out of each mailing you make will be returned to you as undeliverable. In mail order jargon, these pieces are referred to as "nixies." Take pains to check each nixie against your master list. Perhaps the name was misspelled on the label or envelope, the numbers transposed in the address, or the ZIP code

EXHIBIT 14–4 A sampling of mailing list sources

ACT ONE MAILING LIST SERVICES, INC.
188 Pleasant Street, Suite #4
Marblehead, MA 01945
617/639-1919; 800/ACT-LIST

ALL MEDIA, INC.
4965 Preston Park Boulevard, 300
Plano, TX 75093
214/985-4060; 800/466-4061

ALVIN B. ZELLER, INC.
224 Fifth Avenue
New York, NY 10001
212/689-4900; 800/223-0814

AMERICAN BUSINESS LISTS
5711 So. 86th Circle
Omaha, NE 68127
402/331-7169; 800/336-8349

AMERICAN LIST COUNSEL, INC.
88 Orchard Road
Princeton, NJ 08543
908/874-4300; 800/252-5478

AMERICAN STUDENT LIST CO., INC.
330 Old Country Road
Mineola, NY 11501
516/248-6100

COMPILERS PLUS, INC.
466 Main Street
New Rochelle, NY 10801
914/633-5240; 800-431-2914

CPA SERVICES INC.
16800 W. Greenfield Avenue
Brookfield, WI 53005
414/797-9999

CUSTOM LIST SERVICES, INC.
3 Metro Plaza, Suite 107
8300 Professional Place
Landover, MD 20785
301/459-9885

DUN & BRADSTREET INFORMATION SERVICES
3 Sylvan Way
Parsippany, NJ 07054
201/605-6401; 800/624-5669

DUNHILL INTERNATIONAL LIST COMPANY, INC.
1951 N.W. 19th Street
Boca Raton, FL 33431
407/347-0200; 800/DUNHILL

GEORGE MANN ASSOCIATES, INC.
20 Lake Drive
Hightstown, NY 08520
609/443-1330

HUGO DUNHILL MAILING LISTS, INC.
630 Third Avenue
New York, NY 10017
212/682-8030; 800/223-6454

LIST SERVICES CORPORATION
6 Trowbridge Drive
Bethel, CT 06801
203/743-2600

MAIL MARKETING, INC.
171 Terrace Street
Haworth, NJ 07641
201/387-1010

NEW RESI-DATA MARKETING, INC.
101 West Street
Hillsdale, NJ 07642
201/476-1800; 800/221-6293

PCS MAILING LIST COMPANY
85 Constitution Lane
Danvers, MA 01923
508/777-3332; 800/532-LIST

R.L. POLK & COMPANY
6400 Monroe Boulevard
Taylor, MI 48180
313/292-3200; 800/637-7655

RESEARCH PROJECTS CORPORATION
15 E. 26th Street, Suite 1711
New York, NY 10010
212/685-7512; 800/243-4360

THE COOLIDGE COMPANY, INC.
25 W. 43rd Street
New York, NY 10036
212/642-0300

THE KAPLAN AGENCY, INC.
1200 High Ridge Road
Stamford, CT 06905
203/968-8800

THE KLEID COMPANY, INC.
530 Fifth Avenue
New York, NY 10036
212/819-3400

THE SPECIALISTS, LTD.
1200 Lincoln Harbor, 9th floor
Weehauken, NJ 07087
201/865-5800; 800/888-3462

UNI-MAIL LIST CORPORATION
352 Park Avenue South
New York, NY 10010
212/679-7000

was wrong. And, of course, enter any change of address on your master cards, too.

BUILDING AN ORGANIZATIONAL MAILING LIST

If you plan to sell to industry rather than to the individual consumer, check into the many directories available, most of which are published annually. There are directories of manufacturers, retailers, wholesalers, exporters, construction firms, manufacturers' representatives, and the like. These are wonderful resources if you're trying to build a mailing list.

You should also know about several useful directories that can be found in college and university libraries and in many public libraries. (Of course, you can arrange to purchase them yourself if they contain the kinds of names you want.)

There's Dun and Bradstreet's *Million Dollar Directory;* the organizations listed in this reference work are arranged alphabetically, geographically, by product classification, and by line of business. All entries represent businesses with net worths of $1 million or more. The same firm also issues the *Middle Market Directory,* which lists companies with net worths of between one-half and one million dollars. Cumulative supplements to these books are issued during the year.

Another valuable source of information is the *Standard & Poor's Register of Corporations, Directors and Executives.* This useful reference tool lists corporations alphabetically, provides their addresses and telephone numbers, and also gives the names, titles, and functions of officers, directors, and other principals. Also shown are the companies' SIC codes, annual sales volume, number of employees, and other data.

There's also the multivolume *Thomas' Register of American Manufacturers and Thomas' Register Catalog File.* It offers an alphabetical listing of the products and services produced by manufacturing organizations, along with company names and addresses, telephone numbers, branch offices, capital ratings, names of company officials, brand names, and the like. Company catalogs are also made available.

Mail order companies frequently use this reference work to find products for resale.

GET ADDITIONAL INCOME BY RENTING YOUR HOUSE LIST

Although this aspect of list management probably lies several years in the future for you, it won't hurt to know something about it now. Granted continued success in your mail order enterprise, you'll keep building your own mailing list through a combination of media advertising, direct mail, and the testing of outside lists. Eventually, you'll wind up with several thousand names and addresses of people to whom you have sold merchandise or, perhaps, a service. Then you can start thinking about list rental as an additional source of income.

You can try on your own to offer your house list to other mail order firms that you think may be able to sell their products to your customers. Some will be interested in renting your names. They may pay you as much as $80 or more per thousand, for a one-time use. If you have the time, you can arrange to type your names on their envelopes for an extra fee. (If you own a microcomputer and the right software, you'll save lots of time doing the addressing.)

Although the per-thousand rate may not seem to amount to much, bear in mind that you might succeed in renting your list as many as ten or twenty times a year. At the $80 per thousand rate, your list of 5,000 names could bring you $4,000 of extra income, actually extra *profit,* because there's no cost of merchandise involved here as there is when you sell goods through the mails.

It isn't easy for small mail order operators to find companies interested in renting their lists. You would be better off, especially when your house list has grown some more, contacting a list broker or list management company to handle such arrangements. You'll have to pay this representative perhaps 20 percent of what you earn, but it will be worth it. You may also think about computerizing the list when it gets big enough.

SOURCES OF ADDITIONAL INFORMATION

Harper, Rose, *Mailing List Strategies: A Guide to Direct Mail Success.* New York: McGraw-Hill, 1986.

Holtz, Herman, *The Direct Marketer's Workbook.* New York: Wiley, 1986.

Nash, Edward L., *Database Marketing: The Ultimate Marketing Tool.* New York: McGraw-Hill, 1993.

_____ , *The Direct Marketing Handbook,* (2d ed.). New York: McGraw-Hill, 1992.

Stone, Bob, *Successful Direct Marketing Methods,* (5th ed.). Lincolnwood, IL: National Textbook, 1993.

15

Newspapers as a Mail Order Medium

By now you know that success in your own mail order enterprise depends on a blend of the right ingredients, including these interdependent factors:

- The merchandise or service(s) you sell.
- Your offer—and how you present it.
- Your direct mail package.
- The quality of your mailing list.
- Accurate knowledge of your target prospects.

Additional sales will come from increasing the size of your mailing list through, for example, your personal efforts at compiling names and addresses, or by buying or renting lists from other organizations. The print media (newspapers and magazines) represent valuable additional sources, as do the air media (television and radio). In fact, many small mail order firms start in business by placing advertisements in the print media, rather than by attempting a mailing.

This approach is healthy, whether you're trying to sell items directly from your ad or are simply looking to "pull" inquiries. Some ads pay for themselves at the outset; orders with cash or checks enclosed may be sufficient to defray the entire cost of the space. Other ads can be made to pay off by following up inquiries right away with persuasive direct mail literature.

The print media are where people go to read about what's happening now as well as about the past and the future. In this chapter, we discuss the American newspaper. Chapter 16 is devoted to the magazine, followed by coverage of the broadcast media in Chapters 17 and 18.

Of all the mass media, the newspaper attracts the greatest share of the nation's total annual expenditure for media. Television has grown rapidly over the last several decades to where it now occupies a strong second-place position.

Traditionally, most newspaper advertising is retail advertising, placed by department stores and chains, supermarkets and discount houses, theaters, and many other types of local retailers.

There are comparatively few mail order (or direct marketing) advertisements in most newspapers. A few, like the *New York Times* in the Sunday magazine section's "Shopping Guide," do encourage this kind of business. *Grit* and *Capper's* (Topeka, Kansas) are two publications famous for their mail order columns. The lack of mail order advertising should not, however, rule out your use of this medium. It does have value as a proving ground for quickly assessing consumer response to new merchandise and new offers. Variations in art, alternate headlines, and copy changes can be tested readily. You can see your newly created ad published within a day or two and be able to estimate its effectiveness by the time another week has passed. Magazines (see Chapter 16), on the other hand, are different. Each month's issue may be "closed" to an advertiser as early as six to ten weeks before the date of issue. Responses will start to come in over the following weeks but will continue to arrive, perhaps for many months. Thus, it's difficult to project what your total returns are going to be in a time frame much shorter than six or eight weeks after the magazine has been put on sale (or mailed to subscribers).

Newspaper space will cost you less, on the average, than magazine space or television or radio time. And it's certainly cheaper than mounting any direct mail campaign, unless perhaps, you make a limited mailing, using a simple, self-mailing circular.

Moreover, some offers can be quickly tested and evaluated at a modest cost, through the newspaper's classified columns. (Try this whenever you can.)

PLACING MAIL ORDER ADVERTISING IN NEWSPAPERS: ADVANTAGES AND DISADVANTAGES

All advertising media have their good and bad points. To be able to make sensible choices among them, you should familiarize yourself with both the benefits and the drawbacks of every medium you may think of using.

Advantages for the Advertiser

For mail order advertisers, newspapers offer a number of distinct benefits: fast results, rapid ad placement, flexibility, excellent penetration, and so on. Each of these is briefly discussed on the following page.

Fast results. Replies and/or orders begin to arrive a day or two after your advertisement appears. You can expect to receive up to 70 or 75 percent of all responses within the following seven days.

Rapid ad placement. A valuable feature of this medium is the short lead time between ad construction and publication. Closing time for ordering space may run from a few hours to one or two days prior to publication. The newspaper is, therefore, an excellent vehicle for *testing* purposes. You can modify your advertising from one day to the next: new headlines, changes in copy, alternative illustrations, and so forth.

Flexibility. The short lead time gives you the ability to make quick changes you can profit by. For example, if a prolonged heat wave is expected to roll in within the next thirty-six hours, you might decide to insert an ad for a hand-held, battery-operated fan you carry in stock, instead of featuring some other item you had planned to run.

Excellent penetration. Collectively, our daily newspapers reach some seven out of ten adults every day, which means an intensive "reach" or coverage of the community wherever you choose to advertise. Even though, in some locales, the area residents may read a weekly paper because no daily is available, you can still be sure that the majority of homes will be reached.

Geographic selectivity. You can target just about every corner of the land to reach prospective buyers. You can select the largest metropolitan centers, small and medium-size towns, and the remotest of villages. You can reach readers living in lakeside communities, mountain or seashore resorts, or cattle country, anywhere, in fact, where the local newspaper audience is composed of the kinds of people who you believe will be interested in what you have to sell.

Listings of all newspapers, including names and addresses, circulations, rates, and other information, are available from the Standard Rate and Data Service of Wilmette, Illinois. Their publications may be found in the reference rooms of college and university libraries and in many public libraries.

Unhurried reading. People generally read newspapers at a leisurely pace. Morning papers may be read on commuter trains, but certainly, most evening papers are read at home. This means, of course, that advertisements that are interesting are considered carefully by the reader. Often, ads are torn out and held for future action, giving newspapers a significant advantage over radio or television commercials, which are over (and lost) immediately after having been broadcast.

Additional readers. There's an excellent chance that two or more persons will read the same paper, especially the Sunday editions. For example, the magazine section for the Sunday *New York Times* may well stay around the house for an entire week, along with a number of other sections of the paper.

Availability of special position. Newspapers are organized into different departments and sections. You can gain more attention for your display ad by requesting its placement in the section your prospects will be most likely to read with care: the sports pages, the business section, the entertainment or the food pages, and so forth, depending on just what you're selling. Naturally, if the newspaper regularly carries a special mail order section, you'll most likely want your ad to appear with the other mail order ads.

Space advertising is usually purchased on an R.O.P. (run-of-publication) basis. This means that the paper or magazine decides where to position your ad. Often, by paying an additional charge, you can have your ad placed in a preferred position, for example, on page two or page three, on a right-hand page instead of the left-hand side, in the top corner of a page, and the like.

Relatively low production costs. The typical newspaper mail order ad can be prepared inexpensively. You need a layout, some artwork, and copy that is set into position. If you use an advertising agency, their preparation costs are, for the most part, quite low. If you haven't yet expanded to the point where you do employ an agency, note that most newspapers will set your ads free of charge, except, perhaps, for the preparation of a "cut" of your art at a modest fee. (Stock cuts are made available by many papers.) The resulting ad may not, of course, look quite as professional as if it had been created by an ad agency.

Small space ads destined for the classified section of the newspaper pose no difficulties. Not only does the paper set your copy in print but the classified people are also ready to advise on improvements in the copy you have written.

Drawbacks of the Medium

Although the newspaper has its place in the media plans of many mail order companies (usually well behind direct mail and magazines in terms of planned advertising expenditures), the sophisticated direct marketer is well aware of its deficiencies. The major disadvantages of the newspaper follow:

Waste circulation. The typical newspaper is filled with ads placed by local retailers. Supermarkets, department stores, movie houses, restaurants, and other retail firms advertise often in their area papers, and to good avail. Most of the paper's readers reside in these retailers' trading areas; most are logical prospects for the merchandise/services they sell. In your particular case, however, you distribute selected or specialty items (or, perhaps, a special service) by mail. Consequently, many of the newspaper's readers may not be potential users of your offerings. Then, too, a sizable proportion of these people may not be accustomed to buying through the mails.

Short ad life. Consumers buy newspapers, in the main, for the news and features they contain. Although some of the many advertisements do manage to catch the typical reader's attention and may be studied for a few moments, the bulk of such messages are glanced at and dismissed almost simultaneously. Another factor that hurts is that the entire paper may be discarded within thirty or forty minutes—and that ends that!

Clutter. To compound the problem, your ad will be surrounded by other ads. Often, advertisements make up the bulk of the newspaper. Your small ad may be so overpowered by other, much larger ads on the same page that most readers might not even notice yours. And a big ad, say a half-page advertisement (or even a quarter of a page), may be well out of reach of your modest advertising budget. Luckily, there are some tricks of the trade you might resort to in order to make your little advertisement more noticeable, like using bold and heavy margins, a catchy photograph, lettering in reverse (white print against a black background), and so on. (See Chapter 11 for other ideas.)

Involves only one sense. The newspaper ad's capacity for doing the selling job is decidedly limited. It appeals to only one sense of the reader, the sense of sight. Through visual impact alone, it must attract readers to it, stimulate their interest, convince them of the offer's value, and persuade them to act. Contrast the effectiveness of any print advertisement with that of a typical television commercial, for instance. The latter works on two of the viewer's senses, sight and hearing, and is, therefore, far more powerful.

Types of Newspapers

In 1993, more than 11,000 different newspapers were distributed in the United States.[1] Of these, three out of every four were weekly publications; most of the balance were dailies. Evening papers outnumbered morning dailies by nearly two to one.

Daily Newspapers

Many daily newspapers also put out Sunday editions, or, perhaps, a weekend edition. Nearly all dailies are local in nature, being published in a particular city or town and distributed there, in surrounding suburbs, and often to neighboring villages and towns. A few papers, such as *USA Today, The Wall Street Journal,* and the *Christian Science Monitor,* are national in scope.

Best known of all newspapers in the country are those of our major metropolitan areas, such as the *New York Times, Chicago Tribune, Los*

---

[1] Bureau of the Census, *Statistical Abstract of the United States (1993)* (Washington, DC: U.S. Department of Commerce, 1993), 567.

EXHIBIT 15-1   Some major metropolitan Sunday newspapers

City	1993 Population[1] (1,000s)	Newspaper	Circulation[2] (1,000s)
New York	7,323	*New York Times*	1,762
		New York Daily News	983
Los Angeles	3,485	*Los Angeles Times*	1,164
Chicago	2,784	*Chicago Tribune*	1,133
		Chicago Sun-Times	559
Houston	1,631	*Houston Chronicle*	621
		Houston Post	359
Philadelphia	1,586	*Philadelphia Inquirer/News* (combination)	983
San Diego	1,111	*San Diego Union-Tribune*	461
Detroit	1,089	*Detroit News/Free Press* (combination)	1,215

[1] Bureau of the Census, U.S. Department of Commerce, *Statistical Abstract of the United States (1993)* (Washington, DC: Department of Commerce, 1993), 42–44.
[2] From *Gale Directory of Publications and Broadcast Media,* 1994, 126th Edition, edited by Karen Troshynski-Thomas and Deborah M. Burek. Copyright © 1994 by Gale Research, Inc. Reprinted by permission of the publisher.

Angeles Times, and *Philadelphia Inquirer.* These metropolitan dailies boast of circulations in the many hundreds of thousands of readers.

Toward the other end of the measuring stick are the mid-sized dailies, with circulations that hover between 40,000 and 60,000, such newspapers as the *Santa Barbara News-Press* and the *Stockton Record* (both in California), the *Bay City Times* (Michigan), the *Sioux Falls Argus Leader* (South Dakota), the *Ogden Standard Examiner* (Utah), and the *Wilkes-Barre Citizens' Voice* (Pennsylvania).

There are many more daily newspapers with far fewer readers; the *Bennington Banner* (Vermont—circulation 7,700) and the Benton *Courier* (Arizona—circulation 9,700) are two examples.[2]

Sunday Editions. Sunday papers are usually more widely circulated than weekday issues. The Sunday edition of the *Chicago Tribune,* for example, reaches over 54 percent more people than its average daily paper. (See Exhibit 15–1 for Sunday circulation figures of some of the big metropolitan newspapers.) For this reason, and because they're read far more leisurely and usually by several members of the family, advertising in the Sunday newspaper is preferred by many direct marketers. For somewhat similar reasons, the evening paper seems preferable to the morning paper for mail order purposes.

[2] Circulation figures in this section are from *Gale Directory of Publications and Broadcast Media, 1994,* 126th Edition, edited by Karen Troshynski-Thomas and Deborah M. Burek. Copyright © 1994 by Gale Research Inc. Reprinted by permission of the publisher.

Weekly Newspapers

Although, as the name indicates, these papers are generally published once a week regularly throughout the year, some are issued twice weekly or on some other basis. Because they are for the most part more local than the dailies, the tendency today is to label all of these newspapers (weekly or otherwise) *community newspapers.*

Many are distributed in the suburbs of large metropolitan centers and throughout the cities themselves. However, a larger number reach the rural areas, hitting villages and hamlets where a daily newspaper is only occasionally to be found. Localities look forward to each new issue, avidly digesting the news, features, and other items of community interest just as soon as the paper appears.

Among the many small-circulation community papers are such publications as the *Big Horn Country News* (Hardin, Montana—circulation 3,550), the *Lahontan Valley News* (Fallon, Nevada, circulation 4,700), the *Chronotype* (Rice Lake, Wisconsin, circulation 8,700), and the *Rappahannock News* (Washington, Virginia, circulation 3,100).

The agate line rate for these publications and others with similar small circulations may run between 35 and 75 cents. Small enough to test out a few ads if residents of these small rural communities are representative of the kinds of people you have targeted as prime prospects for your merchandise or service(s). But remember, your cost per thousand readers might turn out to be quite a good deal higher this way than you would pay if you placed an ad in a large city daily or Sunday paper.

Special Readership and Other Types of Papers

Special readership newspapers comprise a rather broad classification that includes, among others, papers printed in dozens of foreign languages, college and university papers, newspapers for black readers, and publications aimed at a variety of religious denominations. Their audiences are logical targets, not only for all types of consumer goods and services but also for offerings of special interest to distinct population segments.

Other types of papers include large numbers of shopping papers, both local and regional in scope, distributed throughout the United States. They're referred to as *shoppers, shopping guides, pennysavers,* or *trading papers.* Most are weeklies. Although they can be and are occasionally used for mail order selling, most of the advertisements they carry are placed by area residents and small retailers or service firms.

Sunday Supplements and Comics

Many newspapers supply magazine supplements and comics pages in their Sunday editions. Both types of supplements are used by mail order advertisers. Unfortunately for the smaller firm, space costs may be out of reach where the circulation is substantial. *Parade,* for example, enjoys a circulation in excess of 35 million readers. *Puck—The Comic Weekly* also reaches a huge audience. However, it's distributed through a number of newspaper groups and you may purchase space by the group instead of buying the entire circulation. Nevertheless, except for an occasional—and small—ad in a less widely circulated Sunday supplement, you (as a small mail order operator) probably should shy away from these media.

Somewhat similar to the Sunday supplements as media vehicles for mail order firms are the familiar, high-circulation weeklies known as the *supermarket newspapers*—the *National Enquirer,* the *Sun,* and the *Globe,* among others. Many hundreds of thousands of copies of these papers are purchased each week by supermarket shoppers. They carry a good deal of direct marketing advertising. Because of their national distribution and general makeup, think of these publications more as magazines than as newspapers and consider their possibilities vis-à-vis other magazines.

BUYING NEWSPAPER SPACE

Given the availability of several different media, which should you use? Choices among those media competing for your advertising dollars will involve consideration of the following factors:

- Audience you're trying to reach.
- Effectiveness of the medium for *your* purposes.
- Reach or coverage.
- Costs involved.

The term *reach* is used to measure that portion of the community reached, or covered, by the particular medium; when we talk about the print media, we mean the circulation of the newspaper or magazine.

Newspaper advertisers think also in terms of *frequency* of impressions, that is, how many times the same story is told to the same readers. Repeating the same advertisement two, three, or four times reinforces its effects on readers.

Circulation

Newspaper advertising rates reflect their circulations. As a rule, the greater the circulation, the more you'll be asked to pay for space. The large metropolitan daily newspapers and many of the smaller papers have their circulations audited on a regular basis by the Audit Bureau of Circulations (Schaumburg, Illinois). Those that aren't audited often present sworn statements of their circulation figures to would-be advertisers. (Only copies that are sold are counted, not those distributed free of charge.) Sales include both subscription copies and papers sold at newsstands, stores, vending machines, and other outlets.

It's generally wise to contact whichever newspapers you're thinking of using. Write or call them and request copies of their latest rate cards.

Newspaper Rates

At least two different rates are quoted advertisers by the newspaper. National advertisers pay the national rate, which is the highest rate. Lower rates are available for department stores, supermarkets, and other retailers; for bars and restaurants; for places of amusement; and so on. Mail order firms are granted low rates, too; they can run from 20 to 35 percent (or more) below the national rate.

Rates are typically quoted by the agate line or by the column inch. There are 14 agate lines to the inch. The width of the line or the inch depends, of course, on the width of the newspaper column, which can differ from one paper to the next. Basically, there are two popular newspaper formats, the regular or standard size and the tabloid. Standard papers typically run about 14 to 14½ inches across, are about 23 inches high, and carry six or seven columns to the page. Tabloid dimensions approximate 10×14 inches (plus or minus fractions of inches); these papers average five columns to the page.

Space Contracts

Let's say you decide to place a small display advertisement in your local newspaper. The ad measures 2 columns wide and runs 5 inches deep. This makes for 10 inches in all (2 columns $\times$ 5 inches). The newspaper will charge you their open rate, the basic per-line (or per-inch) charge for a one-time insertion in the paper. (Remember that 10 inches will equal 140 agate lines.) You'll probably pay more per agate line if you want exposure in the Sunday edition, simply because most Sunday papers enjoy greater circulation than weekday editions.

If you expect to place more advertising, you can sign a *bulk space contract* with them and thereby benefit from a lower rate than their open rate. Newspapers, in effect, offer a discount schedule; the more space you buy, the less it costs you. Translated into operational terms for your mail order business, this will result in a lower cost per inquiry or per sale.

Even though you may have contracted for 1,000 lines for the year in order to earn the discount rate, you're not compelled to use that amount of space. If, for example, you have used only 750 lines by the time your contract expires, you'll be *short rated*. Your actual line usage will be computed by the newspaper at the next higher rate. And since you have probably already paid your bills to this point at the rate shown on the contract, you'll be invoiced for the short-rate differential.

Combo Rates and Other Details

Where newspapers distribute both morning and evening editions (usually under separate names), your ad can appear in both, and you'll earn a lower, combination rate for the two. Or, perhaps, you may be offered a combination rate for running your ad on three successive weekdays, several weekdays and the Sunday edition, and so forth.

Many advertisers believe they obtain better results if their advertisements are displayed in the first few pages of the paper, rather than toward the back, or if the ad appears on a right-hand page (instead of the left-hand side), or at the top of a page, or in an "island" position surrounded by news or editorial matter. Newspapers will try to accommodate these and other special positions requested where they're able to, but they do charge additional for this service. In many cases, however, the premium you pay will be modest.

Other possibilities in many newspapers include the use of a second color in the ad, or the insertion of sheets, folders, or other enclosures that have been preprinted by the advertiser. Unfortunately, this latter approach is often well beyond the reach, financially, of the small mail order operator.

Comparison Shop before Deciding Where to Place Your Ad!

Mail order firms constantly face the problem of where best to advertise their products and/or services. Decisions of media selection boil down to (1) selecting the generic medium type to use in any particular case—newspaper, magazine, radio, television, or direct mail, and (2) intertype choice—*which* newspaper (or magazine, or other) to advertise in. Assuming the similarity of audiences, intertype decisions depend for the most part on circulations and costs.

The tool most commonly used by advertisers to compare the costs of advertising in different newspapers is the *milline rate*. This measure is defined as:

$$\text{Milline rate} = \frac{\text{Line rate} \times 1{,}000{,}000}{\text{Total circulation}}$$

As an illustration, let's assume you're considering three different newspapers for your next advertisement. You check their circulations and their latest rates and come up with the information below.

Newspaper	Circulation	Line Rate
A	210,000	$2.20
B	265,000	2.50
C	330,000	3.85

You figure out the milline rate for Paper A by multiplying the line rate of $2.20 by 1,000,000, then dividing the result ($2,200,000) by the circulation, 210,000. This comes to a milline rate of approximately $10.48. You then calculate the milline rates of the other two newspapers to be $9.43 for B and $11.67 for C. Comparing the three, Paper B would be the right choice.

NEWSPAPER CLASSIFIED ADVERTISING CAN PROVE PROFITABLE

Most newspapers carry classified advertising pages. The advertisements in these sections are all similar in appearance, set in the same small type by the newspaper itself. Of course, many carry headlines in somewhat larger type; some ads are longer than others (in numbers of lines used); some employ more white space than others. These all-copy ads are collectively referred to as *general classified* advertising. Many publications also offer *display classified* opportunities for companies wishing to use small units of space. Line cuts and other illustrations may be used in display classified ads. This type of space is generally sold by column inches.

The typical daily paper rarely carries mail order offers in its classified pages. Nevertheless, you might consider trying out an occasional new item, or new proposition, in a small classified ad, especially in some weekly and rural papers. These little ads can often generate inquiries at a very low cost. It really doesn't take too much of a response to pay for the space.

More commonly, mail order firms resort to *magazine classified* sections (discussed in Chapter 16).

SOURCES OF ADDITIONAL INFORMATION

Hahn, Fred, *Do-It-Yourself Advertising: How to Produce Great Ads, Catalogs, Direct Mail, and Much More.* New York: Wiley, 1993.

Gross, Martin, *The Direct Marketer's Idea Book.* New York: AMACOM, 1989.

Miller, Marlene, *Business Guide to Print Promotion.* Laguna Beach, CA: Iris Communication, 1988.

Nash, Edward L., *The Direct Marketing Handbook,* (2d ed.). New York: McGraw-Hill, 1992.

Stone, Bob, *Successful Direct Marketing Methods,* (5th ed.). Lincolnwood, IL: NTC, 1993.

Troshynski-Thomas, Karen and Deborah M. Burek, (Eds.). *1994 Gale Directory of Publications and Broadcast Media,* (126th ed.). Detroit: Gale Research Inc., 1994.

Ward, Dick, *Creative Ad Design and Illustration.* Cincinnati: North Light Books, 1988.

16

Magazines: Print Medium for the Long Pull

Most mail order concerns get their start either through mailing sales literature directly to a list of names or by placing advertisements in selected magazines. Both approaches are often used, because the two really work in tandem. Names obtained through responses to magazine advertisements are added to the firm's mailing list. Follow-up sales efforts, especially when mailed according to a well-planned schedule, result in additional orders. These may also be used to generate more customers.

ADVERTISING IN MAGAZINES: BENEFITS AND DRAWBACKS

Every advertising medium offers both advantages and disadvantages. Magazines are no exception. They can be a valuable component of the direct marketing company's media plan.

Advantages for the Advertiser

Mail order marketers allocate a far greater share of their promotion dollars to magazines than to newspapers. They prefer the magazine for some rather compelling reasons, including:

- Long publication life.
- Secondary readership.

- Reader specificity.
- Reader loyalty.
- Prestige of the medium.
- Special sections for mail order firms.
- Excellent reproduction of photographs and illustrations.

Brief comments about a few of the more significant advantages of magazine advertising follow:

Long publication life. Typically, we toss the daily (or weekly) newspaper into the trash container or recycling bin shortly after finishing it. On the other hand, each new issue of a magazine may be kept around the home, shop, or office for weeks on end. We may pick up the issue time and time again. We read it in spurts and in parts. So, experienced advertisers claim that, although up to one-half of the total number of replies to a magazine advertisement may arrive within the five weeks following the date of issue, responses will continue to trickle in for months. Sometimes, you'll get replies as much as a year later, and even beyond that point. Magazines are more "permanent" than newspapers. In fact, some readers save the several issues of some publications and build home libraries.

Secondary readership. The primary readers of a magazine include both the subscribers and those who purchase copies at newsstands or stores. Yet, many magazines are also read and enjoyed by other members of the families of the primary readers, and by neighbors, friends, people in waiting rooms, visitors to public library branches, and the like. For some publications, the total number of persons who actually read a single issue may exceed their regular, audited average circulation by 300 percent or more.

Reader specificity. In one way, advertising your product(s) or service(s) in this medium has a lot in common with your approaches to direct mail marketing. Success in your direct mail efforts requires keeping in mind a firm image of your likely prospects, then searching for and finding lists of persons (or organizations) whose characteristics most closely resemble that image.

You use much the same strategy when advertising in magazines. Knowing your customer, you canvas the field and select only those publications whose readers are most likely to buy from you. If, for example, you plan to distribute an innovative light filter or an improved attachment for cameras, you would check into magazines such as *American Photo* and *Popular Photography.* Or, if you want to offer a new fishing lure, you might consider publications like *Field and Stream* and *Fishing World.*

There are literally thousands of magazines, yet most appear to cater to a special, even unique, group of readers. Many periodicals research their audiences and have a pretty good idea of what these people are like. They're usually ready to furnish a potential advertiser with their readership profile.

Depending on just what you have to sell, you can choose publications targeted at farmers or businesspeople, young brides or young mothers, chemical engineers or insurance salespersons, lovers of country music or racing car drivers, skiers or joggers, racquetball or soccer fans, home owners or apartment dwellers, corporation executives or proprietors of small businesses, and so forth.

Reader loyalty. Most magazine readers are intensely loyal to their publications. They consume issue after issue, reading from front to back cover. This can be a plus-factor for the mail order advertiser who seeks to enhance results through *ad frequency*—advertising regularly, month after month.

Prestige of the medium. Somewhat tied into loyalty is a psychological factor: the very appearance of your ad in the readers' "beloved" magazine endows your company, and its products and/or services, with elements of prestige and believability. This is probably due to the old adage that suggests we are known by the company we keep.

Special sections for mail order firms. Many magazines devote special sections to merchandise and services that readers may purchase by mail. Some carry classified pages where mail order firms that can't afford to place display ads are able to advertise at a relatively low cost. In either case, you can be sure that regular readers of those pages are likely prospects for you (provided you have selected the right medium in the first place).

Often, these mail order sections or departments carry special names. Here are a few:

American Legion Magazine	"The Legion Shopper"
American Woman	"Best by Mail"
Bride's Magazine	"Shop at Home"
Elks Magazine	"Elks Family Shopper"
Field and Stream	"Sportsman's Shopper"
Good Housekeeping	"Shopping by Mail"
Popular Mechanics	"PM Buyer's Guide"
Popular Science	"Shopper's Showcase"
Redbook	"Shopping with Redbook"
Runner's World	"Marketplace"
Sports Afield	"Sportsman's Showcase"

Excellent Reproduction

Photographs and drawings used to illustrate magazine advertisements reproduce amazingly well because fine screens (110 lines per inch, or more) are employed in preparing the halftones. (Illustrations in newspaper ads often leave much to be desired simply because coarser screens must be used.) This technical consideration is of even more importance in cases where full-color ads are used to enhance a product's appeal. An example is an ad that displays a gift package of assorted imported cheeses. (For more on the four-color process, see Chapter 10.)

Drawbacks

Magazines also hold disadvantages for advertisers. The more significant drawbacks are discussed below:

Limited appeal to the senses. As with the newspaper, the magazine appeals only to the reader's sense of sight. Your ad will need to be compelling enough to attract, interest, convince, and move the reader to act—all through the printed word, along with illustrations, symbols, spacing, and other techniques.

Waste circulation. Again, there's the strong possibility of considerable waste circulation. Many readers of any magazine you might advertise in aren't regular "by mail" shoppers. Nor are they necessarily candidates for those special products or services you're attempting to sell.

Long lead time. A more serious disadvantage is the extraordinary amount of lead time required by this medium. You'll need to reserve space in most publications long in advance of the scheduled date of issue. You'll have to deliver all the requisite components—the ad mechanical, plates, halftones, color separations (if using color), and so on—depending on whether the magazine is produced by letterpress or offset. Closing dates are typically listed on the magazine's rate card; this may read "the first of the second month preceding the date of issue" (a common closing date). Or closing may fall on "the 25th of the third month preceding the date of issue."

The problem is further compounded by the fact that actual issue dates generally precede the dates shown on the covers of these periodicals by anywhere from several days to as much as two weeks, and sometimes more.

TYPES OF MAGAZINES

More than 10,000 different magazines are regularly published in the United States. More than one-third are monthlies; most of the rest are published either weekly, bimonthly, or on a quarterly basis. Collectively, these constitute a tremendous and potentially profitable medium for the mail order firm. Market segmentation possibilities are enormous; you can reach almost any type of audience: old, young, rich, poor, professional and business people, numismatists or stamp collectors, hunters or amateur cooks.

A convenient way of classifying these publications is by dividing them into general consumer magazines; special interest publications; business, trade, and professional magazines; and farm publications.

Special Interest Publications

These periodicals far outnumber those aimed at the general public. When categorized by reader interests, tastes, preferences, or lifestyles, the variety is astounding. In most cases, the titles of these magazines are a strong indication of the types of readers they seek to attract. Here is an abbreviated list:

American Hunter	*Model Railroader*
Black Belt	*Motor Boating & Sailing*
Bowler's Journal	*Outdoor Life*
Casino Player	*PC World*
Children's Digest	*Popular Mechanics*
Country Journal	*Popular Photography*
Crafts Magazine	*Popular Science*
Fishing World	*Railroad Model Craftsman*
Flower & Garden Magazine	*Rider*
Golf Digest	*Skiing*
Guns & Ammo	*Surfer*
Hot Rod	*The Numismatist*

Some publications are of special attraction to the residents of particular cities, such as *Cleveland, Columbus Monthly, Houston Metropolitan Magazine, Los Angeles Magazine,* and so on. Still other special interest periodicals focus on the members of fraternal orders and other organizations, theatergoers and hotel guests, and religious groups.

Business, Trade, and Professional Magazines

Included in this category are a fair number of general business magazines (*Business Week* and *Fortune,* as examples) and a far greater number of specialized periodicals of interest to different industries, trades, professional groups, and technical personnel. As with the special interest magazines, you can readily determine audience composition from the titles. Examples include:

Beverage World	*Chemical Engineering*
Candy Industry	*Cosmetics & Toiletries*
Ceramic Industry	*Flooring*
Chain Store Executive	*Food Management*

Insurance Sales	*Radio World*
Lodging Hospitality	*Restaurant Business*
National Jeweler	*Sales & Marketing Management*
Packaging Digest	*Sporting Goods Business*
Plastics Engineering	*Textile World*
Purchasing Management	*Theatre Journal*

Farm Publications

Some authorities include these magazines with the Business, Trade, and Professional category on the strength of an obvious fact: farming is a vocation. It is, however, also a way of living, a lifestyle for American farmers, ranchers, cattle raisers, and the like. So, these publications do merit a separate classification.

Many farm magazines are circulated only within a given state (rural areas); others may be regional or even national in distribution. A few of the titles follow:

American Fruit Grower	*National Hog Farmer*
Beef	*Ohio Farmer*
Colorado Ranger & Farmer	*Oklahoma Rural News*
Farm Journal	*Progressive Farmer*
Farmer-Stockman	*Rural Georgia*
Hoard's Dairyman	*Rural Missouri*
Hoosier Farmer	*Successful Farming*
Missouri Beef Cattleman	*Texas Agriculture*
Missouri Ruralist	*Wisconsin Agriculturist*

HOW TO BUY SPACE FOR YOUR DISPLAY ADVERTISEMENTS

Magazines, like newspapers, usually offer different rate schedules to different classes of advertisers. The highest rate is the national rate; lower rates are offered to camps, schools, book and record clubs, mail order firms, and some other types of organizations. The typical ad inserted by a mail order company will cost anywhere from 15 to 25 percent less, on the average, than an ad placed by a manufacturer. This is true whether it's to be printed in black and white, in two colors, or in full color. As an example, where a one-page black-and-white advertisement scheduled for a single insertion would cost the national advertiser $17,000, a direct marketing firm might be charged only $13,600.

Fractional Pages and Color

Space in magazines is sold on a fractional or full-page basis and by the column inch. Where the publication offers a special shop-by-mail section, there may be a minimum unit you'll be required to buy. If the magazine carries classified advertising, you'll be charged by the word or agate line, or by the inch if the section admits classified display advertisements.

When analyzed by the total amount of space for your investment, the full-page ad is your best buy. When you require less space for your message, you'll actually be paying proportionately more for every line or every inch you use. The premium you'll pay can run to as much as 20 percent or higher on a half-page ad, for example. Examples of these premiums can be readily seen in Exhibit 16–1.

Check the entries for Magazine A. The space for a single insertion of your one-page mail order ad would cost you $3,000. You might then assume, quite logically, that half a page would cost you $1,500. Yet, the magazine will charge $1,800 for the space; $300 more than you calculated. You'll be asked to pay a premium of 20 percent above what the price theoretically ought to be.

What about the possibility of adding color to your advertisement? Depending on the publication, you'll be charged as little as 10 to 15 percent, or up to 25 percent and more, over the normal black-and-white cost, should you want to add just a single color, provided you use one full page. (See Exhibit 16–2 to confirm this.) Less space than that will cost you proportionately more. In fact, when it comes to full four-color advertising, this differential runs way, way up—to 50 percent and more over the one-page, black-and-white rate.

It should be noted that the majority of magazines that accept four-color advertising won't accept anything smaller than one-third of a page. Some require a minimum space of one-half page or a full page.

EXHIBIT 16–1   Magazine mail order rates: Fractional versus full-page costs*

Magazine	Cost of One Page	One-half Page			One-third Page		
		Cost at Page Rate	Actual Cost	Premium Percentage	Cost at Page Rate	Actual Cost	Premium Percentage
A	$ 3,000	$ 1,500	$ 1,800	+20.0%	$ 1,000	$ 1,200	+20.0%
B	4,239	2,199.50	2,545	+20.0	1,413	1,693	+19.8
C	14,050	7,025	8,570	+22.0	4,683.33	5,620	+20.0
D	16,800	8,400	9,470	+12.7	5,600	6,760	+20.7
E	22,900	11,450	13,700	+19.7	7,633.33	9,200	+20.6
F	28,900	14,450	17,890	+23.8	9,633.33	10,410	+ 8.1
G	42,945	21,472.50	25,775	+20.0	14,315	16,035	+12.0
H	55,240	27,620	34,525	+25.0	18,413.33	22,095	+20.0

*All costs based on publication rate cards received during the first half of 1994.

EXHIBIT 16–2   Magazine mail order rates: Single insertion costs per full page, color versus black and white*

Magazine	Black and White	Two Color	Premium Percentage	Four Color	Premium Percentage
A	$ 3,000	$ 3,585	+19.5%	$ 4,040	+34.7%
B	4,239	5,091	+20.1	6,480	+52.9
C	14,050	17,405	+23.9	20,970	+49.3
D	16,800	18,880	+12.4	25,200	+50.0
E	22,900	27,900	+21.8	32,800	+43.2
F	28,900	33,960	+17.5	41,430	+43.4
G	42,945	50,265	+17.0	56,785	+32.2
H	55,240	68,540	+24.1	85,700	+55.1

*All costs based on publication rate cards received during the first half of 1994.

Space Contracts

Again, just as is the case with the newspaper, magazines offer special frequency rates as well as discounted rates on the total amount of space used within the contract period. Substantial savings can result should the ad be scheduled for three, six, or more issues of the publication.

The short-rate procedure is explained in Chapter 15; should you not use all of the space contracted for, your billings will be recomputed and you'll be expected to pay the differential.

Current Rates

A regular, large-space R.O.P. display advertisement in the more widely distributed consumer magazines is often well beyond the capabilities of the small mail order firm, yet such operators do "take a flyer" from time to time. With circulations in the hundreds of thousands, and some of them up in the millions, such publications may charge anywhere from several thousands of dollars to as much as $40,000 and more for a one-page, black-and-white advertisement, even at the lower mail order rate. However, many magazines contain special sections, or at least pages, devoted to merchandise sold by mail. See page 189 for examples of special mail order sections. Ads in these sections are typically smaller than their R.O.P. counterparts. And space in them can be purchased more readily by the small operator since the magazine accepts minimum-size ads, sometimes as small as a column inch. Some publications run "editorial style" mail order ads; in these instances, there may be a minimum size requirement, such as 27, 33, 42, or 60 lines or more.

Exhibit 16–3 shows a sample listing of publications with each magazine's total circulation, the cost per page for black-and-white mail order advertising, and the computed cost per thousand. This last figure is

EXHIBIT 16–3 Mail order rates: Magazine advertising[1]

Publication	Circulation[2]	B/W Page Rate	Cost per Thousand[3]	Minimum Mail Order Unit	Unit Cost
American Baby	1,300,000	$ 36,900	$28.38	1 inch	$ 1,700
American Legion Magazine	2,900,000	22,670	7.82	1 inch	812
American Woman	160,000	3,000	18.75	1/12 page	600
Better Homes & Gardens	7,600,000	116,040	15.27	1 inch	3,920
Bride's Magazine	338,700	13,610	40.18	1/12 page	2,090
Car and Driver	1,100,000	23,595	21.45	1/3 page	10,005
Cosmopolitan	2,500,000	50,915	20.37	1/12 page	3,860
Country America	1,000,000	22,900	22.90	1/12 page	2,000
Ebony	1,800,000	31,024	17.24	1 inch	1,293
Elks Magazine	1,350,000	7,740	5.73	2 inches	570
Esquire	700,000	20,690	29.56	1/6 page	4,355
Essence	950,000	18,530	19.51	1/6 page	4,188.25
Glamour	2,000,000	42,880	21.44	1/12 page	3,880
Good Housekeeping	5,000,000	73,512	14.70	1 inch	3,052
Harper's Magazine	205,000	4,239	20.68	1/12 page	636
Home Mechanix	1,000,000	16,800	16.80	1/6 page	3,890
Horticulture	330,000	7,180	21.76	1 inch	405
Hot Rod	800,000	18,700	23.37	1 inch	1,029
Inside Sports	675,000	14,050	20.81	1/6 page	2,810
McCall's	4,600,000	57,548	12.51	1 inch	2,491
Mademoiselle	1,100,000	27,330	24.85	1/4 column	2,310
New Body	91,500	2,050	22.40	1/12 page	430
Parents Magazine	1,825,000	36,205	19.84	1 inch	1,520
Popular Mechanics	1,600,000	28,340	17.71	1 inch	1,075
Redbook	3,200,000	42,945	13.42	1 inch	1,515
Self	1,100,000	28,400	25.82	1/3 page	10,830
Seventeen	1,850,000	26,356	14.25	1/12 page	2,196
Skiing Magazine	440,000	15,375	34.94	1/12 page	2,178.75
Vogue	1,100,000	28,900	26.27	1/2 column	5,480

[1] Rates in effect as of 1994.
[2] Circulation rate base in most instances as per magazine rate cards.
[3] Obtained by dividing the cost of a full-page black-and-white advertisement by the circulation.

arrived at by dividing the cost of a full-page black-and-white advertisement, after multiplying this cost by 1,000, by the total circulation of the publication. This approach gives you a basis for comparing media buys. The formula looks like this:

$$\text{Cost per M} = \frac{\text{Black-and-white page rate} \times 1,000}{\text{Total circulation}}$$

Added to the above information, Exhibit 16–3 also gives perhaps more useful data for the smaller firm—the size of the minimum space unit normally accepted by the magazine and the cost of that unit.

Other Pointers

Some of the more widely circulated magazines offer regional editions. Advertisements placed in these editions will, of course, cost far less than if you were to use the entire distribution. However, you'll pay proportionately more for the space on a per-thousand basis.

Split-run possibilities are also available from some publications. This means that the magazine can split its total circulation in two, three, or more segments: northeast, south, mountain states, west coast, and so on, enabling the advertiser to try out alternate advertisements (all of the same size) simultaneously.

For either regional editions or split runs, most magazines will insist that you use a minimum space of at least one-third or one-half of a page.

Special positions for your display advertisement, outside of the regular mail order section, are usually difficult to get. If the publication decides to honor your request, you pay an extra charge. As to your chances of being able to purchase an inside or back cover position, these are next to nil. Some magazines won't take a mail order advertisement in these positions; others will consider only a full-color page. And the cost can be twice, three times, or much more than that of a single black-and-white full-page ad.

On occasion, advertisers will use inserts in connection with their offers. A business reply card is an example. These inserts must be printed and paid for by the advertisers and delivered to the publication for insertion. Their use often dramatically increases the total number of responses. Usually, you'll be required to pay for this service at the rate customarily charged for a full-page black-and-white advertisement.

Some magazines use their own business reply cards to encourage readers to send for information about advertisements carried in the publication. Responses thus obtained are forwarded to the individual advertisers. This is commonly called a magazine *bingo card*.

CLASSIFIED ADS IN MAGAZINES OFTEN PAY OFF

Many magazines have classified sections, just as the newspapers do. These can be very profitable columns for the smaller mail order house. Some advertisers appear in the same publication month after month, for years. Costs are comparatively low when contrasted with the cost of a display ad or even with the cost of a minimum-space mail order unit. After all, what most small firms are looking for is either a low cost-per-inquiry or a low-cost-per-sale; the trick is to have the advertisement pay for itself if at all possible.

An interesting alternative, especially where publications offer no regular classified pages, is the "MarketPlace," handled by Classified, Inc., of 100 E. Ohio Street, Chicago, IL 60611. This is a classified column that the company introduces into a variety of publications. The column is sectioned off from the surrounding text and topped by the "MarketPlace"

EXHIBIT 16–4 Publications with classified sections

Name and Address of Publication	Cost Information for Classified Ads*	
	Regular Classified	Display Classified
American Legion Magazine c/o Fox Associates, Inc. 116 W. Kinzie Street Chicago, IL 60610 800/345-8670	$17 per word; no minimum number of words	1 inch—$868
American Photo 1633 Broadway, 45th floor New York, NY 10019 212/767-6042	$6.90 per word; minimum 15 words	1 inch—$459
Baseball Digest Century Publishing Company 990 Grove Street Evanston, IL 60201 708/491-6440	$1.35 per word; minimum 10 words	——
Boating 1633 Broadway, 45th floor New York, NY 10019 212/767-6042	$4.25 per word; minimum 15 words	1 inch—$348
Better Homes and Gardens c/o Classified, Inc. 100 E. Ohio Street, Suite 632 Chicago, IL 60611 800/424-3090	$43.95 per word; minimum 16 words	——
Capper's P.O. Box 534230 Sarasota, FL 34230 813/366-3003	$2 per word; minimum 10 words	1 inch—$129.50
Car and Driver 1633 Broadway, 45th floor New York, NY 10019 212/767-6042	$10.55 per word; minimum 15 words	1 inch—$950
Country America c/o Classified, Inc. 100 E. Ohio Street, Suite 632 Chicago, IL 60611 800/424-3090	$11.95 per word; minimum 20 words	——

*Rates in effect as of March 1995

EXHIBIT 16–4   *(Continued)*

Name and Address of Publication	Cost Information for Classified Ads*	
	Regular Classified	*Display Classified*
Crafts 'n' Things Clapper Communications Companies 701 Lee Street, Suite 1000 Des Plaines, IL 60016 708/297-7400	$3.25 per word; minimum 20 words	——
Cycle World 1633 Broadway, 45th floor New York, NY 10019 212/767-6042	$4.90 per word; minimum 15 words	1 inch, $320
Ellery Queen, Alfred Hitchcock *Magazines* (combination) Dell Magazines 380 Lexington Avenue New York, NY 10168 212/782-8532	$4.80 per word; minimum $72.00	——
Entrepreneur Magazine P.O. Box 570 Clearwater, FL 34617 800/762-3555	$8.95 per word; minimum 10 words	——
Family Circle 110 Fifth Avenue New York, NY 10011 212/463-1537	$34.00 per word; minimum 15 words	——
Field and Stream 2 Park Avenue New York, NY 10016 212/779-5000	$13.25 per word; minimum 14 words	1 inch—$900
Flying 1633 Broadway, 45th floor New York, NY 10019 212/767-5750	$4.80 per word; minimum 15 words	1 inch—$446
Football Digest Century Publishing Company 990 Grove Street Evanston, IL 60201 708/491-6440	$1.35 per word; minimum 10 words	——

EXHIBIT 16–4 *(Continued)*

Name and Address of Publication	Cost Information for Classified Ads*	
	Regular Classified	*Display Classified*
Golf Magazine 2 Park Avenue New York, NY 10016 212/779-5000	$22.80 per word; minimum 10 words	1 inch—$1,110
Grit P.O. Box 534230 Sarasota, FL 34230 813/366-3003	$2 per word; minimum 10 words	1 inch—$129.50
Home Mechanix 2 Park Avenue New York, NY 10016 212/779-5000	$8.25 per word; minimum 15 words	1 inch—$495
Horticulture 98 No. Washington Street Boston, MA 02114 617/742-5600	$5.25 per word; minimum 15 words	——
Income Opportunities 1500 Broadway, Suite 600 New York, NY 10036 212/642-0600	$7.95 per word; minimum charge, $119.25	——
Independent Business P.O. Box 1510 Clearwater, FL 34617 800/237-9851	$7.30 per word; minimum 10 words	1 inch—$520
Outdoor Life 2 Park Avenue New York, NY 10016 212/779-5000	$11.10 per word; minimum 14 words	1 inch—$735
Popular Mechanics 224 W. 57th Street New York, NY 10019 212/649-2000	$12.60 per word; minimum 10 words	——
Popular Photography 1633 Broadway, 45th floor New York, NY 10019 212/767-5750	$8.45 per word; minimum 15 words	1 inch—$726

EXHIBIT 16–4   *(Continued)*

Name and Address of Publication	Cost Information for Classified Ads*	
	Regular Classified	*Display Classified*
Popular Science 2 Park Avenue New York, NY 10016 212/779-5000	$13.65 per word; minimum 12 words	1 inch—$760
Runner's World 33 E. Minor Street Emmaus, PA 18098 610/967-8316	$200 for 20 words or less; $9.00 each additional word	1 inch—$560
Redbook 224 W. 57th Street New York, NY 10019 212/649-3391	$30 per word; minimum 20 words	——
Ski Magazine 2 Park Avenue New York, NY 10016 212/779-5000	$7.70 per word; minimum 15 words	1 inch—$970
The Atlantic P.O. Box 1510 Clearwater, FL 34617 800/237-9851	$7.95 per word; minimum 15 words	——
VFW Magazine c/o Pabco Representatives, Inc. 169 Lexington Avenue New York, NY 10016 212/532-0660	$11.95 per word; minimum 20 words	1 inch—$539
Working Mother P.O. Box 1510 Clearwater, FL 34617 800/237-9851	$12.70 per word; minimum 10 words	1 inch—$785

masthead. The firm usually sells space in the column for a group of magazines. For example, there's a group of women's magazines that includes, among others, *True Experience, True Story, True Romance,* and *Modern Romances.* The company will also place your classified advertising in other periodicals; *Business Week, Metropolitan Home,* and *Child* are examples.

As noted in Chapter 15, mail order firms and other direct response companies use very little newspaper classified advertising. The opposite is true with magazine classified. These columns are filled with small advertisements from an amazing variety of organizations that seek replies by mail. Some ads offer merchandise directly for sale; these are usually low-cost items that sell for up to $5. Mail order operators often prefer a two-step approach for merchandise that costs more than that. The classified ad will offer a booklet, free details, or other information, perhaps asking the respondent to send a self-addressed stamped envelope (SASE) or a modest amount, perhaps 50¢ or $1, to rule out curiosity seekers. The follow-up material sent by the advertiser tries to sell the respondent. This two-step approach is practically a must for anything priced over $10.

Magazine readers often read the classified pages thoroughly. They have come to expect all sorts of offers that may interest them and answer their needs. Magazines such as *Popular Mechanics* and *Popular Science* contain many pages of such advertisements; some of the ads have been running for years (with changes of copy, of course).

To help the reader locate advertisements that may be of interest, the publication groups these ads under different headings.

As is true in newspaper classified, magazine classified includes both regular (words only) and display classified. Exhibit 16–4 contains a short list of magazines that offer classified space. In addition to providing names, addresses, and telephone numbers of these publications, current rates for regular classified advertising, and, where available, for display classified are shown. Also indicated are the minimum sizes offered by the magazine.

SOURCES OF ADDITIONAL INFORMATION

Davidson, Jeffrey P., *Marketing to Home-Based Businesses*. Homewood, IL: Business One Irwin, 1991.

Gross, Martin, *The Direct Marketer's Idea Book*. New York: AMACOM, 1989.

Hahn, Fred, *Do-It-Yourself Advertising: How to Produce Great Ads, Catalogs, Direct Mail, and Much More*. New York: Wiley, 1993.

Holtz, Herman, *The Direct Marketer's Workbook*. New York: Wiley, 1986.

Miller, Marlene, *Business Guide to Print Promotion*. Laguna Beach, CA: Iris Communication, 1987.

Nash, Edward L., *The Direct Marketing Handbook,* (2d ed.). New York: McGraw-Hill, 1992.

Stone, Bob, *Successful Direct Marketing Methods,* (5th ed.). Lincolnwood, IL: NTC, 1993.

Troshynski-Thomas, Karen and Deborah M. Burek, (Eds.), *1994 Gale Directory of Publications and Broadcast Media,* (126th ed.). Detroit: Gale Research Inc., 1994.

Ward, Dick, *Creative Ad Design and Illustration*. Cincinnati: North Light Books, 1988.

THE BROADCAST MEDIA AND TELEMARKETING

17

Radio and the Direct Marketing Firm

Even though the greater share of their promotion budgets typically goes into direct mail activity and advertising in the print media, many direct marketing companies rely on radio and/or television—the broadcast media—for some of their sales. Each day, somewhere, the air waves carry messages to consumers about long-playing records and tapes, hardware items and kitchen utensils, encyclopedias and magazine subscriptions, garden supplies and burglar alarms, and a host of other products and services.

THE BROADCAST MEDIA

Both radio and television, especially the local variety, are far more widely used by retail and manufacturing businesses than by mail order concerns. Yet, they can play an important role in mail order selling. Radio can be an asset both as an alternative to and in addition to your print advertising and your mailings. Television can be valuable as a medium where the product you want to advertise will enjoy greater sales if it can be demonstrated, or shown in full color.

Media people in advertising agencies like to refer to the broadcast media as "universal" media, in the sense that through either radio or television you can reach most every household in the nation. Radios, often as many as four or more, are found in most homes and in millions of automobiles, trucks, and other vehicles. Most households are equipped with at least one television set, but many have two or more, and color sets are found today in a vast majority of households.

Radio Today

In 1992, more than 9,700 commercial radio stations were in operation across the country. Of these, slightly more than one-half were AM stations.[1]

Most radio stations are independents. Only a small fraction of the total number belongs to a national network, like the American Broadcasting Company (ABC), the National Broadcasting Company (NBC), the Columbia Broadcasting System (CBS), and the Public Broadcasting System (PBS). The typical direct marketing firm uses these networks infrequently because of the cost. More often, such advertisers will use local radio; they advertise on individual stations in selected areas or, perhaps, schedule their announcements on a number of such stations during the same time period.

RADIO'S PLUSES AND MINUSES FOR DIRECT MARKETERS

As an advertising medium, radio attracts retailers for several reasons, and for the same reasons it should interest the mail order company as well:

- Quick consumer reaction.
- Short lead time and flexibility.
- Radio goes everywhere.
- Audience targeting.
- Help in preparing announcements.

Quick Consumer Reaction

People may respond almost instantaneously to offers broadcast over both radio and television. Most direct marketing firms using these media will provide the listener (or viewer) with telephone numbers to call to place orders directly or to give his or her name and address so that information, catalogs, and the like can be mailed to that person. On radio, these numbers are usually repeated several times for the listening audience. Telephone operators or recording machines may stand by twenty-four hours a day, so that even an announcement aired at two or three o'clock in the morning can generate immediate results.

Short Lead Time and Flexibility

Newspapers may require a lead time of one or two days for the advertiser. They have to set the ads up in print, select the pages on which they're to

---

[1] U.S. Department of Commerce, Bureau of the Census, *Statistical Abstract of the United States, 1993,* (113th ed.) (Washington, DC: U.S. Government Printing Office, 1993), 561.

appear, and so on. Radio announcements, on the other hand, can be broadcast within hours after the copy has been delivered. This means exceptional flexibility in copy changes, a definite assist to the advertiser.

Radio Goes Everywhere

Newspapers reach a majority of the households in the nation, but radios can be found in just about every one. Most cars are also equipped with radios, many with FM reception as well. If you advertise on radio, your messages may be heard by people driving to and from work, those on vacation at beaches or in the mountains, bicyclists, and people out for a walk. You'll reach places where newspapers are seldom found.

Audience Targeting

Over time, every successful radio station attracts a solid core of regular listeners. Station audiences are loyal; people often listen to the same radio station hour after hour, day after day without turning the dial (unlike television viewers, who often switch channels). So the possibilities of targeting selected segments of consumers are practically unlimited. You can aim your announcements at listeners who appreciate classical or semiclassical music, at rock fans or country music lovers, at those who prefer talk shows, or at specific nationality groups or certain segments of the population. There are, for instance, hundreds of radio stations targeted at black Americans. You can also reach such large groups as young men and women under twenty-one years of age, many of whom appear not to be oriented toward newspaper readership.

Help in Preparing Announcements

The radio advertiser can count on the station's staff for help in writing copy, selecting background music, and so on.

Disadvantages of Radio

Although radio always has been and is being used successfully by direct marketing companies, this medium does have several significant drawbacks that are briefly discussed below:

Restricted presentation. If you advertise in the print media or on television, you can show your audiences the merchandise you're featuring. Moreover, on TV you can also address the viewers with enthusiasm, reinforcing the visual message with the added force of direct, one-to-one selling. You can't demonstrate your product over the radio. You must rely on sound alone to trigger the listener's imagination—to attract his or her attention, arouse interest, build desire, and secure action. Your only tools are words, music, and perhaps sound effects; with these you need to construct skillfully an impressive picture in the listener's imagination, one strong enough to motivate that person to respond.

Distractions. Even though many people do listen attentively to their radios, in a large percentage of cases, the radio is heard with "half an ear." Often, radio music or talk is little more than background sound for the individual engaged in other activities demanding his or her attention: driving a car, cleaning the house, cooking, speaking to friends, and so on.

Short messages. Typically, the mail order radio announcement runs one minute in length. No sooner has it been broadcast then its message is gone—lost to the listener. There's no way an interested party can refer back to it, as one can with advertisements in magazines or newspapers. Hence the need, in radio advertising, for scheduling repeated airings of your announcements.

Fragmentation. In most areas of the country, anywhere from five to six to as many as two dozen or more radio stations, both AM and FM, may be transmitting at the same time. What this means to the advertiser is clear. Despite radio's practically universal reach (in that it enters over 99 percent of the nation's homes), this massive audience is spread across a number of stations at any one time—day or night, and over the weekend as well. So, your chances of the listeners in a specific locale catching a single announcement of yours aren't much better than poor to fair; all the more reason to think in terms of repetition, of frequency.

HOW TO BUY RADIO TIME

Although national advertisers may sponsor parts of or entire programs on radio, the mail order operator thinks in terms of spot announcements, more precisely, *local* spot radio. These, for the most part, are full one-minute spots; shorter ones can't really get the story across.

Rates on local radio vary according to the time of day or night the advertiser wants his or her announcements to be aired. The twenty-four hours of the day are divided into segments called day parts. Although these may vary somewhat from station to station, the information in Exhibit 17–1 is a fairly accurate representation of these segments.

The Standard Rate and Data Service regularly publishes information regarding rates. You can use their service if you'll be doing a lot of radio advertising. You may also contact those stations you're interested in to request copies of their current rate cards. Ask if they offer special rates for mail order advertisers and about their package plans.

When using this medium, plan to air a series of announcements scheduled over a period of, perhaps, one to three weeks. Frequency of advertising is the key to success here; advertisers look for the cumulative effect of their radio commercials and the cumulative reach attained. The same announcement can be broadcast repeatedly at different times of the day and night and on different days of the week. Or, you can create two or three totally different commercials, all presenting the same

EXHIBIT 17–1   Approximate time classifications for radio stations

Time Class	Description	Hours
AAA	Morning drive time	5:30 A.M. to 10 A.M. (Monday–Saturday)
AA	Daytime	10 A.M. to 3:30 P.M. (Monday–Friday)
A	Evening drive time	3:30 P.M. to 8 P.M. (Monday–Friday)
B	Night time	8 P.M. to Midnight (Monday–Saturday)
C	Late night/Sunday	Midnight to 5:30 A.M. (Monday–Saturday); all day Sunday

proposition, and arrange for them to be rotated by the station as the scheduled times come up. The more you repeat your message over the air, the greater the chance that listeners who have missed earlier broadcasts will be exposed to it. And along with repeated announcements, the chances for customer response increases. (Incidentally, results will be much better if you arrange to use a toll-free 800 number in connection with your advertising message.)

The direct marketing firm generally avoids the more popular time slots, such as morning and evening drive time, because they command the highest prices of all categories. Moreover, it's far easier to obtain off-hours time because Class AAA and Class AA time is snapped up rapidly by the bigger advertisers. In fact, many mail order operators prefer to have their commercials broadcast late at night and on Sundays and Saturdays because most consumers are at home then. The thinking is that listening is so much more relaxed at home and that the audience will have paper and pencil nearby to jot down box numbers, addresses, or telephone numbers as soon as they're broadcast.

HOW TO WRITE EFFECTIVE RADIO ANNOUNCEMENTS

Radio announcements are usually quite inexpensive to write and prepare. Most direct-response commercials are of the straight-offer type, where a station announcer delivers the message in a professional manner. The one-minute spot announcement usually contains somewhere between 110 and 145 or so words. If you haven't engaged the services of an advertising agency, the radio station will often help prepare your radio copy for better results. Sound effects and music (to introduce, end, or accompany a message as background) can also be used, often to good avail.

Often, advertisers rely on other formats for radio announcements. Otto Kleppner, author of an excellent textbook on advertising, mentions techniques such as the customer interview, the slice-of-life, and the two-announcer approach, along with the straight announcement and other types.[2]

Most of the copywriting guidelines for the print media covered in Chapter 11 apply as well to the creation of radio copy. After all, good writing is good writing! But this medium of radio differs radically from the print media, and from television, in two important aspects. First, your listener can't see the item you're trying to sell. Second, you must rely on spoken words, possibly along with music and/or sound effects, to create an image of the product, and *then* do an effective selling job.

That's quite a handicap you'll be working under. What a challenge, though, to your creativity and talent! Of course, if you're lucky enough to afford an ad agency, you can turn over the challenge to them.

To help sharpen your skills at writing radio announcements, refer to the many copy hints in Chapter 11 before you start practicing.

SOURCES OF ADDITIONAL INFORMATION

Book, Albert C., Norman D. Cary, and Stanley I. Tannenbaum, *The Radio and Television Commercial,* (2d ed.). Lincolnwood, IL: NTC Business Books, 1986.

Duffy, Ben, *Advertising Media and Markets.* New York: Garland, 1985.

Gross, Martin, *The Direct Marketer's Idea Book.* New York: AMACOM, 1989.

Holtz, Herman, *The Direct Marketer's Workbook.* New York: Wiley, 1986.

Nash, Edward L., *The Direct Marketing Handbook,* (2d ed.). New York: McGraw-Hill, 1992.

Schulberg, Bob, *Radio Advertising: The Authoritative Guide.* Lincolnwood, IL: NTC Business Books, 1988.

Stone, Bob, *Successful Direct Marketing Methods,* (5th ed.). Lincolnwood, IL: NTC, 1993.

Troshynski-Thomas, Karen and Deborah M. Burek, (Eds.), *1994 Gale Directory of Publications and Broadcast Media,* (126th ed.). Detroit: Gale Research Inc., 1994.

---

[2] Otto Kleppner and Norman A.P. Govoni, *Advertising Procedure,* (7th ed.) (Englewood Cliffs, NJ: Prentice-Hall, Inc., 1979), 433–34.

18

Television and the Direct Marketing Firm

A television commercial is radio and print advertising, and personal selling as well, all wrapped together in one neat, astounding package. It enters the intimacy of most all American homes through "the tube."

There's no more effective advertising medium for persuading the public to buy.

TELEVISION TODAY

In 1992, more than 1,000 commercial television stations (551 VHF and 567 UHF) served the American public.[1] Videocassette recorders could be found in 67 million households, 56 million of which enjoyed programs on cable TV. Some 11,000 cable TV systems were in operation.

Today, advertisers spend more on television (well over $22 billion annually) than on other media, with the sole exception of newspapers.

Many cable TV networks are practically household names; for example:

AMC—American Movie Classics

CMTV—Country Music Television

CNN—Cable News Network

---

[1] U.S. Department of Commerce, Bureau of the Census, *Statistical Abstract of the United States, 1993,* (113th ed.) (Washington, DC: U.S. Government Printing Office, 1993), 561.

DIS—The Disney Channel

ESPN—Entertainment, Sports Programming Network

HBO—Home Box Office

HSN—Home Shopping Network

LIF—Lifetime

MTV—Music Television

NIK—Nickelodeon

QVC—QVC Shopping Network

TNN—The Nashville Network

TNT—Turner Network Television

USA—USA Network

ADVANTAGES AND DISADVANTAGES OF THE MEDIUM

Although chances are you'll not be using television to promote your merchandise or service(s) for some time, it's never too early to begin learning about what this medium can do for you.

Television: Benefits for the Advertiser

Some of the reasons why many advertisers prefer television include:

- *Strongest appeal to the senses.* Because television touches on not one but two of the human senses, sight and sound, its impact is far stronger than those of the other mass media. Then, too, the prevalence of color television in homes today further enhances the impact of a presentation. The medium is tops for any product that needs to be demonstrated. We have all seen the closeups on camera, in full color, of a pair of hands demonstrating a special tool for quickly slicing vegetables into different and appetizing shapes; pots and pans with special nonstick surfaces arrayed attractively over a tablecloth; a running list of song titles accompanied by music and a series of colorful rustic scenes flashed on the screen to advertise a new long-playing record or tape; and so on.

- *Quick response.* As with radio, responses to offers made over television, whether inquiries or actual orders, are immediate. I have been present in a number of telephone rooms for direct marketing companies where a dozen or more salespeople were ready to answer the phones. No sooner is the number to call announced and flashed on the screen than incoming calls begin to light up the switchboard and the room's atmosphere changes from one of subdued anticipation to frenzied excitement.

- *Tremendous reach.* There are far fewer television than radio stations. Many sections of the country are penetrated by only one or two television stations, so audiences are sizable and loyal. In the more populous areas, viewers can easily number in the hundreds of thousands, even millions.

Television: The Negatives

Television is such an attractive medium that you would think the mail order firm would jump into it eagerly. After all, television audiences are sizable and public reaction is quick. Nevertheless, the medium presents several disadvantages that merit careful thought and consideration:

- *High costs.* One problem that's sure to make you think, not twice, but three and four times before approaching a single television station is the cost of television time itself. A single one-minute spot can run from several hundred to a few thousand dollars. Then, there's the cost of *producing* a television commercial. It's practically inane to consider producing one yourself; generally, you need the help of experts, which could mean more thousands.

    You can, of course, do what many direct marketers do—look for nonprime-time buys at every station you're interested in. Even postmidnight spots can generate business.

- *Short life.* Television also presents some of the disadvantages we found in radio. Like the radio announcement, the television commercial must be short, and, as soon as it has been broadcast, the viewer is no longer able to study the offer. Moreover, many people in the audience dislike watching commercials. When one appears, some viewers run to the kitchen for a snack; others may flick the dial to see what other television channels are showing. Still others seem to be able to mentally tune out most commercials.

- *Lack of selectivity.* Another drawback is the fact that most television audiences are broadly heterogeneous. You can't benefit from the selectivity factor as you can with radio and magazine advertising. As a result, thousands of viewers of your commercial won't be proper targets for your messages.

BUYING AIR TIME ON TELEVISION

Because it's so infrequently used by the small mail order company, only a few comments on television marketing are included here. (We direct the interested reader to several of the books listed at the end of this chapter.)

Just as in radio, television time is offered to advertisers according to day parts. Top rates are asked for those hours viewing is traditionally heaviest. These differ, however, from the scheduling of radio stations; class AA time on TV is not drive time, rather, it's the evening hours. These would usually be the hours between 7:30 and 11:00 P.M.

Again, as in radio, direct marketing firms tend to buy spots on local television at times that carry the lowest costs. The commercials are generally 60 seconds in length, although purchasing 90- or 120-second spots is fairly common. Commercials need to be professionally done; the use of technical production companies is common.

Copy for the *audio,* or sound, portion of the commercial script is similar in intent, style, and delivery to radio announcements. There's an additional refinement: it must tie in completely with what the audience will be viewing on their TV sets.

Action for the viewing, or *video,* component is also planned in advance by developing *storyboards,* rough sketches of the various scenes and events, done in sequence as they'll be presented on the screen. Instructions for the camera are also worked out. The final script is divided into halves, with video instructions on the one side and audio copy on the other.

CREATING TELEVISION COMMERCIALS THAT SELL

Advertising your product(s) or service(s) on television can certainly prove effective for your mail order company. As we already know, both the impact and the drawing power of television far exceed that of any other mass medium. Its one big drawback is, of course, the great cost of producing television commercials and purchasing air time.

There are ways to hold down your expenses in both areas. In producing commercials, for example, an advertiser generally works with a production house. The prices asked by the smaller production companies are often lower than those quoted by the larger establishments. Moreover, they tend to watch production costs more closely because they work for small firms for the most part.

You might also ask for assistance at the television station on which you plan to advertise. Some stations have staff that can help you to produce commercials. Another suggestion is that you consider building your commercial around a slide presentation; this can lower your production costs considerably.

When preparing television commercials, it's always helpful to keep the AIDA concept in mind (see Chapter 9). Successful commercials grab the attention of viewers almost instantaneously, quickly arouse their interest, build a desire to have or to own that which is being advertised, and then get action in the form of an order or a telephone call. Indeed, mail order advertisers can and often do benefit by using a toll-free 800 number in conjunction with their commercials.

To hold down your costs, make certain that every second of the commercial counts. Every word that's spoken and every scene that's shot must make its necessary contribution to the whole. Anything extraneous, anything that doesn't make a contribution, should be coldly excised.

As for holding down your costs of air time, check into the special package rates that are available. Think about using late night spots. Occasionally, you may be able to secure some time through a barter house. It is also possible to make deals with some stations on a P.I. (Per Inquiry) basis, where you won't have to pay anything at all up front. In such cases, the station will air your commercials whenever they so choose and as frequently as they choose. To compensate them for this type of promotion, you'll need to pay the station a prearranged sum for each inquiry or order received.

THE PROMISING FIELD OF INTERACTIVE TV

An exciting outgrowth of the electronic revolution has been the development and subsequent evolution of home information systems. Many consumers now enjoy the convenience of doing their banking and readily accessing financial and other kinds of data banks from the privacy of their own homes.

During the 1970s, experiments with "interactive, two-way" information systems were carried on in several European countries and in Canada. Among the more noteworthy installations were those of Teletel (in France), Prestel (Great Britain), Bildshirmtext (Germany), and Telidon (Canada).

Here in the United States, American companies soon followed suit and began promoting their own interactive systems toward the end of the decade and into the 1980s. Early trials included Warner Communications' QUBE, Knight-Ridder's Viewtron, Chemical Bank's Pronto Home Banking, and, later on, JC Penney's Telacton. On-line shopping was strengthened by Comp-U-Card, an organization that offered its members thousands of brand name products at substantially discounted prices. Also making its debut was Sears Roebuck's Prodigy. CompuServe and Prodigy now have several million subscribers who can review well over 100 different catalogs via their computerized databases.

Consumer interest in the new technology that facilitates in-home shopping continues to mount. Retailing organizations were quick to recognize the sales potential inherent in interactive television. Instead of visiting stores in person, consumers can now scan retailers' offerings in their own living rooms, select the merchandise they desire, and order it by computer or telephone. In turn, the retailer fills the order, shipping out the goods by United Parcel Service or by parcel post.

CD-ROMs (compact disks with read-only memory) carry text, sound, and full-color video and can be played in a CD-ROM computer drive. Millions of these have already been installed in computers.

TV shopping networks have also been proliferating. Launched in the mid-1980s, HSN (Home Shopping Network) and QVC (Quality, Value, Convenience) can now be viewed in more than 50 million American households. A number of smaller shopping networks serve several hundred thousand to millions of households; Value-Vision, for example, reaches more than ten million.

Among the newcomers to TV shopping are Spiegel/Time-Warner's Catalog 1, S—The Shopping Network, and TV Macy's.

Before the year 2000, we'll most likely find many more millions of consumers becoming entranced with electronic retailing. Some 500 new TV channels are expected to materialize; many of these will become shopping channels.

SOURCES OF ADDITIONAL INFORMATION

Baldwin, Huntley, *How to Create Effective TV Commercials,* (2d ed.). Lincolnwood, IL: NTC Business Books, 1988.

Book, Albert C., Norman D. Cary, and Stanley I. Tannenbaum, *The Radio and Television Commercial,* (2d ed.). Lincolnwood, IL: NTC Business Books, 1986.

Cohen, William, *Direct Response Marketing.* New York: Wiley, 1984.

Duffy, Ben, *Advertising Media and Markets.* New York: Garland, 1985.

Stone, Bob, *Successful Direct Marketing Methods,* (5th ed.). Lincolnwood, IL: NTC Business Books, 1993.

Troshynski-Thomas, Karen and Deborah M. Burek, (Eds.), *1994 Gale Directory of Publications and Broadcast Media,* (126th ed.). Detroit: Gale Research Inc., 1994.

19

Telemarketing

Mail order firms can often use the telephone to good avail, especially companies that sell industrial goods and/or services by direct mail and through catalog sales. Effectively marketing your offerings over a WATS line can add substantially to your sales volume; installing an 800 number for incoming calls will do much the same.

You can gainfully use the telephone to:

- Acquire additional names and addresses for your mailing list.
- Alert customers to upcoming sales and other promotions.
- Answer inquiries.
- Build goodwill toward your company.
- Contact prospective buyers.
- Inform customers about new merchandise.
- Open customer charge accounts.
- Reactivate dead accounts (customers who haven't bought from you in more than twelve months).
- Research buyers' intentions, preferences, or dislikes.
- Solicit reorders.
- Take new orders.

WHAT TELEMARKETING IS

Telemarketing is a unique method of personal selling that differs from other approaches in that it does not involve personal visits or face-to-face contact. It consists of telephoning consumers and/or organizations, primarily to solicit business. It's also used, of course, to cut down on selling costs as well as increase a firm's revenues. Thus, telemarketing is employed to obtain leads, set up appointments for visits by sales representatives, get orders, elicit survey and other kinds of information, and so on. Across industry, it is a rapidly growing and popular selling approach, especially in business-to-business marketing. Well over four million people are engaged in this exciting field of activity.

If your promotional plans include testing this approach, you can elect to employ an outside telemarketing service or you can do it yourself inside your company.

Inbound and Outbound Telemarketing

Telemarketing can be either inbound or outbound. With the first type, you can expect to receive inquiries and/or orders via the 800 number you list in your print or air media advertising, catalogs, or mailings. In outbound telemarketing, you cold-canvass by telephone numerous individuals and/or organizations most often to offer selling propositions and, occasionally, to gather needed information.

DEVELOPING THE TELEMARKETING PROGRAM

Before attempting to initiate a telephone salesforce, you should work out all details of an effective telemarketing program. Here are the more significant aspects to consider:

- Establishing telemarketing objectives.
- Working up the basic curriculum (product, company, and customer knowledge; developing telemarketing skills; proper delivery of sales presentations; closing sales).
- Determining the training methods to be used.
- Establishing a timetable for the training.
- Choosing one or more instructors.
- Putting the training program into effect.
- Evaluating the program.

Once you have planned your program, you'll need to begin thinking about the following:

- Setting up the telephone room.
- Preparing scripts.

- Hiring and training telemarketers.
- Obtaining leads.
- Making presentations.
- Closing sales.
- Keeping records.

Setting Up the Telephone Room

Shortly after you've initiated a telemarketing operation and judged it successful, you'll probably begin thinking of expanding your salesforce. Before you do so, though, be sure to set up the proper environment for effective telephone-room production. You'll need to work out the right arrangement of desks, chairs, telephones, and paneling—carpeting or other materials should be used to reduce the noise level in the room, so that each telemarketer can both speak and listen to the voice at the other end of the instrument without undue interference.

Preparing Scripts

You'll need lots of time and effort to turn out an effective script for teleprospecting. The script requires a quick, catchy hook right at the beginning—the promise of some benefit that will induce the prospect to keep on listening. Every script should sound thoroughly believable and aimed at building rapport at once between you and the listener. Identify yourself to the prospect and state your reason for calling. Carefully work into the presentation the more significant attributes of the product or service, as well as the product/service benefits your prospect can expect to reap. Also be sure to write in a technique or two for overcoming the more common objections that listeners may raise. Finally, prepare a persuasive closing method for getting the order.

Obtaining Leads

Your telephone company will be glad to sell you lists of telephone subscribers, whether they are consumers or business organizations. (You may, perhaps, find lists of new business start-ups of special interest to you.) Or, you can choose from literally many thousands of lists that are available from compilers, brokers, list managers, and other organizations. (See Chapter 14.)

Making Presentations

Your telemarketing staff will need lots of practice in delivering their sales presentations properly over the telephone. A pleasant, well-modulated speaking voice is essential. So is a deliberate delivery pace so that the listener can absorb and understand what is being said. Ask the more experienced members of your team to give demonstrations. Use role playing; let them role play as prospective buyers while they listen to the newer telemarketers' presentations. Ask them to raise one or more objections along the way.

Closing Sales

Again, use both demonstration and role playing in training your telemarketers how to counter objections and close sales. (See Chapter 9 for more information on these topics.)

Keeping Records

Accurate recordkeeping is a crucial component of all telemarketing activity. You'll need to devise and print many copies of a telephone call form on which to record such information as: the time you made the call, if you reached your prospect (if not, then indicate when to call back to speak to that individual), if you were able to make your entire presentation or the other person disconnected, whether or not the prospect seemed interested in your proposition, what the result of your presentation was, (whether or not you closed the sale), and what action you should take next.

HIRING THE RIGHT PEOPLE FOR THE JOB

Telemarketing is, of course, more of an art than a science. You need to bear in mind the fact that, to prospective buyers, the salesperson on the telephone is only a voice. There's no face-to-face contact to help close the sale.

There's no doubt about it; telemarketing is a tough, challenging profession! The telemarketer must sit for hours behind a desk, typically dialing upwards of 100 telephone calls each day from a list of prospects. (Unless an automatic dialing program is in place!) He or she must try to gain the prospect's attention almost at once, quickly build some modicum of rapport between the two, and attempt to hold that person's interest throughout the entire sales presentation. The caller needs to possess an ironclad constitution, one that's able to withstand frequent rejection. Some respondents will hang up immediately; others will listen for several minutes before bellowing a resounding "I'm not interested!" or "Don't bother me!" and banging down the instrument.

What Effective Telemarketers Are Like

To build an efficient and productive telephone salesforce, you'll need to recruit the right people and then train them well.

Try to hire people to train for telemarketing positions who have an abundance of the following characteristics:

articulate	empathetic
courteous	enthusiastic
dependable	friendly

hardworking   polite

honest   responsible

patient   self-confident

Perhaps the most important qualities to look for when interviewing applicants are a pleasant speaking voice, a friendly personality, a positive attitude, and a firm grasp of what should constitute good interpersonal relations. Of course, newly-hired telemarketers will require thorough training in this unique selling method as well as detailed knowledge of the product(s)/service(s) you offer and other job aspects.

TRAINING THE TELEMARKETER

To develop an outstanding sales team, you'll need to plan an effective training program. Be cautioned, though, that training alone won't do it. You'll also need to devise an appropriate commission-based compensation plan, work up an effective personnel evaluation program, and provide competent supervision for your telemarketing staff.

Among other topics, your training program should cover:

- Sales skills (how to gain attention at once, arouse interest, make a presentation, meet and overcome any objections, and close the sale).
- Company knowledge.
- Product/service knowledge.
- Customer/prospect knowledge.
- Knowledge of competitors' products and services.
- Paperwork and recordkeeping.
- Time management.

SOURCES OF ADDITIONAL INFORMATION

Ambrose, Sandra and Daniel Hellmuth, *Telemarketing Skills Training Manual.* Englewood Cliffs, NJ: Prentice-Hall, 1990.

Davis, Lou Ellen, *Teleprospecting: Warming Up the Cold Call to Increase Sales.* Englewood Cliffs, NJ: Prentice-Hall, 1992.

Fidel, Stanley Leo, *Start-Up Telemarketing: How to Launch a Profitable Sales Operation.* New York: Wiley, 1987.

Freestone, Julie, *Telemarketing Basics.* Los Altos, CA: Janet Cusp Publications, 1989.

Harlan, Raymond C. and Walter B. Woolfson, Jr., *Telemarketing That Works: How to Create a Winning Program for Your Company.* Chicago: Probus, 1991.

McHatton, Robert J., *Total Telemarketing.* New York: Wiley, 1988.

Mahfood, Phillip E., *Teleselling: High Performance Business-to-Business Phone Selling.* Chicago: Probus, 1993.

Masser, Barry Z., *Power Selling by Telephone.* Englewood Cliffs, NJ: Prentice-Hall, 1986.

_____ , *Complete Handbook of All-Purpose Telemarketing Scripts.* Englewood Cliffs, NJ: Prentice-Hall, 1990.

Porterfield, James D., *Selling on the Phone.* New York: Wiley, 1987.

Richardson, Linda, *Selling by Phone: How to Reach and Sell Customers in the Nineties.* New York: McGraw-Hill, 1992.

Slutsky, Jeff, *Streetsmart Teleselling: The 33 Secrets.* Englewood Cliffs, NJ: Prentice-Hall, 1990.

Stone, Bob and John Wyman, *Successful Telemarketing,* (2d ed.). Lincolnwood, IL: National Textbook, 1991.

PART
V

ADDITIONAL INFORMATION FOR THE GROWING FIRM

20

How to Manage Company Finances More Effectively

In Chapter 5, you were offered some insights into the financial side of the business enterprise. Information was presented about the customary sources of funds for starting and running a business. You were introduced to the format and terms of the two major accounting documents: the balance sheet and the income statement. Finally, you were shown how to set selling prices for your goods and services.

In this chapter, you learn how to plan, organize, manage, and control your firm's finances more effectively. You find out how to stay on top of what's happening in your business and how to improve your profit picture by calculating and then analyzing some significant financial ratios. You'll discover a simple procedure for circumventing those distressing cash-flow problems that plague business organizations of all types and sizes. An introduction to the budgeting process then follows; this will be of value to you in planning and controlling your new mail order enterprise. An overview of taxation, at the federal, state, and local levels, concludes the chapter.

STAY ON TRACK BY MONITORING YOUR FINANCIAL RATIOS

Some very useful ratios can be calculated from information readily available in your firm's operating statements (P&Ls) and balance sheets. Once you have grasped the essentials of *ratio analysis,* you can apply this technique to just about every area of business. It can give you valuable information to help you plan, organize, direct, and control your new mail order enterprise. It enables the business owner "to spot trends in a business and to compare its performance and condition with the average performance of similar businesses in the same industry.[1]

To illustrate the technique, let's take another look at the profit and loss statement of Handicrafts by Roslyn, shown in Exhibit 20–1. Note the net sales figure of $204,655 at the top of the P&L. Further down, you'll see the gross margin entry, listed as $120,945. From these two entries on the firm's operating statement, we can form a gross margin-to-sales ratio as indicated below:

$$\text{Gross margin-to-sales ratio} \quad = \quad \frac{\text{Gross margin}}{\text{Sales}} \times 100\%$$

$$= \quad \frac{\$120,945}{\$204,655} \times 100\%$$

$$= \quad 59.1\%[2]$$

How do we interpret the result of our calculations? We see, of course, that Handicrafts by Roslyn was able to retain 59.1 cents out of every dollar taken *after* paying for the goods that were sold and *before* any operating expenses or income taxes were deducted.

What is the value of knowing our gross margin-to-sales ratio? Let's suppose, for example, that the firm's P&L for the prior year showed a ratio of 60.5 percent. When we compare current year results with that percentage, we can readily determine that the company earned 1.4 cents *less* per sales dollar than the year before. In thinking through this situation, management can only conclude that either (1) the firm paid more, percentage-wise, for the goods it sold this year, or (2) consideration needs to be given to increasing the selling prices of some of the merchandise.

Another Illustration

For further clarification of the ratio analysis procedure, let's explore the relationship of the firm's advertising expenses to its net sales, by solving the equation:

$$\text{Advertising expenses-to-sales ratio} \quad = \quad \frac{\text{Advertising expenses}}{\text{Sales}} \times 100\%$$

$$= \quad \frac{\$22,250}{\$204,655} \times 100\%$$

$$= \quad 10.9\%$$

The company spent $10.90 out of every $100 it took in during the year on advertising. Again, deciding whether this percentage is too much, just

---

[1] Linda Howarth Mackay, "Financial Management: How to Make a Go of Your Business," *Small Business Management Series No. 44* (Washington, DC: U.S. Small Business Administration, 1983), 13.

[2] Ratios are often expressed as percentages.

EXHIBIT 20–1   A profit and loss statement

HANDICRAFTS BY ROSLYN
Profit and Loss Statement
For: Year Ended December 31, 1994

Net Sales		$204,655
Less cost of goods sold:		
Opening inventory, January 1	$ 4,830	
Purchases during year	83,890	
Freight charges	880	
Total goods handled	$89,600	
Less ending inventory, December 31	5,890	
Total cost of goods sold		83,710
Gross Margin		$120,945
Less operating expenses		
Salaries and wages	$37,740	
Payroll taxes	4,320	
Utilities	3,980	
Telephone	2,870	
Rent	12,000	
Office supplies	1,830	
Postage	11,270	
Maintenance expenses	3,385	
Insurance	2,200	
Interest expense	770	
Depreciation	3,220	
Advertising	22,250	
Dues and contributions	445	
Miscellaneous expenses	490	
Total operating expenses		106,770
Operating Profit		$ 14,175
Other income		
Dividends on stock	$ 410	
Interest on bank account	505	
Rental of mailing list	1,480	
Total other income		2,395
Total income before income tax		$ 16,570
Less provision for income tax		4,535
Net Profit		$ 12,035

enough, or too little will depend on the firm's past performance or on the percentage that is characteristically assigned to advertising by mail order firms.

Determining Your Firm's Liquidity

One set of financial ratios can tell you how *liquid* your mail order company is. In short, they measure whether your firm owns enough assets to be able to retire all outstanding obligations with ease. The most important liquidity measures are the *current ratio* and the *acid-test,* or *quick, ratio.*

The Current Ratio

The current ratio can be obtained from information listed on your firm's latest balance sheet. To work out the current ratio, divide your total current assets figure by the sum of your current liabilities.

At this point, check the balance sheet for Dinky's Toys & Gadgets that you saw in Chapter 5 and that now appears as Exhibit 20–2. The various current assets (cash, securities, accounts receivable, and both merchandise and supplies inventories) add up to $58,890. The current liabilities (accounts payable, notes payable, and accrued taxes) total $19,525.

Let's apply the equation for calculating the current ratio:

$$\text{Current ratio} \quad = \quad \frac{\text{Current assets}}{\text{Current liabilities}}$$

$$= \quad \frac{\$58,890}{\$19,525}$$

$$= \quad 3.0\text{-to-1}$$

A current ratio of at least 2:1 (or, double the value of the current assets total) is considered, in the majority of cases, a sign that your firm is in a healthy financial position. This may vary somewhat, though, from industry to industry.

A healthy approach that will keep you in close touch with your business is to prepare both basic accounting statements on a quarterly basis. This way, you'll be able to determine your current ratios, as well as other useful data, every three months, rather than wait until the year is over.

The Acid-test Ratio

Quite similar to, but considerably more insightful than the current ratio, is the acid-test, or quick, ratio. The formula for this measure is:

Acid-test ratio =

$$\frac{\text{Cash} + \text{Marketable securities} + \text{Accounts receivable}}{\text{Current liabilities}}$$

The fraction's numerator comprises all current company assets with the exception of inventories. These are omitted because they cannot be quickly converted to cash, as can the other listed assets.

EXHIBIT 20–2   A simple balance sheet

DINKY'S TOYS & GADGETS
Balance Sheet
for Year End December 31, 19XX

ASSETS

CURRENT ASSETS
   Cash on hand and in banks $27,540
   Marketable securities   2,545
   Accounts receivable (less allowance for bad debts)   1,880
   Merchandise inventory   23,210
   Supplies inventory   3,715
      Total Current Assets $58,890

FIXED ASSETS
   Office machinery and equipment (less depreciation)   11,830
   Furniture (less depreciation)   7,760
   Leasehold improvements   4,100
      Total Fixed Assets   23,690
      TOTAL ASSETS $82,580

LIABILITIES AND NET WORTH

CURRENT LIABILITIES
   Accounts payable $13,530
   Notes payable within year   3,585
   Accrued taxes   2,410
      Total Current Liabilities $19,525

LONG-TERM LIABILITIES
   Note payable, 1995   3,300
   Note payable, 1997   3,300
      Total long-term liabilities   6,600
      Total Liabilities $26,125
      Net Worth (Owner's Equity) $56,455
      TOTAL LIABILITIES AND NET WORTH $82,580

Now, let's fill in the required information from the balance sheet in Exhibit 20–2.

$$\text{Acid-test ratio} \ = \ \frac{\$27{,}540 + \$2{,}545 + \$1{,}880}{\$19{,}525}$$

$$= \ \frac{\$31{,}965}{\$19{,}525}$$

$$= \ 1.6\text{-to-}1$$

Healthy enterprises show quick ratios of 1:1 or higher. A ratio lower than 1:1 may be an indication of financial difficulty. Again it would be fruitful not only to compare your quick ratios for several years to watch for trends in direction but also to compare your ratios to those of other firms in your industry.

Profitability Ratios

A second highly useful set of ratios are those that advise you as to how profitable (or unprofitable) your business operation is. Profit, of course, can be measured against a variety of data on both basic accounting statements; sales, net worth, and assets are some examples.

Here are several of the more widely used measures:

$$\text{Profit-to-sales} = \frac{\text{Net profit}}{\text{Net sales}} \times 100\%$$

$$\text{Return on assets} = \frac{\text{Net profit}}{\text{Assets}} \times 100\%$$

$$\text{Return on net worth} = \frac{\text{Net profit}}{\text{Net worth}} \times 100\%$$

$$\text{Sales-to-net worth} = \frac{\text{Net sales}}{\text{Net worth}} \times 100\%$$

Again, by way of illustration, let's work out the profit-to-sales ratio for Handicrafts by Roslyn (Exhibit 20–1).

$$\text{Profit-to-sales} = \frac{\text{Net profit}}{\text{Net sales}} \times 100\%$$

$$= \frac{\$12,035}{\$204,655} \times 100\%$$

$$= 5.9\%$$

Let's translate the resulting percentage into terms that management can readily grasp. Apparently, for that year, the handicrafts firm made 5.9 cents as profit on every sales dollar taken in, after setting money aside for income tax.

HOW TO AVOID CASH FLOW PROBLEMS

Most organizations of all types and sizes may experience occasional cash-flow problems. Small enterprises, especially new firms seeking to secure a foothold in the economy, may encounter cash flow difficulties more frequently. A major contributory factor in such cases is the fact that sales revenues will fluctuate all throughout the year. Generally, each month yields a different percentage of annual sales. In most lines of retailing, for example, sales revenues for the November–December period can run as high as one-third of the entire year's sales, and often higher.

With careful planning, most problems with your cash flow can be avoided. The prescription for avoidance involves working up a logical analysis of your firms's influx and outgo of funds for the twelve months ahead. Using the resultant chart, you'll learn at what times during the year you're most likely to encounter a negative cash position as well as when to expect a strong cash balance. This will give you ample time to arrange for borrowing additional funds to carry you through the draught periods.

Making Your Cash Flow Chart

To prepare your cash flow projection for the coming year, you'll need to borrow the *sales-forecast form* that appeared earlier as Exhibit 2–5 in the second chapter of this book. For your convenience, it is reproduced here as Exhibit 20–3.

Start with the first month of the upcoming year, proceeding to fill in each line, one by one, in the first column of Exhibit 20–3. Some clarification of the items shown is needed. Items 2, 3, 7, 8, and 10 are self-explanatory. Additional information is offered below for the remaining lines in the exhibit:

- *Item 1—Cash in Bank (start of month).* To derive this figure, add any cash you may keep on your premises to the monies you have

EXHIBIT 20–3   Projected sales forecast form

ESTIMATED CASH FORECAST												
	Jan.	Feb.	Mar.	April	May	June	July	Aug.	Sept.	Oct.	Nov.	Dec.
(1) Cash in Bank (Start of Month)												
(2) Petty Cash (Start of Month)												
(3) Total Cash (add 1) and (2)												
(4) Expected Cash Sales												
(5) Expected Collections												
(6) Other Money Expected												
(7) Total Receipts (add 4, 5 and 6)												
(8) Total Cash and Receipts (add 3 and 7)												
(9) All Disbursements (for month)												
(10) Cash Balance at End of Month. in Bank Account and Petty Cash (subtract (9) from (8)*												

*This balance is your starting cash balance for the next month.

Source: Office of Management Assistance, "Business Plan for Retailers," *Small Marketers Aid No. 150* (Washington, DC: U.S. Small Business Administration, 1972), 17.

on deposit in your firm's checking and savings accounts (including any long-term certificates of deposit you may have).

- *Item 4—Expected Cash Sales.* Enter the sum total of all income you believe you'll take in during the month (from your scheduled mailings, print advertising, radio and television commercials, telemarketing, and other sources).
- *Item 5—Expected Collections.* Enter here the sum total of all payments likely to be sent to you by your charge customers (from your accounts receivable).
- *Item 6—Other Money Expected.* For this entry, total up all stock dividends you may be getting in, incoming interest on your firm's bank accounts and company-owned bonds, sums you may collect from renting your house, mailing list, or selling off company property which you no longer can use (for example: typewriters, adding machines, outdated computers, overstocked office supplies, office furniture, and so on).
- *Item 9—All Disbursements (for month).* Review your accounts payable ledger to determine which bills you'll have to pay during the month (merchandise, invoices, salaries, rent, utilities, and the like), then enter your total expected expenditures on this line.

You'll arrive at the cash balance for the January column (line 10) by subtracting line 9 from line 8, as indicated. Next, enter the bottom-line figure for January on line 1 in the February column. Follow the same procedure for the month of February; when you have completed the column, continue across the chart all the way through to the end of the year.

After you have completed your chart, divide the finished form into four quarterly charts—one each for January through March, April through June, July through September, and October through December. The data in your chart for January through March will most likely be more accurate than those in the three later charts. As the year progresses, you may feel the need to make slight adjustments to your figures in advance of each quarter because of tactical changes you may decide to make along the way.

However, even from the original, full-year report, you should be able to determine those months during which you may be tight for money as well as those periods when you can count on a sizable excess of cash. What's more, if you continue to prepare your cash-flow analyses year after year, you'll never have to confront the dire predicament of an unexpected and severe shortage of funds.

USE BUDGETS TO PLAN AND CONTROL YOUR ENTIRE OPERATION

Perhaps the most important management tool of all for businesses of every type and size is the budgeting process. Budgets are useful devices that help you plan for, and control, your firm's future. When preparing a

EXHIBIT 20-4   Magazine advertising budget: January–June

Publication	January	February	March	April	May	June
A	$ 3,570	$2,760	$2,500	$1,880	$1,880	$1,880
B	3,930	3,930	—	2,120	—	—
C	1,715	—	1,715	—	1,715	—
D	1,100	1,100	—	—	—	—
Totals:	$10,315	$7,790	$4,215	$4,000	$3,595	$1,880

budget of any kind, you'll first need to conceptualize some future condition or state that you wish to attain. Once you've clarified your vision sufficiently, you should then be able to specify your objectives and then work out the steps you need to take to reach those objectives. During the process, you may be fortunate enough to foresee the development of an occasional problem and decide, well in advance, how best to cope with it.

You're already familiar with one or two kinds of budgets. The pro forma P&L—the operating statement that projects estimated figures for next season or next year—is a budget. So is the pro forma balance sheet. If you're intent on maintaining adequate control of your business operation, be sure to prepare such projections regularly. Start with estimates of the sales dollars you expect to take in each week or each month, and then prepare from those estimates your overall *sales budget* for the period. Do the same for all expenses (both fixed and variable) you've projected; this will give you your *expense budget.* By following the same procedure, you can—and should—prepare individual budgets for every major segment of your business. Use the data you generate to work up both of your pro forma accounting statements.

As your season (or year) proceeds, you'll need to compare actual results with your budgeted figures. If any of your actual figures deviate too far from those that you've budgeted, you can take steps to help bring results back into line.

Exhibit 20–4 shows how one small firm budgeted its expenditures for magazine advertising space for the first half of next year: (These expenditures are part of the overall budget for media advertising and direct mailings.)

WHAT ARE YOUR TAX OBLIGATIONS?

As we all know only too well, the federal government insists on collecting its just share of our earned income, no matter what form that income takes: salaries, commissions, stock dividends, capital gains on the sale of property, gambling winnings, interest on bank accounts, or profits from operating a business.

Most states also have the same attitude. To further compound the problem, some of our nation's larger cities also impose an income tax.

As the owner of a new mail order company, you'll be liable for income tax on the profits it generates and for various other taxes as well. It would be wise, then, to find out as much as you can about your tax liabilities—and responsibilities—as a business owner, even before you start your business. You need to know what to expect. Remember, the lack of knowledge is no defense (to the Internal Revenue Service, that is).

There's little room here for more than a cursory treatment of the more salient aspects of taxation. For a thorough understanding, a helpful booklet can be obtained from your local office of the Internal Revenue Service. It's called *Publication 334—Tax Guide for Small Business*. (You can have it mailed to you.) The booklet contains detailed instructions regarding accounting methods, how to determine your gross profit and net income or loss, information on the acquisition and disposal of business assets, sample filled-in tax forms (for sole proprietorships, partnerships, and corporations), information about tax credits, and so on.

If you have one or more employees working for you, ask also for the *Employer's Tax Guide, Circular E*. And request a copy of *Publication 534—Tax Information on Depreciation*. This booklet will help in working out depreciation schedules for your firm's assets.

Federal Income Tax

Different legal forms of business call for different approaches to the federal tax on income. If you're the owner of a small business, have no partners, and didn't select the corporate form, you're a *sole proprietor*. Tax laws require you to file annually the same Form 1040 you used while you were working at your job, whether you use your own name for the business or have assumed a trade name (which, of course, you registered). You'll show your company's name on the proper line of Schedule C, Form 1040, where you must report your business results for the year. Schedule C is titled "Profit or Loss from Business (Sole Proprietorship)." (See Appendix for samples of this and other tax forms.)

If you're one of the partners (a principal) in a partnership, you still file Form 1040 at income tax time. On it, you'll report your share of the firm's income. However, Form 1065, "U.S. Partnership Return of Income," must also be sent to the Internal Revenue Service for information purposes only. The income tax is levied against you as an individual, not against the partnership.

Corporations are treated differently. Since they have an existence of their own, they're required to pay taxes on profits directly. Generally, corporations need to submit Form 1120, "U.S. Corporation Income Tax Return" or Form 1120-A, "U.S. Corporation Short-Form Income Tax Return." The short form may be used by corporations that show less than $500,000 in each of three categories: gross receipts, total income, and total assets. (Certain other requirements also must be met.)

Organizations that have elected to operate as a small business, or S corporation, file on Form 1120S, "U.S. Income Tax Return for an S Corporation."

Although the corporation itself will need to pay income tax on its earnings, as an employee of the corporation you still must file Form 1040 and pay your own personal income tax due.

A sole proprietor or a partner generally needs to file a *declaration of estimated tax* (Form 1040ES) along with the Form 1040 and pay any tax due in four installments throughout the year. (The entire amount may be paid in full, if you so desire.) Corporations also must pay estimated tax and deposit the payments at regular intervals.

Other Kinds of Taxes

At the federal level, you must be concerned with your employees' income taxes (and withholding rules), social security tax, Medicare tax, and federal unemployment (FUTA) tax. Both the social security and Medicare taxes are levied on you as well as on your employees. You're required to collect and pay each employee's part of the two taxes and then contribute an equivalent amount from your firm's treasury.

Social Security Tax

In 1994, the tax rate for social security was 6.2 percent of every employee's wages—up to a "wage base limit" of $60,600. (*Note:* The wage base limit is the maximum wage for the year that is subject to the tax.) Employers were required to match the amounts collected; this brought the total to be paid to the federal government to 12.4 percent.

Medicare Tax

The Medicare tax rate for that same year was 1.45 percent each for employee and employer (2.9 percent total). The wage base limit for Medicare tax, which was set at $135,000 in 1993, was dropped in 1994. All wages are now subject to this tax.

Federal Unemployment Tax (FUTA)

The federal unemployment tax (FUTA) system, along with the state systems, provides payments to workers who have lost their jobs. For 1994, the FUTA tax was applied to only the first $7,000 in wages paid to each employee during the year. The rate was set at 6.2 percent of wages—LESS some credit for payments made to state unemployment tax systems. Incidentally, this tax is imposed directly on the employer; not one cent is to be deducted or collected from employee wages.

Self-Employment Tax

If you operate your mail order firm as either a sole proprietorship or a partnership, you need to pay self-employment tax on your earnings in lieu of the social security and Medicare taxes you previously paid as an employee. In 1994, the self-employment tax rate was 15.3 percent of net earnings.

If this tax applies to you, be sure to obtain a copy of IRS *Publication 533,* ("Self-Employment Tax"). You'll need to compute your tax liability on Schedule SE and submit the schedule along with your Form 1040 before the due date of your return.

State Taxes

State taxes differ in regulations, dates of payment, and amounts from one state to the next. There are sales taxes, unemployment taxes, unincorporated business or corporation taxes, and personal income taxes. And, locally, you need to think about real estate taxes and, possibly, sales and/or personal property taxes, too.

Contact all taxing authorities in your area for information. Your accountant can help you tremendously. So can your state department of labor, if you employ help.

SOURCES OF ADDITIONAL INFORMATION

Coltman, Michael M., *Understanding Financial Information: The Non-Financial Manager's Guide,* (2d ed.). Bellingham, WA: Self-Counsel Press, 1990.

Donnahoe, Alan S., *What Every Manager Should Know About Financial Analysis.* New York: Simon & Schuster, 1989.

Fleury, Robert E., *The Small Business Survival Guide: How to Manage Your Cash, Profits, and Taxes.* Naperville, IL: Sourcebooks, 1992.

Glau, Gregory R., *The Small Business Financial Planner.* New York: Wiley, 1989.

Hayes, Rick Stephan, *Business Loans: A Guide to Money Sources and How to Approach Them,* (rev. ed.). New York: Wiley, 1989.

Milling, Bryan E., *Cash Flow Problem Solver,* (2d ed.). Radnor, PA: Chilton, 1984.

O'Hara, Patrick D., *SBA Loans: A Step-by-Step Guide,* (2d ed.). New York: Wiley, 1994.

Scott, Gina Graham, *Positive Cash Flow: Complete Credit and Collections for the Small Business.* Holbrook, MA: Bob Evans, 1990.

Simini, Joseph P., *Budgeting Basics for Nonfinancial Managers.* New York: Wiley, 1989.

Planning Your Organization

It's never too early to start thinking about putting together an organization that can deal effectively with an expanding list of duties and responsibilities. Your organization must be strong enough to ensure the continued and successful growth of your company.

But right from the beginning, be cautious! Hire only when you must; you'll be amazed at how much you need to do in additional sales to cover even the seemingly minor expense of one part-time worker. For the sake of illustration, assume that your end-of-year gross margin percentage is 60 percent of sales. (Recall that gross margin, or gross profit, is what you have earned after subtracting your cost of goods sold from your sales figures.) In concrete terms, this means that only sixty cents of every dollar you take in can be used to cover your overhead expenses and produce some profit. The other forty cents must go to pay for the merchandise you have sold. Now, you consider hiring a full-time, entry-level employee at a modest salary of, say, $300 a week. When you add to this expense the worker's fringe benefits and your contribution to the federal government of a matching percentage of his or her social security tax, your total outlay will most likely exceed $20,000 annually. Putting these together, sixty cents out of every sales dollar and $20,000 a year, you'll need to take in $36,667 more in sales over the year *just to break even* on this cost of adding one employee.

PERSONNEL ADMINISTRATION

These are the major policy areas in which you must make decisions about your personnel:

- Recruitment and selection.
- Employee compensation.
- Training.
- Supervision.
- Management development.
- Compliance with labor legislation.

For more detailed study of these areas, refer to several of the books on human resources administration listed in the bibliography at the end of this chapter.

RECRUITING AND SELECTING PERSONNEL

Analyze the job requirements for each position you anticipate in your firm, then set up job specifications for those positions. In this way, you'll have a clear idea of the kind of individual you should be searching for to fill an opening. Sources of prospective employees include newspaper advertisements (classified for many jobs, display ads for higher level positions), neighborhood schools and colleges, public and private employment agencies, recommendations from other employees, customers, and friends, posted signs, and "walk-ins" or "write-ins."

Introduce some professionalism into your selection procedure. Use these familiar tools: the employment application, the personal interview, and, possibly for some positions, standardized performance tests. You can purchase employment application forms at your local business stationery store. Depending on the nature and level of the job opening, one or more personal interviews may be indicated. These are not only useful for broadening your perceptions of the information shown on the application but also for gaining valuable insights into the applicant's personality, depth of knowledge and/or training, command of the English language, self-control, and other aspects. The interview is also an excellent vehicle for telling the job seeker about your company and what his or her prospects with you may be.

CHOOSING A SUPERIOR COMPENSATION PLAN

You need to devise the kind of pay scale that will appropriately reward your employees for their work. For most workers, this means a daily wage rate or a weekly salary that compares favorably with those earned by persons in equivalent positions with competitive firms. You must strive to keep them satisfied so that they remain in your employ, rather than seek greener pastures elsewhere. Some form of incentive (such as a small commission paid in addition to a basic salary or, in some situations, a straight commission approach) should be built in for salespeople.

Along with the basic pay plan, you must decide on the kinds of fringe benefits to offer that will round out the total employee compensation program.

PLANS FOR TRAINING AND DEVELOPMENT

New employees require indoctrination into the ways of your organization. Among other things, they need to know:

- Your firm's history.
- The kinds and quality of your products and/or service(s).
- Your pricing policies and promotion approaches.
- What their responsibilities will be and to whom they will report.
- Existing personnel policies and procedures.
- Their opportunities for personal growth and promotion.

All this indoctrination should be taken care of immediately after they have been hired. Preferably, you should conduct this initial training personally, at least until the size of your organization is such that a specialist must be hired to take over this function to enable you to devote your time to other aspects of your business.

Consider assigning each new worker to a more experienced person holding the same position; in this way, the job of coaching the newcomer becomes easier. In the larger organization, another valuable assist could come from developing and distributing a good employee handbook.

To ensure organizational flexibility, along with a healthy level of productivity, prepare intermediate and advanced training programs for the future. Use them to broaden the existing skills of your employees, to prepare people for promotion to the supervisory ranks or for transfer to other departments, and to train others to fill your top management slots. Familiarize yourself with management training methods, perhaps by taking one or two relevant courses at a nearby college of business administration or by attending one of the intensive training programs for top managers offered by the American Management Association.

Work on your own self-development, too. Read all the books you can find on personnel administration and on the principles of management. Strive also to improve your own human relations skills; in the final analysis, running a company successfully means working effectively with people to get the required work done.

MOTIVATING AND SUPERVISING EMPLOYEES

During the 1960s, researcher Frederick Herzberg formulated his dual-factor theory, based on his investigations into worker motivation.[1] He found that two sets of factors in the workplace affect worker satisfaction on the job: *motivators* (or "job satisfiers") and *hygiene factors* (or "dissatisfiers"). With regard to the first set, he maintained that employees were motivated primarily by such features as recognition, responsibility, advancement, achievement, and the very nature of the work engaged in. Hygiene factors, such as salary, working conditions, company policy, and one's relations with one's supervisor, do little to motivate workers but can create job dissatisfaction.

Yes, despite a most common preconception, salary by itself doesn't contribute too much to worker motivation!

It might be worthwhile at this point to restate those important motivators:

- Responsibility.
- Recognition.
- Achievement.
- Advancement.
- Nature of the work.

Supervisors: What They Are and What They Do

The structure of the typical business organization is hierarchical, much like one face of a pyramid. At the apex of the pyramid is the owner or the chief executive officer. Below this individual on an organizational chart may be several vice presidents, then department managers, then their assistants—all the way down to the rank and file, at the base of the pyramid. To the personnel at lower levels in the hierarchy, their supervisors represent the firm's management. Supervisors are conduits for communication between them and management.

Supervisory Tasks

Regardless of the type and size of the business organization, the supervisory personnel engage in most of the following activities:

- Building and sustaining morale.
- Clarifying company policy.
- Coaching.

---

[1] For further insights into the dual-factor theory, see: Frederick Herzberg, *Work and the Nature of Man* (New York: Thomas Y. Crowell, 1966); Frederick Herzberg, "One More Time: How Do You Motivate Employees?" *Harvard Business Review 46* (January-February 1968), 53–62.

- Delegating tasks and responsibilities.
- Encouraging worker initiative.
- Establishing priorities.
- Giving orders.
- Setting goals.
- Taking disciplinary steps when necessary.
- Training.

Significant Supervisory Attributes

To do their job well, supervisors should:

- Avoid reprimanding an employee in front of others.
- Be able communicators.
- Be adept at motivating others.
- Be reasonable.
- Deal fairly with all.
- Demonstrate interest in others.
- Encourage new ideas.
- Exercise good judgment.
- Give credit when due.
- Give praise when deserved.
- Invite subordinates to participate in decision making.
- Keep subordinates well informed.
- Know about individual differences.
- Listen attentively to others.
- Practice good interpersonal relations.
- Reward outstanding performance.
- Set logical goals.
- Show consideration to others.
- Understand both individual and group psychology.
- Welcome suggestions.

LABOR LEGISLATION

Seek your attorney's counsel regarding the many labor laws and regulations with which you'll need to comply. If you employ people, you're bound to both state and federal legislation and regulated by local ordinances as well. At the very least, you should become familiar with the major provisions, and their implications for your company, of the federal laws briefly summarized in Exhibit 21–1.

EXHIBIT 21–1   Federal labor legislation

Year	Title	Major Thrust
1935	The National Labor Relations Act (also called the Wagner Act)	Designed to counter unfair practices on the part of employers (in the Depression years) and to reduce industrial unrest, this law gave employees the right to organize and to engage in collective bargaining. It also established the National Labor Relations Board.
1938	The Fair Labor Standards Act (once known as the Federal Wages and Hours Law)	This established federal regulation of wages and hours, a minimum wage, provision for overtime pay, and constraints on child labor. A notable exemption here is administrative and executive personnel.
1947	The Labor-Management Relations Act (also known as the Taft-Hartley Act)	This law banned the closed shop and created the Federal Mediation and Conciliation Service.
1963	The Equal Pay Act	This act established the premise of equal pay for men and women who do the same work. It prohibited discrimination against employees on the basis of sex.
1964	The Civil Rights Act	This piece of legislation created the Equal Employment Opportunity Commission. Along with subsequent amendments, it prohibits discrimination among employees on the basis of race, religion, sex, or national origin in hiring practices, compensation levels or advancement opportunities.
1967	The Age Discrimination in Employment Act	Similar to the Civil Rights Act in its intent, this law bars discrimination in businesses engaged in interstate commerce against persons between the ages of forty and sixty-five on the basis of age. (A subsequent

EXHIBIT 21–1   *(Continued)*

Year	Title	Major Thrust
		amendment raised the top age to seventy.)
1970	The Occupational Safety and Health Act (OSHA)	This law seeks to assure safe working conditions for employees. Businesses must comply with safety and health standards and keep accurate records pertinent to this area. They are also subject to inspections designed to monitor compliance with the provisions of this act.
1972	The Equal Employment Opportunity Act	An amendment to the Civil Rights Act of 1964, this legislation extended its provisions to include employees of local and state governments, educational institutions (both public and private), and others.
1973	The Vocational Rehabilitation Act	Along with subsequent amendments, this law outlawed employment discrimination against handicapped persons who are able to fulfill their work responsibilities.
1974	The Employee Retirement Income Security Act (ERISA)	Designed to protect the retirement income rights of employees, this law assures vesting rights and specifies the proper funding of retirement plans.
1978	The Mandatory Retirement Act	This legislation eliminated the practice of requiring a worker's retirement at age sixty-five.
1983	The Job Training Partnership Act	This law replaced the earlier CETA (Comprehensive Education and Training Act) of 1978 and provides grants to individual states for the training of unemployed and economically disadvantaged persons.

Source: Irving Burstiner, *The Small Business Handbook,* (rev. ed.) (New York: Simon & Schuster, 1994), 120–21. © 1989 by Irving Burstiner. Reprinted by permission of Simon & Schuster.

Other pertinent Federal laws not mentioned in Exhibit 21–1 above are:

- Pregnancy Discrimination Act (1978)—Prohibits discrimination against women on account of pregnancy, childbirth, or a related health condition.
- Older Workers' Benefit Protection Act (1990)—Bars discrimination based on age with regard to employee benefits.
- Americans with Disabilities Act (1991)—Prohibits discrimination in employment practices because of physical or mental disability.

SOURCES OF ADDITIONAL INFORMATION

Aldag, Ramon J. and Timothy M. Stearns, *Management,* (2d ed.). Cincinnati: South-Western, 1991.

Beach, Dale S., *Personnel: The Management of People at Work,* (6th ed.). New York: Macmillan, 1991.

Catt, Stephen E. and Donald S. Miller, *Supervision: Working with People,* (2d ed.). Homewood, IL: Irwin, 1991.

Donnelly, James H., James L. Gibson, and John M. Ivancevich, *Fundamentals of Management,* (7th ed.). Homewood, IL: Irwin, 1990.

Hilgert, Raymond and Theo Haimann, *Supervision: Concepts and Practices of Management,* (5th ed.). Cincinnati: South-Western, 1991.

Hodgetts, Richard M. and Donald F. Kuratko, *Management,* (3rd ed.). San Diego, CA: Harcourt Brace Jovanovich, 1991.

Holton, Bill and Cher Holton, *The Manager's Short Course.* New York: Wiley, 1992.

Mosley, Donald C., Leon C. Megginson, and Paul H. Pietry, Jr., *Supervisory Management: Empowering and Developing People,* (3rd ed.). Cincinnati: South-Western, 1992.

Sherman, Arthur W. and George W. Bohlander, *Managing Human Resources.* Cincinnati: South-Western, 1992.

Stoner, James and R. Edward Freeman, *Management,* (5th ed.). Englewood Cliffs, NJ: Prentice-Hall, 1991.

Looking Forward in Time

Congratulations on your success! Through effort and persistence, you have managed to establish and build a strong, exciting new business. It may have taken you only a year, but more likely, three to five years to arrive at this stage. Each day brings bundles of mail, many pieces with checks or money orders. Activity at your place is constant: opening the mail, sorting orders from inquiries and other correspondence, typing shipping labels, pulling merchandise from the selves to be wrapped for mailing, carting packages to the post office, and so on.

Along the way, you have developed a profitable catalog business, set up a toll-free telephone number for your customers to call in their orders, instituted a good customer credit program to encourage more buying, experimented with telephone selling to increase catalog distribution, and perhaps even gone into drop shipping some of your merchandise items for other mail order companies.

By now, you may be so intoxicated with your success that you're thinking "Where do I go from here?"

ALTERNATIVE PATHWAYS TO GROWTH AND EXPANSION

Exactly at this point you need to ponder alternatives. Would it be best to continue concentrating on mail order selling, perhaps moving to larger quarters and automating your handling and processing methods? Should you consider the benefits and drawbacks in seeking more precipitous

EXHIBIT 22-1   Tips on time management

1. Consolidate similar tasks.

2. Tackle tough jobs first.

3. Delegate and develop others.

4. Learn to use idle time.

5. Get control of the paper flow.

6. Avoid the cluttered-desk syndrome.

7. Get started immediately on important tasks.

8. Reduce meeting time.

9. Take time to plan.

10. Learn to say "no."

Source: H. Kent Baker, "Techniques of Time Management," *Management Aids No. 239* (Washington, DC: U.S. Small Business Administration, January 1979), 5-6.

growth through acquisition of one or more mail order firms? Would a merger make more sense?

You might think of *integrating backward* a single step, forming your own wholesale business so that you can buy your merchandise at lower cost. This move might also enable you to sell your goods to other mail order houses or to retail stores. Or, you could take two steps backward and set up your own manufacturing facility.

EXHIBIT 22-2   Twenty major time wasters

External Time Wasters

Telephone interruptions	Excessive paperwork
Meetings	Communication breakdown
Visitors	Lack of policies and procedure
Socializing	Lack of competent personnel
Lack of information	Red tape

Internal Time Wasters

Procrastination	Failure to plan
Failure to delegate	Poor scheduling
Unclear objectives	Lack of self-discipline
Failure to set priorities	Attempting to do too much at once
Crisis management	Lack of relevant skills

Source: H. Kent Baker, "Techniques of Time Management," *Management Aids No. 239* (Washington, DC: U.S. Small Business Administration, January 1979), 3.

Another choice, and one that merits serious thought, is to open a retail store in conjunction with your mail order business.

But before you decide on any major change of direction, make sure that your *current* business is in excellent shape and that you have done everything you can to tone it up so that it runs smoothly without your close personal supervision. Moreover, you need to free yourself from needless interruptions and unimportant daily chores. The information presented in Exhibits 22–1 and 22–2 may help you with time management.

IT'S ESSENTIAL TO REVIEW YOUR FINANCES

Whether you plan to expand your present business, seek to acquire other mail order operations, or set out in an entirely new direction, one ingredient above all else is essential: *money*. Growth capital isn't easy to come by.

You may be determined to plough back repeatedly every cent of your earned profits to enlarge your firm's treasury over a period of time. This can be done, but it usually takes at least a few years before you can accumulate enough funds to attempt a new direction.

A sizable bank loan is a distinct possibility. (It wouldn't be if you hadn't already been running a business successfully for some time. Banks are wary of the entrepreneur without a track record.) If you present the bank official with a well-structured growth plan, one that details your realistic appraisal of the opportunities and includes both past and projected income statements and balance sheets, you may well expect your loan application to be approved. The problem here, however, is the high interest rate you have to pay for your indebtedness and the strain on your business assets caused by having to return the principal in installments.

You might consider, instead, searching for investment capital. There are people and organizations willing to invest in companies that show promise, in return for some ownership percentage. These venture capitalists include private individuals, partnerships, investment banking firms, small business investment companies (licensed by the Small Business Administration), and professionally managed firms that work with institutional monies. (See Exhibit 22–3 for a listing of the contents of the usual venture proposal to be submitted to venture capitalists.)

EXPLORING OPPORTUNITIES IN WHOLESALING

Only a modest percentage of manufacturers sell their products directly to consumers or to organizational buyers. Most prefer to concentrate their energies and assets on the production of goods and leave the problems associated with distribution to intermediaries. These latter firms are specialists who act as go-betweens between producer and purchaser: brokers, wholesalers, and retailers. Each type performs (and is compensated for) its particular function along the marketing channel, that theoretical passageway through which the goods will travel to their end users.

EXHIBIT 22–3   Elements of a venture proposal

Purpose and objectives—a summary of the what and why of the project;

Proposed financing—the amount of money you'll need from the beginning to the maturity of the project proposed, how the proceeds will be used, how you plan to structure the financing, and why the amount designated is required;

Marketing—a description of the market segment you've got now or plan to get, the competition, the characteristics of the market, and your plans (with costs) for getting or holding the market segment you're aiming at;

History of the firm—a summary of significant financial and organizational milestones, description of employees and employee relations, explanations of banking relationships, recounting of major services or products your firm has offered during its existence, and the like;

Description of the product or service—a full description of the product (process) or service offered by the firm and the costs associated with it in detail;

Financial statements—both for the past few years and pro forma projections (balance sheets, income statements, and cash flows) for the next 3 to 5 years, showing the effect anticipated if the project is undertaken and if the financing is secured (This should include an analysis of key variables affecting financial performance, showing what would happen if the projected level of revenue is not attained.);

Capitalization—a list of shareholders, how much is invested to date, and in what form (equity/debt);

Biographical sketches—the work histories and qualifications of key owners/employees.

Principal suppliers and customers

Problems anticipated and other pertinent information—a candid discussion of any contingent liabilities, pending litigation, tax or patent difficulties, and any other contingencies that might affect the project you're proposing;

Advantages—a discussion of what's special about your product, service, marketing plans or channels that gives your project unique leverage.

Source: LaRue Tone Hosmer, "A Venture Capital Primer for Small Business," *Management Aids No. 235* (Washington, DC: U.S. Small Business Administration, 1978), 3.

Also known as distributors and jobbers, most wholesalers buy products in large quantities at sizable trade discounts from manufacturers, either directly or sometimes through the services of a broker. They take possession of the goods, storing them in warehouses to be held against future orders. Typically, the wholesale establishment needs enough warehouse space to store merchandise for literally hundreds of accounts. And the stock may represent hundreds, and perhaps thousands, of different items, depending on the nature of the lines carried. They sell, of course, to retail stores and to door-to-door direct sales organizations, fund-raising firms, and mail order companies. Some also supply commercial and industrial firms, government agencies and departments, utilities, hospitals, school systems, and other types of organizations.

All of which means—if you should select this avenue—a heavy capital investment for the warehouse (along with its equipment and complement of personnel) and for the inventory you'll need to maintain. And that's without mentioning the need for sales representation to take orders for the goods! Moreover, the wholesale firm typically must extend credit to its customers, so you'll need sufficient financial strength to be able to maintain hundreds of unpaid balances at all times in your accounts receivable ledger for periods of up to ninety days, and occasionally longer, without fear of jeopardizing your operation.

Additional requirements for success in the wholesale trades include an efficient order handling and billing system, tight inventory control (usually with the aid of data processing equipment), and effective warehouse supervision.

Several types of wholesaling firms normally do not maintain warehouses of their own, nor do they call for too heavy an initial investment. Among others, these include the truck jobber and the rack merchandiser. The first type is generally found in the food industry, visiting supermarkets and groceries regularly to deliver dairy products, fresh fruits and vegetables, and other perishable goods. The rack merchandiser places display stands or racks in various types of stores, fills the racks with merchandise, then periodically services the displays for the retailer. Both types of distributors seldom extend credit; their customers pay them on delivery. Both load their trucks or vans each day with goods, at the producer's or distributor's warehouse, then make their deliveries.

For further information regarding particular wholesale trades, find out the name and address of the trade association and contact that organization's secretary.

BECOMING A MANUFACTURER

Although they fulfill somewhat different needs in the distribution sector, both wholesalers and retailers buy finished products, store them for a time, and then resell them. Their major contribution to the economy is that they help propel manufactured goods along the marketing channels toward the end user.

The manufacturing company represents a different type of business. A manufacturer is a producer; that is to say, a firm that makes, forms, constructs, fabricates, or even assembles the parts and finished products that distributors and retail outlets make available to all of us. In effect, they are the sources of supply that provide the momentum to keep our economy humming.

A typical producer purchases raw materials, semiprocessed or semifinished goods, and/or components. Within the company plant, certain operations are performed with or on these ingredients. Examples include extruding, stamping, welding, pressing, shaping, turning, mixing, cutting, and so on. Most often, these processes involve machinery, although frequently, operations are performed by hand. The outcome of this activity is finished goods. Subsequently, the products may be packaged, placed into cartons, transferred to the plant's finished goods inventory, and eventually sent to the shipping department from which they depart for their destinations.

Why should the mail order firm consider this avenue? Occasionally, the company will come across a product, or a line of products, that enjoys an immediate and resounding sales success. Its potential seems exciting. It may be that by investing in a piece of equipment the item can be produced internally at a much lower cost per unit than the firm has been paying the supplier. Moreover, the same machine might be able to produce other salable products. A big benefit here is that your company controls the supply of this merchandise. You need not worry about being out of stock or obtaining the kind of markup on your goods that you need. Then, too, if you can manufacture greater quantities than you can use, there's the opportunity of selling your excess production to other mail order dealers or to retail stores.

Indeed, you may already be in some phase of manufacturing. If you have been selling handicrafts, bagging or packing merchandise, making rubber stamps, mixing chemicals, cutting patterns, or stringing beads for bracelets and necklaces, you're already a producer. Bringing in machinery or equipment may eventually cut your costs and sharply increase your output.

Setting yourself up properly in manufacturing typically calls for a considerable investment in a suitable plant; for machinery, equipment, and supplies; in the materials you'll need for producing your line of merchandise; and perhaps for skilled or semiskilled workers to operate the machines. You must think about plant layout, production scheduling and control (including setting production standards), and efficient stock-keeping procedures.

The following short list of manufacturing possibilities may give you some worthwhile ideas:

Advertising specialties	Canned preserves
Apparel	Ceramic items/supplies
Athletic equipment	Chemicals
Athletic goods	Cleaning compounds
Automotive care products	Cosmetics
Baked goods	Curtains and draperies
Bathroom accessories	Decorative accessories
Beaded novelties	Dolls
Beauty aids and supplies	Electrical supplies
Books	Embroidery
Business cards	Foods

Furniture

Garden supplies

Giftware

Glassware

Greeting cards

Handicrafts

Health foods

Health-related equipment

Hobby kits/supplies

Household furnishings

Jewelry

Kitchen utensils

Knitting supplies

Lighting fixtures

Lubricants

Machinery and equipment

Marine supplies

Maternity clothes

Metal products

Models and kits

Molded novelties

Monogrammed items

Neckties

Needlework kits

Paints

Paper goods

Party supplies

Pet supplies

Photographic supplies
and equipment

Plastic products

Pool chemicals

Printed specialties

Printing

Religious articles

Signs and posters

Slippers

Sporting goods

Sports equipment

Toiletries

Tools

Toys

OPENING A RETAIL STORE

A common route for the successful mail order company, especially one that deals in consumer products, is to establish a retail store. This is a natural direction for growth because in selling merchandise by mail you're already involved in running a retail operation. You sell individual items to individual consumers—a "store by mail."

This type of expansion has its advantages. You can continue your mail order activity at the store address, given a large room or, even better, several rooms in the back of your store, or in the basement. This means your *two* businesses will then share *one* rent along with other overhead costs. Your store operation will complement your mail order business in other ways, and vice versa. You'll be able to use some merchandise in both, turn slow-sellers into fast-movers by running special in-store promotions, add the names and addresses of store shoppers to your mailing list to increase your overall sales, order goods in larger quantities to obtain greater discounts, and so on.

You should, however, try to keep separate records. By regarding each enterprise as a distinct profit center, you can keep on top of what's happening and make the kinds of decisions that will ensure end-of-year profits in both businesses.

The Exciting World of Independent Retailing

You know little about running a store, you say? Nonsense! You haven't owned one before? So what?

How many different stores have you visited or shopped in during your lifetime? So many that you must be aware by now of what shoppers expect to see and find in a store, and the kinds of attention and service they want from the retail merchant.

Although they account for a sizable share of total annual retail sales in the country, department stores, supermarkets, and chain stores are numerically in the minority. The vast majority of American stores are small, single-unit establishments run by independent merchants. These people are a hardy, courageous lot. They work long hours, diligently applying their energies and talents to the daily decisions that must be made. Some prosper indeed; most earn a good livelihood, managing to keep their businesses in the black year after year despite the inroads of inflation, economic downturns, and the pressure of ever-present competition.

These are the people you'll be joining.

Naturally, you would seek a location for your new store where you can attract enough of the kinds of shoppers who will buy your merchandise and where the competition is light or nonexistent.

It's often best to carry over into your new store operation the kinds of goods you have had success with in mail order. If, for instance, you have been selling books by mail (a popular line for direct marketers), opening a traditional bookstore or even a used-book exchange would seem a logical choice. Following along the same line of reasoning, mail order experience with giftwares or household items ought to lead to the launching of a souvenir and gift shop, a variety store, or even a hardware store. Compatible or complementary lines may, of course, be added to your basic merchandise assortment.

Only a cursory treatment of the salient aspects of store retailing can be accorded here. Check into the references listed at the end of this chapter.

Prepare a Retail Business Plan

Chapter 2 outlined a design to help you work up a business plan for your new mail order enterprise. Granted, it was hard work preparing all the details, but it allowed you to chart the course that established you in mail order marketing.

Now you're faced with the problem of generating a second plan. Starting a retail store is another, and quite different, business. Nevertheless, if you want to improve your chances for succeeding in this new venture, plug away at it. And do it well!

Find the Right Location

Like many other aspiring mail order entrepreneurs, you most likely initiated your business from your home and in your spare time. Then, when business activity outgrew the limited confines of your attic, basement, or spare room, you rented an office nearby. Location wasn't too important at the time, so long as it was convenient for you and the landlord proposed a rental figure that you could tolerate. Finding a store location is another matter entirely. The majority of store types depends heavily on the traffic that passes by. Mostly, this is pedestrian traffic, although vehicular traffic can also be important in many situations. You need to go where the traffic is, for location is often the *single most important factor* in a store's success or failure.

Choosing a location involves three sequential decisions:

1. Picking out the right town or city for your business and for *you*
2. Determining the right retail area in that town or city
3. Getting the right store site within that area.

The City's Retail Structure

Although you can readily find an occasional store sitting all by itself in any city of your choice, as is the case with some furniture stores or discount outlets located along major highways, most experienced retailers prefer to go where the action is. They know that surrounding stores act as magnets, drawing shoppers to a particular area. The greater the number and the better the mix of stores, the heavier the traffic will be. They benefit by this increase, for many of the shoppers may visit their stores, too.

A convenient way of categorizing the retail sections within any city is to break them down, first of all, into two main classifications: the old type or unplanned groupings and the more modern planned retail centers. The former term embraces the downtown area's business section, secondary business districts, neighborhood shopping streets, and small store clusters. These types grew over the decades without the benefit of any overall coordination, in the sense that many different landlords and builders may have been involved in their development.

Unplanned Retail Areas

In the downtown section, the central business district (CBD) is where the department stores, banks, largest buildings, and main branches of chain stores are generally found. Both pedestrian and automobile traffic are heavy, and store rents are exceedingly high. (Of course, this may not be true where the area has been seriously depressed or has deteriorated badly.) Usually found along the main roads leading out of the downtown area toward the outskirts of the city, there may be several secondary business districts. Stores there are much like those of the CBD. They are, however, ordinarily smaller in size, have less window frontage, and carry a more limited selection of merchandise than their counterparts downtown. The streets are normally busy during the daytime, and the merchants fare nicely. Rents run high but are considerably less than those of the CBD.

Neighborhood shopping streets are found throughout the city and its suburbs. They attract shoppers from surrounding apartment houses and homes up to a few city blocks away in all directions. Although there are some specialty and shopping goods stores in these areas, as in the business districts, a greater percentage of the shops sell convenience goods. Here are fruit and vegetable stands, bakeries, pizza parlors, meat stores, independent pharmacies, hardware stores, and so on; also a number of service retailers, such as laundromats, beauty parlors, barber shops, and the like.

A final type characterizing the older retail structure of the city is the store cluster. There may be many of these, each cluster a grouping of as few as three or four stores to as many as eight or ten. Usually, they're nestled among rows of private homes or in a block of large apartment buildings.

Planned Shopping Centers

Shopping center locations, the newer types, are of three basic kinds. Smallest of all is the neighborhood shopping center (or strip center) where one typically finds a row of small stores, usually with one larger, "traffic builder" outlet at one end. Often, this is a supermarket, variety store, or drugstore. Neighborhood centers have parking facilities for anywhere from several dozen to as many as 150 automobiles or more. They may be L- or U-shaped in design.

A larger variety, the community shopping center, may run anywhere from 100,000 to 150,000 square feet. As contrasted with the neighborhood type of center, more of the stores carry specialty or shopping goods. There are also several larger stores; these may include one or more discount or general merchandise outlets (such as a Kmart or Wal-Mart), and, perhaps, a junior department store or large specialty store. These centers have a more extended trading area; they'll draw shoppers from as far away as twenty minutes by car.

The real giants are the so-called regional shopping centers. They're large complexes that contain, in addition to as many as 50 to 100 and more stores, one to five branches of department stores, movie houses, banks, fast-food shops and regular restaurants, offices, and so on. Most of these centers are fully enclosed, climate-controlled shopping malls that attract crowds the year round, from 9:30 in the morning to 9:30 at night. Their draw is tremendous; shoppers drive to these centers from as far away as forty-five or fifty minutes by car. Some of the regionals run as big as half a million or three quarters of a million square feet in total area.

Setting Up Your Store

The sculptor readily perceives the extraordinary aesthetic possibilities in an ordinary block of stone. The artist regards the blank canvas stretched across the easel as a challenge to create a masterpiece. And the poet is invited by a single sheet of paper to weave words together so intriguingly as to evoke the emotions.

That place you plan to lease for your new retail enterprise merits no less spirit—or soul, as the case may be—on your part. Often, you rent little more than four bare walls, a floor and a ceiling, and an outside show window, with entrance alongside. From this raw material, you must shape a suitable and attractive environment that will invite shoppers to enter, make their purchases, and leave satisfied so that they'll return again and again. You would be wise to seek professional assistance; hire a store designer to help you lay out and decorate your store.

Here are the major facets you need to be concerned with:

- The store front.
- The interior (decor, layout, fixturization).
- Proper lighting, heating, and air conditioning.
- Displays.

The Store Front

Your store front is, of course, the first contact that passersby will have with your new business. Overhead sign, front decor, and entrance must all carry through the kind of image you want to project. The show window(s) should be kept attractively trimmed and spotlessly clean. Merchandise displayed should be representative of the kind and quality of goods carried in the store so that the public is attracted to the window(s) and then invited to come in. Merchandise and trim should be changed regularly; for most types of stores, changes every two or three weeks are recommended.

The Interior

You may even have been fortunate enough to have found premises that need little redecorating, with suitably finished ceiling, flooring, and walls. Usually, however, that isn't the case. If you're handy, you may be able to save a substantial amount of money by doing some of the decorating yourself, for example, laying an asphalt tile floor, putting up wallpaper, or painting. Many kinds of floor coverings are available; select one that not only is attractive and fits the overall decor, but is also durable and needs little maintenance. Ceilings may be dropped low to convey a sense of intimacy or left high, perhaps covered with acoustical tile so that the store inside looks spacious.

As with store decorating, laying out the interior should be done with professional guidance. Selling and work areas must be separated. Ample space should be left for unimpeded shopper traffic. Aisles behind counters and showcases need to be planned so that sales personnel may pass easily. Fixtures must be moved into place; you can use simple drawings of the store interior to locate display cases, back bars, shelves, register, and so on.

Proper Lighting, Heating, and Air Conditioning

To illuminate the interior, use fluorescent lighting. It does a better job of brightening than incandescent lighting and is more efficient (your electrical bills will be lower). You may want to place incandescent bulbs (or "spots") here and there to highlight one or more sections of the store and to show merchandise more effectively.

You should also realize that today's consumers expect to be able to shop in relative comfort all year round. Thus, suitable air conditioning and heating equipment need to be installed in your store.

Displays

Both show window and interior displays are also essential elements that merit the close attention of most store retailers. These are discussed in some detail later in this chapter in the section on sales promotion.

Buying and Merchandising

Like the two sides of a single coin, buying and merchandising are complementary activities essential to successful store operation. Proper buying and merchandising will mean that you have the right goods on hand, at the right prices and in the right quantities, at the right time. Both elements involve considerable planning and continuous attention. Because your store inventory represents a major investment, as well as a means of earning profit, an overriding objective is to maintain as lean a stock at all times as is possible. It should be sufficient to satisfy customer needs without needlessly tying up your capital.

Buying Merchandise

You have already had some experience buying merchandise for resale in your earlier mail order business. Now you need to seek out other sources, suppliers who can provide the kinds of goods that are ordinarily sold in your particular type of store. You'll certainly be visited by sales representatives from various wholesale and manufacturing establishments. These salespeople will be quick to show you their lines, extend the usual trade credit, and vie generally for your orders. You can gain information about other sources from the trade association in your field, whether you own a hardware store, gift shop, furniture outlet, women's wear or menswear store, or variety store. (There seems to be such an association for nearly every retail line.) You should also check whether there's an independent buying office that services your type of store; these organizations, located in the major metropolitan areas, may be able to represent you for a relatively low annual fee. Their buyers will scout the market continually, looking for items you can sell in your store and even placing orders on your behalf. In this way, if your store is located far from the market, you can be assured of the latest styles, prices, deals, and the like without the need to make a business trip several times a year.

If your store is to be properly stocked, you'll be involved in:

- Determining the needs and wants of your shoppers.
- Anticipating demand and deciding on quantities needed.
- Locating suppliers who are reliable and with whom you can work.
- Negotiating good prices and favorable terms.
- Scheduling deliveries.
- Receiving and checking the merchandise.
- Maintaining a careful inventory control.

Both merchandising and buying are important to you. There's lots of money to be saved—and some headaches, too—each year by developing expertise in these fields. You can profit by a thorough study of several of the books on these topics listed at the end of this chapter.

Controlling Your Store Merchandise

A store's inventory typically consists of one or more broad merchandise lines that represent the kinds of goods its customers would normally expect to find in an outlet of that type. As a familiar example, today's supermarket carries such lines as dairy products, meats, produce, groceries, household items, drugs, and several others. Each of these broad categories is, of course, broken down into literally hundreds of products. A children's wear retailer would carry both everyday and play clothes, sleepwear, outerwear, and so forth.

Managing your inventory encompasses, first of all, selecting the major lines you ought to carry, and then developing the desired breadth of assortment you need to stock within each of the lines. Personal visits to several representative stores should acquaint you with the kinds of items that are traditionally offered. Your trade association can probably provide you with a detailed list of products that should form the basic stock assortment for your kind of store. In some instances, you may even be able to learn the more popular styles, materials, colors, and sizes of these items.

Deciding how much inventory to carry is a different problem. Well in advance, you'll need to anticipate the amount of business you'll be doing, and then translate the expected dollar volume into your stock requirements. Retailers quickly learn about *stockturn,* how fast or how slow their inventory sells, or "turns over." It's expressed by the ratio of sales to average stock, as shown in the following formula:

$$\text{Stockturn} = \frac{\text{Sales}}{\text{Average stock}}$$

Here's an example. Assume you plan for first-year sales of $120,000. From your trade association (or from another source, such as Dun and Bradstreet's), you find that the typical stock, or inventory, turnover rate for your kind of merchandise is 2.5 times per year, at retail. Plug the knowns into the formula, and you come up with:

$$\text{Stockturn} = \frac{\$120,000}{x}$$

Or:

$$x = \frac{\$120,000}{2.5}$$

The x represents the one unknown quantity, the average stock. To solve the equation, divide the $120,000 by 2.5, to find an average inventory figure of $48,000. This tells us that you must maintain, on the average, an inventory valued at $48,000 at *retail* prices. Of course, you'll need to convert this valuation to cost figures in order to know how much you'll have to spend for the stock. If you work on a *keystone* markup, that is, you double your cost of an item to arrive at its retail selling price, you'll need to purchase an inventory of some $24,000 at cost.

Bear in mind, though, that this is an average figure. During certain months or seasons, you'll carry less in inventory; other times, such as during December, you may need to stock far more.

Inventory and record keeping are required elements of effective inventory control. Keep a close watch on fast-moving products. Get rid of slow movers through special promotions and sales or by marking down their prices. Keep track of all items by units, rather than by their overall dollar volume. Take physical inventory at least quarterly, and preferably each month. Work up a simple inventory form: list all items you carry on ruled sheets of paper, arrange them by classifications of merchandise and by product variants within the categories, show each item's price, leave space to enter figures as the counting is being done, and provide space for extension of inventory values. As you gain experience in merchandise management, develop minimum and maximum inventory levels for every item in your store, taking into account the necessary lead time for ordering and delivery.

Retail Promotion

In retailing, it's said that nothing happens until the sale is made. You may have a beautiful store laden with all kinds of goodies for shoppers, but until you can get them to come in—and buy—your cash register will be bare.

Retailers communicate with prospective customers through three complex sets of activities: advertising, personal selling, and sales promotion. Let's take a brief look at each of these categories in the so-called promotion mix.

Advertising

Most retail merchants allocate far fewer dollars from their promotion budgets to media advertising than to either sales promotion or personal selling. They prefer to rely more on their window displays to attract consumers into the store and on their salespeople and interior displays to sell these shoppers. The typical independent store owner spends somewhere between 1 and 2 percent of annual sales for advertising.

Of course, it depends on the type of store you have. Retailers who sell "hard goods"—refrigerators, washing machines, television sets, and the like—may allot as much as 5 to 10 percent of their sales volume to the media, especially if they're highly promotional stores.

If you're planning a first-year sales volume of $200,000, and you limit your advertising expense to the median store expenditure of, say, 1.5 percent, you'll have only about $3,000 available for the entire year for advertising purposes. (You should realize, too, that your sales estimate is rather ambitious; it's well above the average for many store types!) Where will you spend this amount? If you try to spread the sum equally across all twelve months, you'll have about $250 each month to plunge into media advertising. With that kind of money, you certainly couldn't afford even the briefest television commercial! Seldom, however, is an annual advertising budget broken down into such equal segments. Usually, the retailer tries to assign monthly percentages that roughly correspond with monthly sales. In this way, more money is available for advertising when shopper interest is brisk, and less during the slow periods of the year.

A new store needs lots of promotion. There's a great need to let the public know where the store's located, what it stands for, the kinds of merchandise it offers, and the types of customers it seeks to attract. You should spend no less than *twice* the average of an established retail business during your first year of operation. Even 5 or 6 percent of your anticipated sales mightn't do the job!

Review again the suggestions in Chapter 11 and in Chapters 15 through 18 for help in planning, creating, and placing your retail advertising.

Personal Selling

Every salesperson working for you should always present a pleasant, helpful personality to your shoppers. However, this alone won't assure a profitable business. Your employees must be trained from the very first day you hire them. They need to know the store merchandise well and where every item is located. They need to be taught that customer servicing comes before all other activities in the store. They need to learn the prices of the goods as well as the selling points of every article. But, above all, they need to be trained in *how to sell.* The ability to sell isn't born with us; it's developed through training and practice on the job.

With thought and effort, it shouldn't be too difficult for you to work up a modest sales training program for your newly hired sales personnel. Review Chapter 9, and refer to several of the sources listed at the end of this chapter.

Such a program ought to encompass, at the very minimum, these subjects:

- How to meet and greet the shopper.
- How to determine what the shopper is looking for.

- How to present the merchandise effectively (and involve the shopper in the presentation).
- How to meet and counter objections.
- How to close the sale.
- How to increase sales through "suggestive selling."

Sales Promotion

The term *sales promotion* merits some elaboration. It includes just about every kind of communication with the public that the retailer can bring into play, except for personal selling and advertising. Both window and interior display are included. Indeed, these two constitute the heart of sales promotion activity in the retail store. Added to these two basics is a wide range of other techniques: sampling, demonstrations, premiums, giveaways, special sales events, contests, publicity stunts, and so on.

Display

Display is the key element in your sales promotion efforts. Your show window is a powerful promotional tool. It represents the shopper's first exposure to your store and to your store's merchandise and pricing. Frequent window changes have already been suggested. Plan your windows well in advance so that you can prepare and, if necessary, purchase beforehand any materials, signing, or decorations you may need. When ready to trim the window, make sure you have already laid out all props, window posters, merchandise, display stands, sign tickets, and the like. Select the merchandise items for display with care; goods shown should be both timely and in demand. Group your items attractively and allow plenty of "air space" between groups. Use combinations of different sizes of stands and pedestals, along with shelves (of glass or wood), to help group the merchandise and to raise your displays to various heights.

The window center is its most compelling space. Center features should be selected with care and presented effectively, even dramatically. Try to show merchandise in use whenever you can. Small signs and large posters may accent the window theme. For example, one or two posters depicting foreign countries may be borrowed from a neighboring travel agency to lend authenticity and weight to a vacation time theme. Indeed, every new window display should have a theme, for this makes the display more powerful and integrated.

A helpful practice is to prepare, with the aid of a calendar, a six-month schedule and timetable for all window changes. You then choose appropriate themes around which the windows are to be constructed, selecting from the many standard ones such as Washington's Birthday, Halloween, back-to-school, winter holiday, and so on and by using your own creativity to devise new and exciting themes. Finally, list all the supplies, merchandise, fixtures, and signs that will be needed to dress each window. Thus, you end up with a complete window-dressing plan for half a year.

Many small store owners hire the services of a part-time window trimmer for a more professional job than they could do themselves.

Interior Displays

Displays inside the store need the same attention as your windows do, but their purpose is different. Where the show window is designed primarily to stop passersby and induce them to come in, interior displays help to add to the shoppers' interest and perhaps convince them to make purchases. They complement the efforts of the salesclerks.

Other Aspects of Store Management

Other important facets of retail store operation must be explored by the neophyte merchant, including such areas as sales and expense control, personnel management, store maintenance, and problems of security (shoplifting, money handling procedures, avoidance of theft, and so on).

Such information, however, more properly belongs in an entire book devoted to independent retailing. Read several such books thoroughly before embarking on your retail venture.

SOURCES OF ADDITIONAL INFORMATION

Benson, Benjamin, et al., *Your Family Business: A Success Guide for Growth and Survival.* Homewood, IL: Dow Jones-Irwin, 1990.

Burstiner, Irving, *Basic Retailing,* (2d ed.). Homewood, IL: Irwin, 1991.

_____ , *How to Start and Run Your Own Retail Business.* New York: Citadel Press, 1994.

Coltman, Michael M., *Buying and Selling a Small Business,* (2d ed.). Bellingham, WA: Self-Counsel Press, 1990.

Ernst & Young, *Mergers and Acquisitions,* (2d ed.). New York: Wiley, 1994.

Jacobson, Ruth, *Your Own Shop.* Blue Ridge Summit, PA: TAB Books, 1990.

Justis, Robert T. and Richard J. Judd, *Franchising.* Cincinnati: South-Western, 1989.

Krallinger, Joseph, *How to Acquire the Perfect Business for Your Company.* New York: Wiley, 1991.

Lea, James W., *Keeping It in the Family: Successful Succession of the Family Business.* New York: Wiley, 1991.

Levy, Michael and Barton A. Weitz, *Retailing Management.* Homewood, IL: Irwin, 1992.

Lewison, Dale M. and M. Wayne DeLozier, *Retailing,* (3rd ed.). Columbus, OH: Merrill Publishing, 1989.

Mirvis, Philip H. and Mitchell L. Marks, *Managing the Merger: Making It Work.* Englewood Cliffs, NJ: Prentice-Hall, 1991.

Reed, Stanley Foster and Lane & Edson, P.C., *The Art of M&A: A Merger/ Acquisition/Buyout Guide*. Homewood, IL: Business One Irwin, 1989.

Rust, Herbert, *Owning Your Own Franchise*. Englewood Cliffs, NJ: Prentice-Hall, 1991.

Scharf, Charles A., Edward E. Shea, and George C. Beck, *Acquisitions, Mergers, Sales, Buyouts, Takeovers: A Handbook with Forms*. Englewood Cliffs, NJ: Prentice-Hall, 1991.

Schuch, Milton L., *Retail Buying and Merchandising*. Englewood Cliffs, NJ: Prentice-Hall, 1988.

Siegel, Joel E., Jae K. Shim, and David Minars, *The Financial Trouble-Shooter: Spotting and Solving Financial Problems in Your Company*. New York: McGraw-Hill, 1993.

SAMPLE FEDERAL INCOME TAX FORMS

EXHIBIT A–1   Schedule C (Form 1040)

SCHEDULE C (Form 1040)	**Profit or Loss From Business** (Sole Proprietorship)	OMB No. 1545-0074
Department of the Treasury Internal Revenue Service (T)	▶ Partnerships, joint ventures, etc., must file Form 1065. ▶ Attach to Form 1040 or Form 1041. ▶ See Instructions for Schedule C (Form 1040).	19**94** Attachment Sequence No. **09**

Name of proprietor	Social security number (SSN)
Susan J. Brown	111 00 111

A Principal business or profession, including product or service (see page C-1)
Retail, ladies' apparel

B Enter principal business code (see page C-6) ▶ 3 9 1 1 3

C Business name. If no separate business name, leave blank.
Milady Fashions

D Employer ID number (EIN), if any
1 0 1 2 3 4 5 6 7

E Business address (including suite or room no.) ▶ 725 Big Sur Drive
City, town or post office, state, and ZIP code   Franklin, NY 18725

F Accounting method: (1) ☐ Cash   (2) ☑ Accrual   (3) ☐ Other (specify) ▶ ....

G Method(s) used to value closing inventory: (1) ☑ Cost   (2) ☐ Lower of cost or market   (3) ☐ Other (attach explanation)   (4) ☐ Does not apply (if checked, skip line H) | Yes | No |

H Was there any change in determining quantities, costs, or valuations between opening and closing inventory? If "Yes," attach explanation | | ✔ |

I Did you "materially participate" in the operation of this business during 1994? If "No," see page C-2 for limit on losses. | ✔ | |

J If you started or acquired this business during 1994, check here   ▶ ☐

Part I   Income

1	Gross receipts or sales. **Caution:** If this income was reported to you on Form W-2 and the "Statutory employee" box on that form was checked, see page C-2 and check here ▶ ☐	1	397,742
2	Returns and allowances	2	1,442
3	Subtract line 2 from line 1	3	396,300
4	Cost of goods sold (from line 40 on page 2)	4	239,349
5	**Gross profit.** Subtract line 4 from line 3	5	156,951
6	Other income, including Federal and state gasoline or fuel tax credit or refund (see page C-2)	6	0
7	**Gross income.** Add lines 5 and 6 ▶	7	156,951

Part II   Expenses. Enter expenses for business use of your home **only** on line 30.

8	Advertising	8	3,500	19	Pension and profit-sharing plans	19	
9	Bad debts from sales or services (see page C-3)	9	479	20	Rent or lease (see page C-4):		
				a	Vehicles, machinery, and equipment	20a	
10	Car and truck expenses (see page C-3)	10	3,850	b	Other business property	20b	12,000
11	Commissions and fees	11		21	Repairs and maintenance	21	964
12	Depletion	12		22	Supplies (not included in Part III)	22	1,203
13	Depreciation and section 179 expense deduction (not included in Part III) (see page C-3)	13	2,731	23	Taxes and licenses	23	5,727
				24	Travel, meals, and entertainment:		
				a	Travel	24a	
14	Employee benefit programs (other than on line 19)	14		b	Meals and entertainment		
15	Insurance (other than health)	15	238	c	Enter 50% of line 24b subject to limitations (see page C-4)		
16	Interest:						
a	Mortgage (paid to banks, etc.)	16a		d	Subtract line 24c from line 24b	24d	
b	Other	16b	2,633	25	Utilities	25	3,570
17	Legal and professional services	17		26	Wages (less employment credits)	26	59,050
18	Office expense	18	216	27	Other expenses (from line 46 on page 2)	27	8,078

28	**Total expenses** before expenses for business use of home. Add lines 8 through 27 in columns. ▶	28	104,239
29	Tentative profit (loss). Subtract line 28 from line 7	29	52,712
30	Expenses for business use of your home. Attach **Form 8829**	30	
31	**Net profit or (loss).** Subtract line 30 from line 29. • If a profit, enter on **Form 1040, line 12**, and ALSO on **Schedule SE, line 2** (statutory employees, see page C-5). Estates and trusts, enter on Form 1041, line 3. • If a loss, you MUST go on to line 32.	31	52,712
32	If you have a loss, check the box that describes your investment in this activity (see page C-5). • If you checked 32a, enter the loss on **Form 1040, line 12**, and ALSO on **Schedule SE, line 2** (statutory employees, see page C-5). Estates and trusts, enter on Form 1041, line 3. • If you checked 32b, you MUST attach **Form 6198.**	32a ☐ All investment is at risk. 32b ☐ Some investment is not at risk.	

For Paperwork Reduction Act Notice, see Form 1040 instructions.   Cat. No. 11334P   Schedule C (Form 1040) 1994

Source: "Tax Guide for Small Business, 1994," *Publication 334* (Washington, DC: Internal Revenue Service, revised November 1994), 196–97.

EXHIBIT A–1   *(Continued)*

Schedule C (Form 1040) 1994   Page **2**

Part III   **Cost of Goods Sold** (see page C-5)

33	Inventory at beginning of year. If different from last year's closing inventory, attach explanation . .	33	42,843
34	Purchases less cost of items withdrawn for personal use	34	240,252
35	Cost of labor. Do not include salary paid to yourself	35	0
36	Materials and supplies	36	0
37	Other costs	37	0
38	Add lines 33 through 37	38	283,095
39	Inventory at end of year	39	43,746
40	**Cost of goods sold.** Subtract line 39 from line 38. Enter the result here and on page 1, line 4 . .	40	239,349

Part IV   **Information on Your Vehicle.** Complete this part **ONLY** if you are claiming car or truck expenses on line 10 and are not required to file Form 4562 for this business. See the instructions for line 13 on page C-3 to find out if you must file.

41   When did you place your vehicle in service for business purposes? (month, day, year) ▶ ..../........./....... .

42   Of the total number of miles you drove your vehicle during 1994, enter the number of miles you used your vehicle for:

a   Business .... b Commuting .... c Other ....

43	Do you (or your spouse) have another vehicle available for personal use?	☐ Yes	☐ No
44	Was your vehicle available for use during off-duty hours?	☐ Yes	☐ No
45a	Do you have evidence to support your deduction?	☐ Yes	☐ No
b	If "Yes," is the evidence written?	☐ Yes	☐ No

Part V   **Other Expenses.** List below business expenses not included on lines 8–26 or line 30.

Bank service charges		180
Chamber of Commerce		60
Free Credit Card Co.		6,000
Trash removal		1,600
Window washing		238
46	**Total other expenses.** Enter here and on page 1, line 27	46	8,078

EXHIBIT A–2 Form 4562

Form **4562**	**Depreciation and Amortization** (Including Information on Listed Property)	OMB No. 1545-0172
Department of the Treasury Internal Revenue Service (T)	▶ See separate instructions. ▶ Attach this form to your return.	19**94** Attachment Sequence No. **67**

Name(s) shown on return   *Susan J. Brown*

Identifying number   *111-00-1111*

Business or activity to which this form relates   *Milady Fashions*

Part I Election To Expense Certain Tangible Property (Section 179) (Note: *If you have any "Listed Property," complete Part V before you complete Part I.)*

1	Maximum dollar limitation (If an enterprise zone business, see instructions.)	1	$17,500
2	Total cost of section 179 property placed in service during the tax year (see instructions) . .	2	*7500*
3	Threshold cost of section 179 property before reduction in limitation	3	$200,000
4	Reduction in limitation. Subtract line 3 from line 2. If zero or less, enter -0-	4	*0*
5	Dollar limitation for tax year. Subtract line 4 from line 1. If zero or less, enter -0-. (If married filing separately, see instructions.).	5	*17,500*

(a) Description of property	(b) Cost	(c) Elected cost	
6 *Adding machine*	*200*	*200*	

7	Listed property. Enter amount from line 26.	7 *0*		
8	Total elected cost of section 179 property. Add amounts in column (c), lines 6 and 7 . . .	8	*200*
9	Tentative deduction. Enter the smaller of line 5 or line 8	9	*200*
10	Carryover of disallowed deduction from 1993 (see instructions).	10	*0*
11	Taxable income limitation. Enter the smaller of taxable income (not less than zero) or line 5 (see instructions)	11	*17,500*
12	Section 179 expense deduction. Add lines 9 and 10, but do not enter more than line 11 . .	12	*200*
13	Carryover of disallowed deduction to 1995. Add lines 9 and 10, less line 12 ▶	13	

Note: *Do not use Part II or Part III below for listed property (automobiles, certain other vehicles, cellular telephones, certain computers, or property used for entertainment, recreation, or amusement). Instead, use Part V for listed property.*

Part II MACRS Depreciation For Assets Placed in Service ONLY During Your 1994 Tax Year (Do Not Include Listed Property)

(a) Classification of property	(b) Month and year placed in service	(c) Basis for depreciation (business/investment use only—see instructions)	(d) Recovery period	(e) Convention	(f) Method	(g) Depreciation deduction
Section A—General Depreciation System (GDS) (see instructions)						
14a 3-year property						
b 5-year property						
c 7-year property		*800*	*7*	*HY*	*200 DB*	*114*
d 10-year property						
e 15-year property						
f 20-year property						
g Residential rental property			27.5 yrs.	MM	S/L	
			27.5 yrs.	MM	S/L	
h Nonresidential real property			39 yrs.	MM	S/L	
				MM	S/L	
Section B—Alternative Depreciation System (ADS) (see instructions)						
15a Class life					S/L	
b 12-year			12 yrs.		S/L	
c 40-year			40 yrs.	MM	S/L	

Part III Other Depreciation (Do Not Include Listed Property)

16	GDS and ADS deductions for assets placed in service in tax years beginning before 1994 (see instructions)	16	
17	Property subject to section 168(f)(1) election (see instructions)	17	
18	ACRS and other depreciation (see instructions)	18	*1,117*

Part IV Summary

19	Listed property. Enter amount from line 25.	19	*1,300*
20	**Total.** Add deductions on line 12, lines 14 and 15 in column (g), and lines 16 through 19. Enter here and on the appropriate lines of your return. (Partnerships and S corporations—see instructions)	20	*2,731*
21	For assets shown above and placed in service during the current year, enter the portion of the basis attributable to section 263A costs (see instructions)	21	

For Paperwork Reduction Act Notice, see page 1 of the separate instructions.   Cat. No. 12906N   Form **4562** (1994)

Source: "Tax Guide for Small Business, 1994," *Publication 334* (Washington, DC: Internal Revenue Service, revised November 1994), 198–99.

EXHIBIT A-2 *(Continued)*

Form 4562 (1994)   Page **2**

Part V   **Listed Property—Automobiles, Certain Other Vehicles, Cellular Telephones, Certain Computers, and Property Used for Entertainment, Recreation, or Amusement**

*For any vehicle for which you are using the standard mileage rate or deducting lease expense, complete **only** 22a, 22b, columns (a) through (c) of Section A, all of Section B, and Section C if applicable.*

Section A—Depreciation and Other Information (Caution: See instructions for limitations for automobiles.)

22a   Do you have evidence to support the business/investment use claimed? ☒ **Yes** ☐ **No**   22b   If "Yes," is the evidence written? ☒ **Yes** ☐ **No**

(a) Type of property (list vehicles first)	(b) Date placed in service	(c) Business/ investment use percentage	(d) Cost or other basis	(e) Basis for depreciation (business/investment use only)	(f) Recovery period	(g) Method/ Convention	(h) Depreciation deduction	(i) Elected section 179 cost
23 Property used more than 50% in a qualified business use (see instructions):								
USA 280 Van	3/20/94	75 %	8,667	6,500	5 yrs.	200DB/HY	1300	0
		%						
		%						
24 Property used 50% or less in a qualified business use (see instructions):								
		%				S/L –		
		%				S/L –		
		%				S/L –		

25 Add amounts in column (h). Enter the total here and on line 19, page 1 . . . . . | 25 | 1300 |

26 Add amounts in column (i). Enter the total here and on line 7, page 1 . . . . | 26 | 0 |

Section B—Information on Use of Vehicles—If you deduct expenses for vehicles:

- *Always complete this section for vehicles used by a sole proprietor, partner, or other "more than 5% owner," or related person.*
- *If you provided vehicles to your employees, first answer the questions in Section C to see if you meet an exception to completing this section for those vehicles.*

		(a) Vehicle 1		(b) Vehicle 2		(c) Vehicle 3		(d) Vehicle 4		(e) Vehicle 5		(f) Vehicle 6	
27	Total business/investment miles driven during the year (DO NOT include commuting miles)	7,500											
28	Total commuting miles driven during the year	2,025											
29	Total other personal (noncommuting) miles driven	475											
30	Total miles driven during the year. Add lines 27 through 29	10,000											
		Yes	No	Yes	No	Yes	No	Yes	No	Yes	No	Yes	No
31	Was the vehicle available for personal use during off-duty hours?	✔											
32	Was the vehicle used primarily by a more than 5% owner or related person?	✔											
33	Is another vehicle available for personal use?	✔											

Section C—Questions for Employers Who Provide Vehicles for Use by Their Employees

Answer these questions to determine if you meet an exception to completing Section B. **Note:** *Section B must always be completed for vehicles used by sole proprietors, partners, or other more than 5% owners or related persons.*

		Yes	No
34	Do you maintain a written policy statement that prohibits all personal use of vehicles, including commuting, by your employees?		
35	Do you maintain a written policy statement that prohibits personal use of vehicles, except commuting, by your employees? (See instructions for vehicles used by corporate officers, directors, or 1% or more owners.)		
36	Do you treat all use of vehicles by employees as personal use?		
37	Do you provide more than five vehicles to your employees and retain the information received from your employees concerning the use of the vehicles?		
38	Do you meet the requirements concerning qualified automobile demonstration use (see instructions)? . .		

Note: *If your answer to 34, 35, 36, 37, or 38 is "Yes," you need not complete Section B for the covered vehicles.*

Part VI   **Amortization**

(a) Description of costs	(b) Date amortization begins	(c) Amortizable amount	(d) Code section	(e) Amortization period or percentage	(f) Amortization for this year
39 Amortization of costs that begins during your 1994 tax year:					
40 Amortization of costs that began before 1994				40	
41 **Total.** Enter here and on "Other Deductions" or "Other Expenses" line of your return . . .				41	

EXHIBIT A–3   Schedule SE (Form 1040)

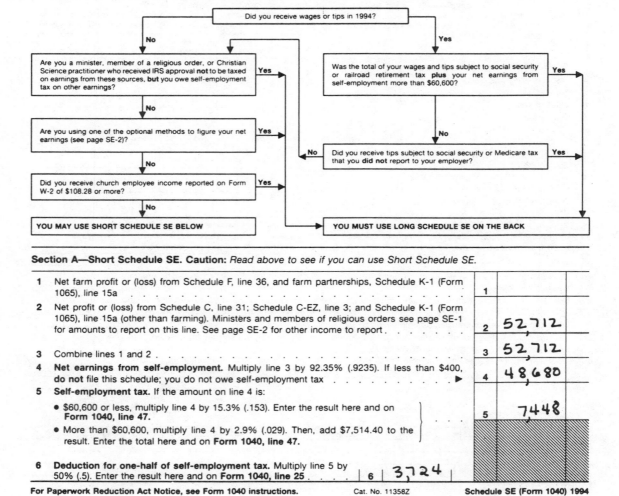

SCHEDULE SE	Self-Employment Tax	OMB No. 1545-0074
(Form 1040)	▶ See Instructions for Schedule SE (Form 1040).	19**94**
Department of the Treasury Internal Revenue Service (T)	▶ Attach to Form 1040.	Attachment Sequence No. **17**

Name of person with **self-employment** income (as shown on Form 1040)
  Susan J. Brown

Social security number of person with **self-employment** income ▶   111 : 00 : 1111

Who Must File Schedule SE

You must file Schedule SE if:

- You had net earnings from self-employment from other than church employee income (line 4 of Short Schedule SE or line 4c of Long Schedule SE) of $400 or more, **OR**
- You had church employee income of $108.28 or more. Income from services you performed as a minister or a member of a religious order **is not** church employee income. See page SE-1.

Note: *Even if you have a loss or a small amount of income from self-employment, it may be to your benefit to file Schedule SE and use either "optional method" in Part II of Long Schedule SE. See page SE-2.*

Exception. If your only self-employment income was from earnings as a minister, member of a religious order, or Christian Science practitioner, **and** you filed Form 4361 and received IRS approval not to be taxed on those earnings, **do not** file Schedule SE. Instead, write "Exempt–Form 4361" on Form 1040, line 47.

May I Use Short Schedule SE or MUST I Use Long Schedule SE?

Did you receive wages or tips in 1994?

No → Are you a minister, member of a religious order, or Christian Science practitioner who received IRS approval **not** to be taxed on earnings from these sources, **but** you owe self-employment tax on other earnings? — **Yes** →

No ↓

Are you using one of the optional methods to figure your net earnings (see page SE-2)? — **Yes** →

No ↓

Did you receive church employee income reported on Form W-2 of $108.28 or more? — **Yes** →

No ↓

Yes → Was the total of your wages and tips subject to social security or railroad retirement tax **plus** your net earnings from self-employment more than $60,600? — **Yes** →

No ↓

Did you receive tips subject to social security or Medicare tax that you **did not** report to your employer? — **Yes** →

No →

YOU MAY USE SHORT SCHEDULE SE BELOW

YOU MUST USE LONG SCHEDULE SE ON THE BACK

Section A—Short Schedule SE. Caution: *Read above to see if you can use Short Schedule SE.*

1	Net farm profit or (loss) from Schedule F, line 36, and farm partnerships, Schedule K-1 (Form 1065), line 15a	1	
2	Net profit or (loss) from Schedule C, line 31; Schedule C-EZ, line 3; and Schedule K-1 (Form 1065), line 15a (other than farming). Ministers and members of religious orders see page SE-1 for amounts to report on this line. See page SE-2 for other income to report	2	52,712
3	Combine lines 1 and 2	3	52,712
4	**Net earnings from self-employment.** Multiply line 3 by 92.35% (.9235). If less than $400, **do not** file this schedule; you do not owe self-employment tax . . . . ▶	4	48,680
5	**Self-employment tax.** If the amount on line 4 is:		
	• $60,600 or less, multiply line 4 by 15.3% (.153). Enter the result here and on **Form 1040, line 47.**	5	7,448
	• More than $60,600, multiply line 4 by 2.9% (.029). Then, add $7,514.40 to the result. Enter the total here and on **Form 1040, line 47.**		
6	**Deduction for one-half of self-employment tax.** Multiply line 5 by 50% (.5). Enter the result here and on **Form 1040, line 25**	6 3,724	

For Paperwork Reduction Act Notice, see Form 1040 instructions.   Cat. No. 11358Z   Schedule SE (Form 1040) 1994

Source: "Tax Guide for Small Business, 1994," *Publication 334* (Washington, DC: Internal Revenue Service, revised November 1994), 200.

EXHIBIT A–4 Form 1065

Form **1065**
Department of the Treasury
Internal Revenue Service

U.S. Partnership Return of Income

For calendar year 1994, or tax year beginning .... , 1994, and ending .... , 19 .....
▶ See separate instructions.

OMB No. 1545-0099

1994

A Principal business activity: Retail	Use the IRS label. Otherwise, please print or type. 10-9876543 DEC94 D71 AbleBaker Book Store 334 West Main Street Orange, MD 20904	D Employer identification number
B Principal product or service: Books		E Date business started: 10-1-79
C Business code number: 5942		F Total assets (see Specific Instructions): $ 45,391

G Check applicable boxes: (1) ☐ Initial return (2) ☐ Final return (3) ☐ Change in address (4) ☐ Amended return

H Check accounting method: (1) ☐ Cash (2) ☑ Accrual (3) ☐ Other (specify) ▶

I Number of Schedules K-1. Attach one for each person who was a partner at any time during the tax year ▶ 2

Caution: *Include **only** trade or business income and expenses on lines 1a through 22 below. See the instructions for more information.*

Section	Line	Description	Sub-line	Sub-amount	Line	Amount
Income	1a	Gross receipts or sales	1a	409,465		
	b	Less returns and allowances	1b	3,365	1c	406,100
	2	Cost of goods sold (Schedule A, line 8)			2	267,641
	3	Gross profit. Subtract line 2 from line 1c			3	138,459
	4	Ordinary income (loss) from other partnerships, estates, and trusts *(attach schedule)*			4	
	5	Net farm profit (loss) *(attach Schedule F (Form 1040))*			5	
	6	Net gain (loss) from Form 4797, Part II, line 20			6	
	7	Other income (loss) (see instructions) *(attach schedule)*			7	559
	8	**Total income (loss).** Combine lines 3 through 7			8	139,018
Deductions (see instructions for limitations)	9	Salaries and wages (other than to partners) (less employment credits)			9	29,350
	10	Guaranteed payments to partners			10	25,000
	11	Repairs and maintenance			11	1,125
	12	Bad debts			12	250
	13	Rent			13	20,000
	14	Taxes and licenses			14	3,295
	15	Interest			15	1,451
	16a	Depreciation (see instructions)	16a	1,174		
	b	Less depreciation reported on Schedule A and elsewhere on return	16b		16c	1,174
	17	Depletion **(Do not deduct oil and gas depletion.)**			17	
	18	Retirement plans, etc.			18	
	19	Employee benefit programs			19	
	20	Other deductions *(attach schedule)*			20	8,003
	21	**Total deductions.** Add the amounts shown in the far right column for lines 9 through 20			21	89,648
	22	**Ordinary income (loss)** from trade or business activities. Subtract line 21 from line 8			22	49,370

Please Sign Here

Under penalties of perjury, I declare that I have examined this return, including accompanying schedules and statements, and to the best of my knowledge and belief, it is true, correct, and complete. Declaration of preparer (other than general partner) is based on all information of which preparer has any knowledge.

▶ Frank W. Able — Signature of general partner or limited liability company member

▶ 3-12-95 — Date

Paid Preparer's Use Only

Preparer's signature ▶	Date	Check if self-employed ▶ ☐	Preparer's social security no.
Firm's name (or yours if self-employed) and address ▶		E.I. No. ▶	
		ZIP code ▶	

For Paperwork Reduction Act Notice, see page 1 of separate instructions. Cat. No. 11390Z Form **1065** (1994)

Source: "Tax Guide for Small Business, 1994," *Publication 334* (Washington, DC: Internal Revenue Service, revised November 1994), 203–6.

EXHIBIT A–4   *(Continued)*

Form 1065 (1994)   Page **2**

Schedule A	Cost of Goods Sold

1	Inventory at beginning of year	1	18,125
2	Purchases less cost of items withdrawn for personal use	2	268,741
3	Cost of labor	3	–0–
4	Additional section 263A costs (see instructions) *(attach schedule)*	4	–0–
5	Other costs *(attach schedule)*	5	–0–
6	**Total.** Add lines 1 through 5	6	286,866
7	Inventory at end of year	7	19,225
8	**Cost of goods sold.** Subtract line 7 from line 6. Enter here and on page 1, line 2	8	267,641

9a Check all methods used for valuing closing inventory:

(i) ☐ Cost

(ii) ☑ Lower of cost or market as described in Regulations section 1.471-4

(iii) ☐ Writedown of "subnormal" goods as described in Regulations section 1.471-2(c)

(iv) ☐ Other (specify method used and attach explanation) ▶ ....

b Check this box if the LIFO inventory method was adopted this tax year for any goods *(if checked, attach Form 970)* . . ▶ ☐

c Do the rules of section 263A (for property produced or acquired for resale) apply to the partnership? . . ☐ **Yes** ☑ **No**

d Was there any change in determining quantities, cost, or valuations between opening and closing inventory? ☐ **Yes** ☑ **No**
If "Yes," attach explanation.

Schedule B	Other Information

		Yes	No
1	What type of entity is filing this return? Check the applicable box ▶ ☑ General partnership ☐ Limited partnership ☐ Limited liability company		
2	Are any partners in this partnership also partnerships?		✓
3	Is this partnership a partner in another partnership?		✓
4	Is this partnership subject to the consolidated audit procedures of sections 6221 through 6233? If "Yes," see **Designation of Tax Matters Partner** below		✓
5	Does this partnership meet **ALL THREE** of the following requirements?		
a	The partnership's total receipts for the tax year were less than $250,000;		
b	The partnership's total assets at the end of the tax year were less than $600,000; **AND**		
c	Schedules K-1 are filed with the return and furnished to the partners on or before the due date (including extensions) for the partnership return. If "Yes," the partnership is not required to complete Schedules L, M-1, and M-2; Item F on page 1 of Form 1065; or Item J on Schedule K-1		✓
6	Does this partnership have any foreign partners?		✓
7	Is this partnership a publicly traded partnership as defined in section 469(k)(2)?		✓
8	Has this partnership filed, or is it required to file, **Form 8264,** Application for Registration of a Tax Shelter? . .		✓
9	At any time during calendar year 1994, did the partnership have an interest in or a signature or other authority over a financial account in a foreign country (such as a bank account, securities account, or other financial account)? (See the instructions for exceptions and filing requirements for Form TD F 90-22.1.) If "Yes," enter the name of the foreign country. ▶		✓
10	Was the partnership the grantor of, or transferor to, a foreign trust that existed during the current tax year, whether or not the partnership or any partner has any beneficial interest in it? If "Yes," you may have to file Forms 3520, 3520-A, or 926		✓
11	Was there a distribution of property or a transfer (e.g., by sale or death) of a partnership interest during the tax year? If "Yes," you may elect to adjust the basis of the partnership's assets under section 754 by attaching the statement described under **Elections Made By the Partnership**		✓

Designation of Tax Matters Partner (See instructions.)

Enter below the general partner designated as the tax matters partner (TMP) for the tax year of this return:

Name of
designated TMP ▶ _____   Identifying
number of TMP ▶ _____

Address of
designated TMP ▶ _____

EXHIBIT A–4   *(Continued)*

Form 1065 (1994)   Page **3**

Schedule K	Partners' Shares of Income, Credits, Deductions, etc.		

	(a) Distributive share items		(b) Total amount

<table>
<tr><td rowspan="16">Income (Loss)</td><td>1</td><td>Ordinary income (loss) from trade or business activities (page 1, line 22) . . . .</td><td>1</td><td>49,370</td></tr>
<tr><td>2</td><td>Net income (loss) from rental real estate activities (attach Form 8825) . .</td><td>2</td><td></td></tr>
<tr><td>3a</td><td>Gross income from other rental activities . . . . 3a</td><td></td><td></td></tr>
<tr><td>b</td><td>Expenses from other rental activities (attach schedule) . . . . 3b</td><td></td><td></td></tr>
<tr><td>c</td><td>Net income (loss) from other rental activities. Subtract line 3b from line 3a . . . . .</td><td>3c</td><td></td></tr>
<tr><td>4</td><td>Portfolio income (loss) (see instructions): a Interest income . . . .</td><td>4a</td><td></td></tr>
<tr><td>b</td><td>Dividend income . . . .</td><td>4b</td><td>150</td></tr>
<tr><td>c</td><td>Royalty income . . . .</td><td>4c</td><td></td></tr>
<tr><td>d</td><td>Net short-term capital gain (loss) (attach Schedule D (Form 1065)) . . . .</td><td>4d</td><td></td></tr>
<tr><td>e</td><td>Net long-term capital gain (loss) (attach Schedule D (Form 1065)) . . . .</td><td>4e</td><td></td></tr>
<tr><td>f</td><td>Other portfolio income (loss) (attach schedule) . . . .</td><td>4f</td><td></td></tr>
<tr><td>5</td><td>Guaranteed payments to partners . . . .</td><td>5</td><td>25,000</td></tr>
<tr><td>6</td><td>Net gain (loss) under section 1231 (other than due to casualty or theft) (attach Form 4797)</td><td>6</td><td></td></tr>
<tr><td>7</td><td>Other income (loss) (attach schedule) . . . .</td><td>7</td><td></td></tr>
<tr><td rowspan="4">Deduc-tions</td><td>8</td><td>Charitable contributions (see instructions) (attach schedule) . . . .</td><td>8</td><td>650</td></tr>
<tr><td>9</td><td>Section 179 expense deduction (attach Form 4562) . . . .</td><td>9</td><td></td></tr>
<tr><td>10</td><td>Deductions related to portfolio income (see instructions) (itemize) . . . .</td><td>10</td><td></td></tr>
<tr><td>11</td><td>Other deductions (attach schedule) . . . .</td><td>11</td><td></td></tr>
<tr><td rowspan="3">Invest-ment Interest</td><td>12a</td><td>Interest expense on investment debts . . . .</td><td>12a</td><td></td></tr>
<tr><td>b</td><td>(1) Investment income included on lines 4a, 4b, 4c, and 4f above . . . .</td><td>12b(1)</td><td>150</td></tr>
<tr><td></td><td>(2) Investment expenses included on line 10 above . . . .</td><td>12b(2)</td><td></td></tr>
<tr><td rowspan="9">Credits</td><td>13a</td><td>Credit for income tax withheld . . . .</td><td>13a</td><td></td></tr>
<tr><td>b</td><td>Low-income housing credit (see instructions):</td><td></td><td></td></tr>
<tr><td></td><td>(1) From partnerships to which section 42(j)(5) applies for property placed in service before 1990 . .</td><td>13b(1)</td><td></td></tr>
<tr><td></td><td>(2) Other than on line 13b(1) for property placed in service before 1990 . . . . .</td><td>13b(2)</td><td></td></tr>
<tr><td></td><td>(3) From partnerships to which section 42(j)(5) applies for property placed in service after 1989</td><td>13b(3)</td><td></td></tr>
<tr><td></td><td>(4) Other than on line 13b(3) for property placed in service after 1989 . . . .</td><td>13b(4)</td><td></td></tr>
<tr><td>c</td><td>Qualified rehabilitation expenditures related to rental real estate activities (attach Form 3468)</td><td>13c</td><td></td></tr>
<tr><td>d</td><td>Credits (other than credits shown on lines 13b and 13c) related to rental real estate activities (see instructions)</td><td>13d</td><td></td></tr>
<tr><td>e</td><td>Credits related to other rental activities (see instructions) . . . .</td><td>13e</td><td></td></tr>
<tr><td>Credits</td><td>14</td><td>Other credits (see instructions) . . . .</td><td>14</td><td></td></tr>
<tr><td rowspan="3">Self-Employ-ment</td><td>15a</td><td>Net earnings (loss) from self-employment . . . .</td><td>15a</td><td>74,370</td></tr>
<tr><td>b</td><td>Gross farming or fishing income . . . .</td><td>15b</td><td></td></tr>
<tr><td>c</td><td>Gross nonfarm income . . . .</td><td>15c</td><td></td></tr>
<tr><td rowspan="7">Adjustments and Tax Preference Items</td><td>16a</td><td>Depreciation adjustment on property placed in service after 1986 . . . .</td><td>16a</td><td></td></tr>
<tr><td>b</td><td>Adjusted gain or loss . . . .</td><td>16b</td><td></td></tr>
<tr><td>c</td><td>Depletion (other than oil and gas) . . . .</td><td>16c</td><td></td></tr>
<tr><td>d</td><td>(1) Gross income from oil, gas, and geothermal properties . . . .</td><td>16d(1)</td><td></td></tr>
<tr><td></td><td>(2) Deductions allocable to oil, gas, and geothermal properties . . . .</td><td>16d(2)</td><td></td></tr>
<tr><td>e</td><td>Other adjustments and tax preference items (attach schedule) . . . .</td><td>16e</td><td></td></tr>
<tr><td></td><td></td><td></td><td></td></tr>
<tr><td rowspan="7">Foreign Taxes</td><td>17a</td><td>Type of income ▶ . . . . b Foreign country or U.S. possession ▶ . . . .</td><td></td><td></td></tr>
<tr><td>c</td><td>Total gross income from sources outside the United States (attach schedule). . . . .</td><td>17c</td><td></td></tr>
<tr><td>d</td><td>Total applicable deductions and losses (attach schedule) . . . .</td><td>17d</td><td></td></tr>
<tr><td>e</td><td>Total foreign taxes (check one): ▶ ☐ Paid ☐ Accrued . . . .</td><td>17e</td><td></td></tr>
<tr><td>f</td><td>Reduction in taxes available for credit (attach schedule) . . . .</td><td>17f</td><td></td></tr>
<tr><td>g</td><td>Other foreign tax information (attach schedule) . . . .</td><td>17g</td><td></td></tr>
<tr><td></td><td></td><td></td><td></td></tr>
<tr><td rowspan="6">Other</td><td>18a</td><td>Total expenditures to which a section 59(e) election may apply . . . .</td><td>18a</td><td></td></tr>
<tr><td>b</td><td>Type of expenditures ▶. . . . .</td><td></td><td></td></tr>
<tr><td>19</td><td>Tax-exempt interest income . . . .</td><td>19</td><td>50</td></tr>
<tr><td>20</td><td>Other tax-exempt income . . . .</td><td>20</td><td></td></tr>
<tr><td>21</td><td>Nondeductible expenses . . . .</td><td>21</td><td></td></tr>
<tr><td>22</td><td>Other items and amounts required to be reported separately to partners (see instructions) (attach schedule)</td><td></td><td></td></tr>
</table>

Analysis	23a	Income (loss). Combine lines 1 through 7 in column (b). From the result, subtract the sum of lines 8 through 12a, 17e, and 18a	23a	73,870

	b Analysis by type of partner:	(a) Corporate	(b) Individual		(c) Partnership	(d) Exempt organization	(e) Nominee/Other
			i. Active	ii. Passive			
	(1) General partners		73,870				
	(2) Limited partners						

EXHIBIT A–4   *(Continued)*

Form 1065 (1994)   Page **4**

Note: *If Question 5 of Schedule B is answered "Yes," the partnership is not required to complete Schedules L, M-1, and M-2.*

Schedule L   **Balance Sheets**

Assets	Beginning of tax year (a)	(b)	End of tax year (c)	(d)
1 Cash		3,455		3,350
2a Trade notes and accounts receivable	7,150		10,990	
b Less allowance for bad debts		7,150		10,990
3 Inventories		18,125		19,225
4 U.S. government obligations				
5 Tax-exempt securities		1,000		1,000
6 Other current assets (attach schedule)				
7 Mortgage and real estate loans				
8 Other investments (attach schedule)		1,000		1,000
9a Buildings and other depreciable assets	15,000		15,000	
b Less accumulated depreciation	4,000	11,000	5,174	9,826
10a Depletable assets				
b Less accumulated depletion				
11 Land (net of any amortization)				
12a Intangible assets (amortizable only)				
b Less accumulated amortization				
13 Other assets (attach schedule)				
14 Total assets		41,730		45,391
Liabilities and Capital				
15 Accounts payable		10,180		10,462
16 Mortgages, notes, bonds payable in less than 1 year		4,000		3,600
17 Other current liabilities (attach schedule)				
18 All nonrecourse loans				
19 Mortgages, notes, bonds payable in 1 year or more				7,739
20 Other liabilities (attach schedule)				
21 Partners' capital accounts		27,550		23,590
22 Total liabilities and capital		41,730		45,391

Schedule M-1   **Reconciliation of Income (Loss) per Books With Income (Loss) per Return** (see instructions)

1 Net income (loss) per books	48,920	6 Income recorded on books this year not included on Schedule K, lines 1 through 7 (itemize):	
2 Income included on Schedule K, lines 1 through 4, 6, and 7, not recorded on books this year (itemize):		a Tax-exempt interest $	
		....	50
3 Guaranteed payments (other than health insurance)	25,000	7 Deductions included on Schedule K, lines 1 through 12a, 17e, and 18a, not charged against book income this year (itemize):	
4 Expenses recorded on books this year not included on Schedule K, lines 1 through 12a, 17e, and 18a (itemize):		a Depreciation $	
a Depreciation $		....	
b Travel and entertainment $		....	
....		8 Add lines 6 and 7	50
		9 Income (loss) (Schedule K, line 23a). Subtract line 8 from line 5	
5 Add lines 1 through 4	73,920		73,870

Schedule M-2   **Analysis of Partners' Capital Accounts**

1 Balance at beginning of year	27,550	6 Distributions: a Cash	52,880
2 Capital contributed during year		b Property	
3 Net income (loss) per books	48,920	7 Other decreases (itemize):	
4 Other increases (itemize):		....	
....		8 Add lines 6 and 7	52,880
5 Add lines 1 through 4	76,470	9 Balance at end of year. Subtract line 8 from line 5	23,590

EXHIBIT A–5   Schedule K-1 (Form 1065)

SCHEDULE K-1 (Form 1065)	Partner's Share of Income, Credits, Deductions, etc.	OMB No. 1545-0099
Department of the Treasury Internal Revenue Service	▶ See separate instructions. For calendar year 1994 or tax year beginning , 1994, and ending , 19	1994

Partner's identifying number ▶ *123-00-6789*

Partnership's identifying number ▶ *10:9876543*

Partner's name, address, and ZIP code
*Frank W. Able
10 Green Street
Orange, MD 20904*

Partnership's name, address, and ZIP code
*Able Baker Book Store
334 West Main Street
Orange, MD 20904*

A This partner is a ☑ general partner ☐ limited partner
☐ limited liability company member
B What type of entity is this partner? ▶ *Individual*
C Is this partner a ☑ domestic or a ☐ foreign partner?
D Enter partner's percentage of: (i) Before change or termination / (ii) End of year
Profit sharing ..... % *50* %
Loss sharing ..... % *50* %
Ownership of capital ..... % *50* %
E IRS Center where partnership filed return: *Philadelphia*

F Partner's share of liabilities (see instructions):
Nonrecourse ..... $ ....
Qualified nonrecourse financing . $ ....
Other ..... $ *10,900*
G Tax shelter registration number . ▶ *N/A*
H Check here if this partnership is a publicly traded partnership as defined in section 469(k)(2) .... ☐
I Check applicable boxes: (1) ☐ Final K-1 (2) ☐ Amended K-1

J Analysis of partner's capital account:

(a) Capital account at beginning of year	(b) Capital contributed during year	(c) Partner's share of lines 3, 4, and 7, Form 1065, Schedule M-2	(d) Withdrawals and distributions	(e) Capital account at end of year (combine columns (a) through (d))
14,050	24,460		(26,440)	12,070

	(a) Distributive share item		(b) Amount	(c) 1040 filers enter the amount in column (b) on:
Income (Loss)	1 Ordinary income (loss) from trade or business activities	1	24,685	See Partner's Instructions for Schedule K-1 (Form 1065).
	2 Net income (loss) from rental real estate activities	2		
	3 Net income (loss) from other rental activities	3		
	4 Portfolio income (loss):			
	a Interest	4a		Sch. B, Part I, line 1
	b Dividends	4b	75	Sch. B, Part II, line 5
	c Royalties	4c		Sch. E, Part I, line 4
	d Net short-term capital gain (loss)	4d		Sch. D, line 5, col. (f) or (g)
	e Net long-term capital gain (loss)	4e		Sch. D, line 13, col. (f) or (g)
	f Other portfolio income (loss) (attach schedule)	4f		Enter on applicable line of your return
	5 Guaranteed payments to partner	5	20,000	See Partner's Instructions for Schedule K-1 (Form 1065).
	6 Net gain (loss) under section 1231 (other than due to casualty or theft)	6		
	7 Other income (loss) (attach schedule)	7		Enter on applicable line of your return
Deductions	8 Charitable contributions (see instructions) (attach schedule)	8	325	Sch. A, line 15 or 16
	9 Section 179 expense deduction	9		See Partner's Instructions for Schedule K-1 (Form 1065).
	10 Deductions related to portfolio income (attach schedule)	10		
	11 Other deductions (attach schedule)	11		
Investment Interest	12a Interest expense on investment debts	12a		Form 4952, line 1
	b (1) Investment income included on lines 4a, 4b, 4c, and 4f above	b(1)	75	See Partner's Instructions for Schedule K-1 (Form 1065).
	(2) Investment expenses included on line 10 above	b(2)		
Credits	13a Credit for income tax withheld	13a		See Partner's Instructions for Schedule K-1 (Form 1065).
	b Low-income housing credit:			
	(1) From section 42(j)(5) partnerships for property placed in service before 1990	b(1)		
	(2) Other than on line 13b(1) for property placed in service before 1990	b(2)		
	(3) From section 42(j)(5) partnerships for property placed in service after 1989	b(3)		Form 8586, line 5
	(4) Other than on line 13b(3) for property placed in service after 1989	b(4)		
	c Qualified rehabilitation expenditures related to rental real estate activities (see instructions)	13c		
	d Credits (other than credits shown on lines 13b and 13c) related to rental real estate activities (see instructions)	13d		See Partner's Instructions for Schedule K-1 (Form 1065).
	e Credits related to other rental activities (see instructions)	13e		
	14 Other credits (see instructions)	14		

For Paperwork Reduction Act Notice, see Instructions for Form 1065.   Cat. No. 11394R   Schedule K-1 (Form 1065) 1994

Source: "Tax Guide for Small Business, 1994," *Publication 334* (Washington, DC: Internal Revenue Service, revised November 1994), 207–8.

EXHIBIT A–5   (Continued)

Schedule K-1 (Form 1065) 1994   Page **2**

		(a) Distributive share item	(b) Amount	(c) 1040 filers enter the amount in column (b) on:
Self-em- ployment	**15a**	Net earnings (loss) from self-employment	**15a** 44,685	Sch. SE, Section A or B
	b	Gross farming or fishing income.	**15b**	See Partner's Instructions for
	c	Gross nonfarm income.	**15c**	Schedule K-1 (Form 1065).
Adjustments and Tax Preference Items	**16a**	Depreciation adjustment on property placed in service after 1986	**16a**	
	b	Adjusted gain or loss	**16b**	See Partner's Instructions for Schedule K-1 (Form 1065) and Instructions for Form 6251.
	c	Depletion (other than oil and gas)	**16c**	
	d	(1) Gross income from oil, gas, and geothermal properties . .	**d(1)**	
		(2) Deductions allocable to oil, gas, and geothermal properties . .	**d(2)**	
	e	Other adjustments and tax preference items (attach schedule) . .	**16e**	
Foreign Taxes	**17a**	Type of income ▶		Form 1116, check boxes
	b	Name of foreign country or U.S. possession ▶		
	c	Total gross income from sources outside the United States (attach schedule)	**17c**	Form 1116, Part I
	d	Total applicable deductions and losses (attach schedule). . .	**17d**	
	e	Total foreign taxes (check one): ▶ ☐ Paid ☐ Accrued . .	**17e**	Form 1116, Part II
	f	Reduction in taxes available for credit (attach schedule) . . .	**17f**	Form 1116, Part III
	g	Other foreign tax information (attach schedule)	**17g**	See Instructions for Form 1116.
Other	**18a**	Total expenditures to which a section 59(e) election may apply	**18a**	See Partner's Instructions for Schedule K-1 (Form 1065).
	b	Type of expenditures ▶		
	19	Tax-exempt interest income	**19** 25	Form 1040, line 8b
	20	Other tax-exempt income.	**20**	See Partner's Instructions for Schedule K-1 (Form 1065).
	21	Nondeductible expenses	**21**	
	22	Recapture of low-income housing credit:		
	a	From section 42(j)(5) partnerships	**22a**	Form 8611, line 8
	b	Other than on line 22a.	**22b**	

Supplemental Information

23   Supplemental information required to be reported separately to each partner (attach additional schedules.if more space is needed):

....

....

....

....

....

....

....

....

....

....

....

....

....

....

....

EXHIBIT A–6   Form 1120A

| Form **1120-A**
Department of the Treasury
Internal Revenue Service | **U.S. Corporation Short-Form Income Tax Return**
See separate instructions to make sure the corporation qualifies to file Form 1120-A.
For calendar year 1994 or tax year beginning ...., 1994, ending ...., 19..... | OMB No. 1545-0890
1994 |

A Check this box if the corp. is a personal service corp. (as defined in Temporary Regs. section 1.441-4T—see instructions) ▶ ☐

Use IRS label. Otherwise, please print or type.

10-2134567   DEC94   5995
Rose Flower Shop, Inc.
38 Superior Lane
Fair City, MD   20715

B Employer identification number

C Date incorporated
7-1-82

D Total assets (see Specific Instructions)
$ 65,987

E Check applicable boxes: (1) ☐ Initial return (2) ☐ Change of address
F Check method of accounting: (1) ☐ Cash (2) ☑ Accrual (3) ☐ Other (specify) .... ▶

Income			
1a Gross receipts or sales 248,000	b Less returns and allowances 7,500	c Balance ▶	1c	240,500
2 Cost of goods sold (see instructions)		2	144,000
3 Gross profit. Subtract line 2 from line 1c		3	96,500
4 Domestic corporation dividends subject to the 70% deduction		4	
5 Interest		5	942
6 Gross rents		6	
7 Gross royalties		7	
8 Capital gain net income (attach Schedule D (Form 1120))		8	
9 Net gain or (loss) from Form 4797, Part II, line 20 (attach Form 4797)		9	
10 Other income (see instructions)		10	
11 Total income. Add lines 3 through 10 ▶		11	97,442

Deductions (See instructions for limitations on deductions.)		
12 Compensation of officers (see instructions)	12	23,000
13 Salaries and wages (less employment credits)	13	24,320
14 Repairs and maintenance	14	
15 Bad debts	15	
16 Rents	16	6,000
17 Taxes and licenses	17	3,320
18 Interest	18	1,340
19 Charitable contributions (see instructions for 10% limitation)	19	1,820
20 Depreciation (attach Form 4562) ... 20		
21 Less depreciation claimed elsewhere on return ... 21a	21b	
22 Other deductions (attach schedule) Advertising	22	3,000
23 Total deductions. Add lines 12 through 22 ▶	23	62,800
24 Taxable income before net operating loss deduction and special deductions. Subtract line 23 from line 11	24	34,642
25 Less: a Net operating loss deduction (see instructions) ... 25a		
b Special deductions (see instructions) ... 25b	25c	

Tax and Payments		
26 Taxable income. Subtract line 25c from line 24	26	34,642
27 Total tax (from page 2, Part I, line 7)	27	5,196
28 Payments:		
a 1993 overpayment credited to 1994 ... 28a		
b 1994 estimated tax payments ... 28b 6,000		
c Less 1994 refund applied for on Form 4466 ... 28c ( ) Bal ▶ 28d 6,000		
e Tax deposited with Form 7004 ... 28e		
f Credit from regulated investment companies (attach Form 2439) ... 28f		
g Credit for Federal tax on fuels (attach Form 4136). See instructions ... 28g		
h Total payments. Add lines 28d through 28g	28h	6,000
29 Estimated tax penalty (see instructions). Check if Form 2220 is attached ▶ ☐	29	
30 Tax due. If line 28h is smaller than the total of lines 27 and 29, enter amount owed	30	
31 Overpayment. If line 28h is larger than the total of lines 27 and 29, enter amount overpaid ▶	31	804
32 Enter amount of line 31 you want: Credited to 1995 estimated tax ▶ 804 Refunded ▶	32	

Please Sign Here

Under penalties of perjury, I declare that I have examined this return, including accompanying schedules and statements, and to the best of my knowledge and belief, it is true, correct, and complete. Declaration of preparer (other than taxpayer) is based on all information of which preparer has any knowledge.

▶ *George Rose*   2-15-95   ▶ President
Signature of officer   Date   Title

Paid Preparer's Use Only

Preparer's signature ▶	Date	Check if self-employed ▶ ☐	Preparer's social security number
Firm's name (or yours if self-employed) and address ▶		E.I. No. ▶	ZIP code ▶

For Paperwork Reduction Act Notice, see page 1 of the instructions.   Cat. No. 11456E   Form **1120-A** (1994)

Source: "Tax Guide for Small Business, 1994," *Publication 334* (Washington, DC: Internal Revenue Service, revised November 1994), 210–11.

EXHIBIT A–6 *(Continued)*

Form 1120-A (1994)   Page **2**

Part I	**Tax Computation** (See instructions.)			

1 Income tax. If the corporation is a qualified personal service corporation (see page 14), check here ▶ ☐ | **1** | *5,196* |

2a General business credit. Check if from: ☐ Form 3800 ☐ Form 3468 ☐ Form 5884
☐ Form 6478 ☐ Form 6765 ☐ Form 8586 ☐ Form 8830 ☐ Form 8826 ☐ Form 8835
☐ Form 8844 ☐ Form 8845 ☐ Form 8846 ☐ Form 8847 . . . . | **2a** |

b Credit for prior year minimum tax (attach Form 8827) . . . . . | **2b** |

3 **Total credits.** Add lines 2a and 2b . . . . | **3** |
4 Subtract line 3 from line 1 . . . . | **4** | *5,196* |
5 Recapture taxes. Check if from: ☐ Form 4255 ☐ Form 8611 . . . . | **5** |
6 Alternative minimum tax (attach Form 4626) . . . . | **6** |
7 **Total tax.** Add lines 4 through 6. Enter here and on line 27, page 1 . . . . | **7** | *5,196* |

Part II	**Other Information** (See instructions.)

1 Refer to page 19 of the instructions and state the principal:
 a Business activity code no. ▶ *5995*
 b Business activity ▶ *Flower shop*
 c Product or service ▶ *Flowers*

2 Did any individual, partnership, estate, or trust at the end of the tax year own, directly or indirectly, 50% or more of the corporation's voting stock? (For rules of attribution, see section 267(c).) *Schedule not shown.* ☑ Yes ☐ No

 If "Yes," attach a schedule showing name and identifying number.

3 Enter the amount of tax-exempt interest received or accrued during the tax year . . . ▶ $ *–0–*

4 Enter amount of cash distributions and the book value of property (other than cash) distributions made in this tax year . . . . ▶ $ *–0–*

5a If an amount is entered on line 2, page 1, see the worksheet on page 12 for amounts to enter below:
 (1) Purchases . . . . | *134,014* |
 (2) Additional sec. 263A costs (see instructions—attach schedule) . |
 (3) Other costs (attach schedule) . | *9,466* |

b Do the rules of section 263A (for property produced or acquired for resale) apply to the corporation? . . . . . . ☐ Yes ☑ No

6 At any time during the 1994 calendar year, did the corporation have an interest in or a signature or other authority over a financial account in a foreign country (such as a bank account, securities account, or other financial account)? If "Yes," the corporation may have to file Form TD F 90-22.1 . . . . ☐ Yes ☑ No
If "Yes," enter the name of the foreign country ▶ ....

Part III	**Balance Sheets**	**(a)** Beginning of tax year		**(b)** End of tax year	
Assets	**1** Cash	*20,540*		*18,498*	
	2a Trade notes and accounts receivable				
	b Less allowance for bad debts	( )		( )	
	3 Inventories	*2,530*		*2,010*	
	4 U.S. government obligations	*13,807*		*45,479*	
	5 Tax-exempt securities (see instructions)				
	6 Other current assets (attach schedule) . . .				
	7 Loans to stockholders				
	8 Mortgage and real estate loans				
	9a Depreciable, depletable, and intangible assets . .				
	b Less accumulated depreciation, depletion, and amortization	( )		( )	
	10 Land (net of any amortization)				
	11 Other assets (attach schedule)				
	12 Total assets	*36,877*		*65,987*	
Liabilities and Stockholders' Equity	**13** Accounts payable	*6,415*		*6,079*	
	14 Other current liabilities (attach schedule) . . .				
	15 Loans from stockholders				
	16 Mortgages, notes, bonds payable				
	17 Other liabilities (attach schedule)				
	18 Capital stock (preferred and common stock) . .	*20,000*		*20,000*	
	19 Paid-in or capital surplus				
	20 Retained earnings	*10,462*		*39,908*	
	21 Less cost of treasury stock	( )		( )	
	22 Total liabilities and stockholders' equity . .	*36,877*		*65,987*	

Part IV	**Reconciliation of Income (Loss) per Books With Income per Return** *(You are not required to complete Part IV if the total assets on line 12, column (b), Part III are less than $25,000.)*

1 Net income (loss) per books . . . . . | *29,446* |
2 Federal income tax . . . . | *5,196* |
3 Excess of capital losses over capital gains . .
4 Income subject to tax not recorded on books this year (itemize) ....
5 Expenses recorded on books this year not deducted on this return (itemize) .

6 Income recorded on books this year not included on this return (itemize) ....
7 Deductions on this return not charged against book income this year (itemize) ....
....
8 Income (line 24, page 1). Enter the sum of lines 1 through 5 less the sum of lines 6 and 7 . . . | *34,642* |

EXHIBIT A–7 Form 1120

Form **1120**				OMB No. 1545-0123

U.S. Corporation Income Tax Return

Department of the Treasury
Internal Revenue Service

For calendar year 1994 or tax year beginning .... , 1994, ending .... , 19 ...
▶ Instructions are separate. See page 1 for Paperwork Reduction Act Notice.

19 94

A Check if a:
1 Consolidated return (attach Form 851) ☐
2 Personal holding co. (attach Sch. PH) ☐
3 Personal service corp. (as defined in Temporary Regs. sec. 1.441-4T— see instructions) ☐

Use IRS label. Otherwise, please print or type.

10-0395674   DEC94   071   3998
Tentex Toys, Inc.
36 Division Street
Anytown, IL   60930

B Employer identification number

C Date incorporated
3-1-72

D Total assets (see Specific Instructions)
$ 879,417

E Check applicable boxes: (1) ☐ Initial return   (2) ☐ Final return   (3) ☐ Change of address

Income	1a	Gross receipts or sales 2,010,000 b Less returns and allowances 20,000 c Bal ▶	1c	1,990,000
	2	Cost of goods sold (Schedule A, line 8)	2	1,520,000
	3	Gross profit. Subtract line 2 from line 1c	3	470,000
	4	Dividends (Schedule C, line 19)	4	10,000
	5	Interest	5	5,500
	6	Gross rents	6	
	7	Gross royalties	7	
	8	Capital gain net income (attach Schedule D (Form 1120))	8	
	9	Net gain or (loss) from Form 4797, Part II, line 20 (attach Form 4797)	9	
	10	Other income (see instructions—attach schedule)	10	
	11	**Total income.** Add lines 3 through 10 ▶	11	485,500
Deductions (See instructions for limitations on deductions.)	12	Compensation of officers (Schedule E, line 4)	12	70,000
	13	Salaries and wages (less employment credits)	13	38,000
	14	Repairs and maintenance	14	800
	15	Bad debts	15	1,600
	16	Rents	16	9,200
	17	Taxes and licenses	17	15,000
	18	Interest	18	27,200
	19	Charitable contributions (see instructions for 10% limitation)	19	23,150
	20	Depreciation (attach Form 4562) 20 17,600		
	21	Less depreciation claimed on Schedule A and elsewhere on return 21a 12,400	21b	5,200
	22	Depletion	22	
	23	Advertising	23	8,700
	24	Pension, profit-sharing, etc., plans	24	
	25	Employee benefit programs	25	
	26	Other deductions (attach schedule)	26	78,300
	27	**Total deductions.** Add lines 12 through 26 ▶	27	277,150
	28	Taxable income before net operating loss deduction and special deductions. Subtract line 27 from line 11	28	208,350
	29	**Less:** a Net operating loss deduction (see instructions) 29a		
		b Special deductions (Schedule C, line 20) 29b 8,000	29c	8,000
Tax and Payments	30	**Taxable income.** Subtract line 29c from line 28	30	200,350
	31	**Total tax** (Schedule J, line 10)	31	55,387
	32	**Payments:** a 1993 overpayment credited to 1994 32a		
	b	1994 estimated tax payments 32b 69,117		
	c	Less 1994 refund applied for on Form 4466 32c ( ) d Bal ▶ 32d 69,117		
	e	Tax deposited with Form 7004 32e		
	f	Credit from regulated investment companies (attach Form 2439) 32f		
	g	Credit for Federal tax on fuels (attach Form 4136). See instructions 32g	32h	69,117
	33	Estimated tax penalty (see instructions). Check if Form 2220 is attached ▶ ☐	33	
	34	**Tax due.** If line 32h is smaller than the total of lines 31 and 33, enter amount owed	34	
	35	**Overpayment.** If line 32h is larger than the total of lines 31 and 33, enter amount overpaid	35	13,730
	36	Enter amount of line 35 you want: **Credited to 1995 estimated tax** ▶ 13,730 Refunded ▶	36	

Please Sign Here
Under penalties of perjury, I declare that I have examined this return, including accompanying schedules and statements, and to the best of my knowledge and belief, it is true, correct, and complete. Declaration of preparer (other than taxpayer) is based on all information of which preparer has any knowledge.

▶ James O. Barclay
Signature of officer

3-7-95
Date

▶ President
Title

Paid Preparer's Use Only

Preparer's signature ▶		Date	Check if self-employed ☐	Preparer's social security number
Firm's name (or yours if self-employed) and address ▶			E.I. No. ▶	
			ZIP code ▶	

Cat. No. 11450Q

Source: "Tax Guide for Small Business, 1994," *Publication 334* (Washington, DC: Internal Revenue Service, revised November 1994), 215–18.

EXHIBIT A–7   *(Continued)*

Form 1120 (1994)   Page **2**

Schedule A	**Cost of Goods Sold** (See instructions.)			
1	Inventory at beginning of year	1	126,000	
2	Purchases	2	1,127,100	
3	Cost of labor	3	402,000	
4	Additional section 263A costs (attach schedule)	4	40,000	
5	Other costs (attach schedule)	5	123,300	
6	**Total.** Add lines 1 through 5	6	1,818,400	
7	Inventory at end of year	7	298,400	
8	**Cost of goods sold.** Subtract line 7 from line 6. Enter here and on page 1, line 2	8	1,520,000	

9a   Check all methods used for valuing closing inventory:
- [ ] Cost
- [✓] Lower of cost or market as described in Regulations section 1.471-4
- [ ] Writedown of subnormal goods as described in Regulations section 1.471-2(c)
- [ ] Other (Specify method used and attach explanation.) ▶ ....

b   Check if the LIFO inventory method was adopted this tax year for any goods (if checked, attach Form 970) . . . . . ▶ [ ]

c   If the LIFO inventory method was used for this tax year, enter percentage (or amounts) of closing inventory computed under LIFO . . . . | 9c | |

d   Do the rules of section 263A (for property produced or acquired for resale) apply to the corporation? . . . . . [✓] Yes   [ ] No

e   Was there any change in determining quantities, cost, or valuations between opening and closing inventory? If "Yes," attach explanation . . . . [ ] Yes   [✓] No

Schedule C	**Dividends and Special Deductions** (See instructions.)	(a) Dividends received	(b) %	(c) Special deductions (a) × (b)
1	Dividends from less-than-20%-owned domestic corporations that are subject to the 70% deduction (other than debt-financed stock)		70	
2	Dividends from 20%-or-more-owned domestic corporations that are subject to the 80% deduction (other than debt-financed stock)	10,000	80 see instructions	8,000
3	Dividends on debt-financed stock of domestic and foreign corporations (section 246A)			
4	Dividends on certain preferred stock of less-than-20%-owned public utilities		42	
5	Dividends on certain preferred stock of 20%-or-more-owned public utilities		48	
6	Dividends from less-than-20%-owned foreign corporations and certain FSCs that are subject to the 70% deduction		70	
7	Dividends from 20%-or-more-owned foreign corporations and certain FSCs that are subject to the 80% deduction		80	
8	Dividends from wholly owned foreign subsidiaries subject to the 100% deduction (section 245(b))		100	
9	**Total.** Add lines 1 through 8. See instructions for limitation			8,000
10	Dividends from domestic corporations received by a small business investment company operating under the Small Business Investment Act of 1958		100	
11	Dividends from certain FSCs that are subject to the 100% deduction (section 245(c)(1))		100	
12	Dividends from affiliated group members subject to the 100% deduction (section 243(a)(3))		100	
13	Other dividends from foreign corporations not included on lines 3, 6, 7, 8, or 11			
14	Income from controlled foreign corporations under subpart F (attach Form(s) 5471)			
15	Foreign dividend gross-up (section 78)			
16	IC-DISC and former DISC dividends not included on lines 1, 2, or 3 (section 246(d))			
17	Other dividends			
18	Deduction for dividends paid on certain preferred stock of public utilities			
19	**Total dividends.** Add lines 1 through 17. Enter here and on line 4, page 1 . . ▶	10,000		
20	**Total special deductions.** Add lines 9, 10, 11, 12, and 18. Enter here and on line 29b, page 1 . . . . ▶			8,000

Schedule E	**Compensation of Officers** (See instructions for line 12, page 1.)					

Complete Schedule E only if total receipts (line 1a plus lines 4 through 10 on page 1, Form 1120) are $500,000 or more.

(a) Name of officer	(b) Social security number	(c) Percent of time devoted to business	(d) Common	(e) Preferred	(f) Amount of compensation
1 James O. Barclay	581-00-0936	100 %	45 %	%	55,000
		%	%	%	
George M. Collins	447-00-2604	100 %	15 %	%	31,000
		%	%	%	
Samuel Adams	401-00-2611	50 %	2 %	%	14,000
2	Total compensation of officers				100,000
3	Compensation of officers claimed on Schedule A and elsewhere on return				30,000
4	Subtract line 3 from line 2. Enter the result here and on line 12, page 1				70,000

EXHIBIT A–7   *(Continued)*

Form 1120 (1994)   Page **3**

Schedule J   Tax Computation (See instructions.)

1   Check if the corporation is a member of a controlled group (see sections 1561 and 1563) . . . . ▶ ☐

2a If the box on line 1 is checked, enter the corporation's share of the $50,000, $25,000, and $9,925,000 taxable income brackets (in that order):

(1) $|_____| (2) $|_____| (3) $|_____|

b   Enter the corporation's share of:

(1) Additional 5% tax (not more than $11,750) $|_____|
(2) Additional 3% tax (not more than $100,000) $|_____|

3   Income tax. Check this box if the corporation is a qualified personal service corporation as defined in section 448(d)(2) (see instructions on page 14). . . . . ▶ ☐   **3**   61,387

4a Foreign tax credit (attach Form 1118)	**4a**	
b Possessions tax credit (attach Form 5735)	**4b**	
c Orphan drug credit (attach Form 6765)	**4c**	
d Check: ☐ Nonconventional source fuel credit ☐ QEV credit (attach Form 8834)	**4d**	

e   General business credit. Enter here and check which forms are attached:

☐ 3800 ☐ 3468 ☑ 5884 ☐ 6478 ☐ 6765 ☐ 8586 ☐ 8830
☐ 8826 ☐ 8835 ☐ 8844 ☐ 8845 ☐ 8846 ☐ 8847   **4e** 6,000

f   Credit for prior year minimum tax (attach Form 8827) **4f**

5 **Total credits.** Add lines 4a through 4f	**5**	6,000
6 Subtract line 5 from line 3	**6**	55,387
7 Personal holding company tax (attach Schedule PH (Form 1120))	**7**	
8 Recapture taxes. Check if from: ☐ Form 4255 ☐ Form 8611	**8**	
9a Alternative minimum tax (attach Form 4626)	**9a**	
b Environmental tax (attach Form 4626)	**9b**	
10 **Total tax.** Add lines 6 through 9b. Enter here and on line 31, page 1	**10**	55,387

Schedule K   Other Information (See pages 17 and 18 of instructions.)

		Yes	No
1	Check method of accounting: a ☐ Cash b ☑ Accrual c ☐ Other (specify) ▶		
2	Refer to page 19 of the instructions and state the principal:		
a	Business activity code no. ▶ 3998		
b	Business activity ▶ Manufacturing		
c	Product or service ▶ Toys		
3	Did the corporation at the end of the tax year own, directly or indirectly, 50% or more of the voting stock of a domestic corporation? (For rules of attribution, see section 267(c).)		✓
	If "Yes," attach a schedule showing: (a) name and identifying number, (b) percentage owned, and (c) taxable income or (loss) before NOL and special deductions of such corporation for the tax year ending with or within your tax year.		
4	Is the corporation a subsidiary in an affiliated group or a parent-subsidiary controlled group?		✓
	If "Yes," enter employer identification number and name of the parent corporation ▶		
5	Did any individual, partnership, corporation, estate or trust at the end of the tax year own, directly or indirectly, 50% or more of the corporation's voting stock? (For rules of attribution, see section 267(c).)	✓	
	If "Yes," attach a schedule showing name and identifying number. (Do not include any information already entered in 4 above.) Enter percentage owned ▶		
6	During this tax year, did the corporation pay dividends (other than stock dividends and distributions in exchange for stock) in excess of the corporation's current and accumulated earnings and profits? (See secs. 301 and 316.)		✓
	If "Yes," file Form 5452. If this is a consolidated return, answer here for the parent corporation and on **Form 851,** Affiliations Schedule, for each subsidiary.		

		Yes	No
7	Was the corporation a U.S. shareholder of any controlled foreign corporation? (See sections 951 and 957.) . . .		✓
	If "Yes," attach Form 5471 for each such corporation. Enter number of Forms 5471 attached ▶		
8	At any time during the 1994 calendar year, did the corporation have an interest in or a signature or other authority over a financial account in a foreign country (such as a bank account, securities account, or other financial account)?		✓
	If "Yes," the corporation may have to file Form TD F 90-22.1. If "Yes," enter name of foreign country ▶		
9	Was the corporation the grantor of, or transferor to, a foreign trust that existed during the current tax year, whether or not the corporation has any beneficial interest in it? If "Yes," the corporation may have to file Forms 926, 3520, or 3520-A		✓
10	Did one foreign person at any time during the tax year own, directly or indirectly, at least 25% of: (a) the total voting power of all classes of stock of the corporation entitled to vote, or (b) the total value of all classes of stock of the corporation? If "Yes,"		✓
a	Enter percentage owned ▶		
b	Enter owner's country ▶		
c	The corporation may have to file Form 5472. Enter number of Forms 5472 attached ▶		
11	Check this box if the corporation issued publicly offered debt instruments with original issue discount . ▶ ☐		
	If so, the corporation may have to file Form 8281.		
12	Enter the amount of tax-exempt interest received or accrued during the tax year ▶ $ 5,000		
13	If there were 35 or fewer shareholders at the end of the tax year, enter the number ▶		
14	If the corporation has an NOL for the tax year and is electing to forego the carryback period, check here ▶ ☐		
15	Enter the available NOL carryover from prior tax years (Do not reduce it by any deduction on line 29a.) ▶ $		

EXHIBIT A–7 *(Continued)*

Form 1120 (1994)   Page **4**

Schedule L	Balance Sheets	Beginning of tax year		End of tax year	
	Assets	**(a)**	**(b)**	**(c)**	**(d)**
1	Cash		14,700		28,331
2a	Trade notes and accounts receivable	98,400		103,700	
b	Less allowance for bad debts	( )	98,400	( )	103,700
3	Inventories		126,000		298,400
4	U.S. government obligations				
5	Tax-exempt securities (see instructions)		100,000		120,000
6	Other current assets (attach schedule)		26,300		17,266
7	Loans to stockholders				
8	Mortgage and real estate loans				
9	Other investments (attach schedule)		100,000		80,000
10a	Buildings and other depreciable assets	272,400		296,700	
b	Less accumulated depreciation	(88,300)	184,100	(104,280)	192,400
11a	Depletable assets				
b	Less accumulated depletion	( )		( )	
12	Land (net of any amortization)		20,000		20,000
13a	Intangible assets (amortizable only)				
b	Less accumulated amortization	( )		( )	
14	Other assets (attach schedule)		14,800		19,300
15	Total assets		684,300		879,417
	Liabilities and Stockholders' Equity				
16	Accounts payable		28,500		34,834
17	Mortgages, notes, bonds payable in less than 1 year		4,300		4,300
18	Other current liabilities (attach schedule)		6,800		7,400
19	Loans from stockholders				
20	Mortgages, notes, bonds payable in 1 year or more		176,700		264,100
21	Other liabilities (attach schedule)				
22	Capital stock: a Preferred stock				
	b Common stock	200,000	200,000	200,000	200,000
23	Paid-in or capital surplus				
24	Retained earnings—Appropriated (attach schedule)		30,000		40,000
25	Retained earnings—Unappropriated		238,000		328,783
26	Less cost of treasury stock	( )		( )	
27	Total liabilities and stockholders' equity		684,300		879,417

Note: You are not required to complete Schedules M-1 and M-2 below if the total assets on line 15, column (d) of Schedule L are less than $25,000.

Schedule M-1	Reconciliation of Income (Loss) per Books With Income per Return (See instructions.)				
1	Net income (loss) per books	147,783	7	Income recorded on books this year not included on this return (itemize):	
2	Federal income tax	55,387			
3	Excess of capital losses over capital gains	3,600		Tax-exempt interest $ 5,000	
4	Income subject to tax not recorded on books this year (itemize):			Insurance proceeds – 9,500	14,500
5	Expenses recorded on books this year not deducted on this return (itemize):		8	Deductions on this return not charged against book income this year (itemize):	
a	Depreciation $		a	Depreciation . . . . . $ 1,620	
b	Contributions carryover $ 850		b	Contributions carryover $	
c	Travel and entertainment $ See itemized statement attached (not shown) – 16,850	17,700			1,620
			9	Add lines 7 and 8	16,120
6	Add lines 1 through 5	224,470	10	Income (line 28, page 1)—line 6 less line 9	208,350

Schedule M-2	Analysis of Unappropriated Retained Earnings per Books (Line 25, Schedule L)				
1	Balance at beginning of year	238,000	5	Distributions: a Cash	65,000
2	Net income (loss) per books	147,783		b Stock	
3	Other increases (itemize): .... Refund of 1991 income tax due to IRS examination			c Property	
			6	Other decreases (itemize): .... Reserve for contingencies	10,000
		18,000	7	Add lines 5 and 6	75,000
4	Add lines 1, 2, and 3	403,783	8	Balance at end of year (line 4 less line 7)	328,783

EXHIBIT A–8 Form 1120S

Form **1120S**	U.S. Income Tax Return for an S Corporation	OMB No. 1545-0130
Department of the Treasury Internal Revenue Service	▶ Do not file this form unless the corporation has timely filed Form 2553 to elect to be an S corporation. ▶ See separate instructions.	19**94**

For calendar year 1994, or tax year beginning _____ , 1994, and ending _____ , 19 ___

A Date of election as an S corporation **12-1-93**	Use IRS label. Other-wise, please print or type.	10-4487965 DEC94 D74 3070 StratoTech, Inc. 482 Winston Street Metro City, OH 43705	C Employer identification number **10 4487965**
B Business code no. (see Specific Instructions) **5008**			D Date incorporated **3-1-75**
			E Total assets (see Specific Instructions) **$ 771,334**

F Check applicable boxes: (1) ☑ Initial return (2) ☐ Final return (3) ☐ Change in address (4) ☐ Amended return
G Check this box if this S corporation is subject to the consolidated audit procedures of sections 6241 through 6245 (see instructions before checking this box) ▶ ☐
H Enter number of shareholders in the corporation at end of the tax year ▶ **6**

Caution: Include only trade or business income and expenses on lines 1a through 21. See the instructions for more information.

Income

1a	Gross receipts or sales **1,545,700**	b Less returns and allowances **21,000**	c Bal ▶ 1c **1,524,700**
2	Cost of goods sold (Schedule A, line 8)		2 **954,700**
3	Gross profit. Subtract line 2 from line 1c		3 **570,000**
4	Net gain (loss) from Form 4797, Part II, line 20 (attach Form 4797)		4
5	Other income (loss) (see instructions) (attach schedule)		5
6	**Total income (loss).** Combine lines 3 through 5 ▶		6 **570,000**

Deductions (See instructions for limitations.)

7	Compensation of officers		7 **170,000**
8	Salaries and wages (less employment credits)		8 **138,000**
9	Repairs and maintenance		9 **800**
10	Bad debts		10 **1,600**
11	Rents		11 **9,200**
12	Taxes and licenses		12 **15,000**
13	Interest		13 **14,200**
14a	Depreciation (see instructions)	14a **15,200**	
b	Depreciation claimed on Schedule A and elsewhere on return	14b	
c	Subtract line 14b from line 14a		14c **15,200**
15	Depletion (**Do not deduct oil and gas depletion.**)		15
16	Advertising		16 **8,700**
17	Pension, profit-sharing, etc., plans		17
18	Employee benefit programs		18
19	Other deductions (see instructions) (attach schedule)		19 **78,300**
20	**Total deductions.** Add the amounts shown in the far right column for lines 7 through 19 ▶		20 **451,000**
21	Ordinary income (loss) from trade or business activities. Subtract line 20 from line 6		21 **119,000**

Tax and Payments

22	**Tax: a** Excess net passive income tax (attach schedule)	22a	
b	Tax from Schedule D (Form 1120S)	22b	
c	Add lines 22a and 22b (see instructions for additional taxes)		22c
23	**Payments: a** 1994 estimated tax payments and amount applied from 1993 return	23a	
b	Tax deposited with Form 7004	23b	
c	Credit for Federal tax paid on fuels (attach Form 4136)	23c	
d	Add lines 23a through 23c		23d
24	Estimated tax penalty (see instructions). Check if Form 2220 is attached ▶ ☐		24
25	**Tax due.** If the total of lines 22c and 24 is larger than line 23d, enter amount owed. See instructions for depositary method of payment ▶		25
26	**Overpayment.** If line 23d is larger than the total of lines 22c and 24, enter amount overpaid ▶		26
27	Enter amount of line 26 you want: **Credited to 1995 estimated tax** ▶ _____	Refunded ▶	27

Please Sign Here

Under penalties of perjury, I declare that I have examined this return, including accompanying schedules and statements, and to the best of my knowledge and belief, it is true, correct, and complete. Declaration of preparer (other than taxpayer) is based on all information of which preparer has any knowledge

▶ *John H. Green*   Signature of officer   Date **3-10-95**   ▶ Title **President**

Paid Preparer's Use Only

Preparer's signature ▶	Date	Check if self-employed ▶ ☐	Preparer's social security number
Firm's name (or yours if self-employed) and address ▶		E.I. No. ▶	
		ZIP code ▶	

For Paperwork Reduction Act Notice, see page 1 of separate instructions.   Cat. No. 11510H   Form **1120S** (1994)

Source: "Tax Guide for Small Business, 1994," *Publication 334* (Washington, DC: Internal Revenue Service, revised November 1994), 222–25.

EXHIBIT A–8 *(Continued)*

Form 1120S (1994)   Page **2**

Schedule A	Cost of Goods Sold (See instructions.)		
1	Inventory at beginning of year	1	126,000
2	Purchases	2	1,127,100
3	Cost of labor	3	
4	Additional section 263A costs (see instructions) *(attach schedule)*	4	
5	Other costs *(attach schedule)*	5	
6	**Total.** Add lines 1 through 5	6	1,253,100
7	Inventory at end of year	7	298,400
8	**Cost of goods sold.** Subtract line 7 from line 6. Enter here and on page 1, line 2	8	954,700

9a Check all methods used for valuing closing inventory:

    (i) ☐ Cost

    (ii) ☑ Lower of cost or market as described in Regulations section 1.471-4

    (iii) ☐ Writedown of "subnormal" goods as described in Regulations section 1.471-2(c)

    (iv) ☐ Other (specify method used and attach explanation) ▶ ....

  b Check if the LIFO inventory method was adopted this tax year for any goods *(if checked, attach Form 970)*.   ▶ ☐

  c If the LIFO inventory method was used for this tax year, enter percentage (or amounts) of closing inventory computed under LIFO | 9c | |

  d Do the rules of section 263A (for property produced or acquired for resale) apply to the corporation?   ☐ Yes ☑ No

  e Was there any change in determining quantities, cost, or valuations between opening and closing inventory?   ☐ Yes ☑ No

    If "Yes," attach explanation.

Schedule B	Other Information		

		Yes	No
1	Check method of accounting: **(a)** ☐ Cash **(b)** ☑ Accrual **(c)** ☐ Other (specify) ▶		
2	Refer to the list in the instructions and state the corporation's principal: **(a)** Business activity ▶ 5008 Distributor **(b)** Product or service ▶ heavy equipment		
3	Did the corporation at the end of the tax year own, directly or indirectly, 50% or more of the voting stock of a domestic corporation? (For rules of attribution, see section 267(c).) If "Yes," attach a schedule showing: **(a)** name, address, and employer identification number and **(b)** percentage owned.		✔
4	Was the corporation a member of a controlled group subject to the provisions of section 1561?		✔
5	At any time during calendar year 1994, did the corporation have an interest in or a signature or other authority over a financial account in a foreign country (such as a bank account, securities account, or other financial account)? (See instructions for exceptions and filing requirements for Form TD F 90-22.1.) If "Yes," enter the name of the foreign country ▶		✔
6	Was the corporation the grantor of, or transferor to, a foreign trust that existed during the current tax year, whether or not the corporation has any beneficial interest in it? If "Yes," the corporation may have to file Forms 3520, 3520-A, or 926		✔
7	Check this box if the corporation has filed or is required to file **Form 8264**, Application for Registration of a Tax Shelter ▶ ☐		
8	Check this box if the corporation issued publicly offered debt instruments with original issue discount ▶ ☐ If so, the corporation may have to file **Form 8281**, Information Return for Publicly Offered Original Issue Discount Instruments.		
9	If the corporation: **(a)** filed its election to be an S corporation after 1986, **(b)** was a C corporation before it elected to be an S corporation **or** the corporation acquired an asset with a basis determined by reference to its basis (or the basis of any other property) in the hands of a C corporation, and **(c)** has net unrealized built-in gain (defined in section 1374(d)(1)) in excess of the net recognized built-in gain from prior years, enter the net unrealized built-in gain reduced by net recognized built-in gain from prior years (see instructions) ▶ $ 37,200		
10	Check this box if the corporation had subchapter C earnings and profits at the close of the tax year (see instructions) ▶ ☐		

Designation of Tax Matters Person (See instructions.)

Enter below the shareholder designated as the tax matters person (TMP) for the tax year of this return:

Name of designated TMP ▶ John H. Green

Identifying number of TMP ▶ 458-00-0327

Address of designated TMP ▶ 4340 Holmes Parkway, Metro City, OH 43704

EXHIBIT A–8   *(Continued)*

Form 1120S (1994)   Page **3**

Schedule K	Shareholders' Shares of Income, Credits, Deductions, etc.		
	(a) Pro rata share items		**(b)** Total amount

1	Ordinary income (loss) from trade or business activities (page 1, line 21)	**1**	119,000
2	Net income (loss) from rental real estate activities *(attach Form 8825)*	**2**	
3a	Gross income from other rental activities **3a**		
b	Expenses from other rental activities *(attach schedule)*. **3b**		
c	Net income (loss) from other rental activities. Subtract line 3b from line 3a	**3c**	
4	Portfolio income (loss):		
a	Interest income	**4a**	4,000
b	Dividend income	**4b**	16,000
c	Royalty income	**4c**	
d	Net short-term capital gain (loss) *(attach Schedule D (Form 1120S))*	**4d**	
e	Net long-term capital gain (loss) *(attach Schedule D (Form 1120S))*	**4e**	
f	Other portfolio income (loss) *(attach schedule)*	**4f**	
5	Net gain (loss) under section 1231 (other than due to casualty or theft) *(attach Form 4797)*	**5**	
6	Other income (loss) *(attach schedule)*	**6**	
7	Charitable contributions (see instructions) *(attach schedule)*	**7**	24,000
8	Section 179 expense deduction *(attach Form 4562)*.	**8**	
9	Deductions related to portfolio income (loss) (see instructions) (itemize)	**9**	
10	Other deductions *(attach schedule)*	**10**	
11a	Interest expense on investment debts	**11a**	3,000
b (1)	Investment income included on lines 4a, 4b, 4c, and 4f above	**11b(1)**	20,000
(2)	Investment expenses included on line 9 above	**11b(2)**	
12a	Credit for alcohol used as a fuel *(attach Form 6478)*	**12a**	
b	Low-income housing credit (see instructions):		
(1)	From partnerships to which section 42(j)(5) applies for property placed in service before 1990	**12b(1)**	
(2)	Other than on line 12b(1) for property placed in service before 1990.	**12b(2)**	
(3)	From partnerships to which section 42(j)(5) applies for property placed in service after 1989	**12b(3)**	
(4)	Other than on line 12b(3) for property placed in service after 1989	**12b(4)**	
c	Qualified rehabilitation expenditures related to rental real estate activities *(attach Form 3468)*	**12c**	
d	Credits (other than credits shown on lines 12b and 12c) related to rental real estate activities (see instructions).	**12d**	
e	Credits related to other rental activities (see instructions)	**12e**	
13	Other credits (see instructions)	**13**	6,000
14a	Depreciation adjustment on property placed in service after 1986	**14a**	
b	Adjusted gain or loss	**14b**	
c	Depletion (other than oil and gas)	**14c**	
d (1)	Gross income from oil, gas, or geothermal properties	**14d(1)**	
(2)	Deductions allocable to oil, gas, or geothermal properties	**14d(2)**	
e	Other adjustments and tax preference items *(attach schedule)*	**14e**	
15a	Type of income ▶		
b	Name of foreign country or U.S. possession ▶		
c	Total gross income from sources outside the United States *(attach schedule)* . . .	**15c**	
d	Total applicable deductions and losses *(attach schedule)*	**15d**	
e	Total foreign taxes (check one): ▶ ☐ Paid ☐ Accrued	**15e**	
f	Reduction in taxes available for credit *(attach schedule)*	**15f**	
g	Other foreign tax information *(attach schedule)*	**15g**	
16a	Total expenditures to which a section 59(e) election may apply	**16a**	
b	Type of expenditures ▶		
17	Tax-exempt interest income	**17**	5,000
18	Other tax-exempt income	**18**	
19	Nondeductible expenses	**19**	16,350
20	Total property distributions (including cash) other than dividends reported on line 22 below	**20**	65,000
21	Other items and amounts required to be reported separately to shareholders (see instructions) *(attach schedule)*		
22	Total dividend distributions paid from accumulated earnings and profits	**22**	
23	**Income (loss).** (Required only if Schedule M-1 must be completed.) Combine lines 1 through 6 in column (b). From the result, subtract the sum of lines 7 through 11a, 15e, and 16a	**23**	112,000

Left margin section labels: Income (Loss); Deductions; Investment Interest; Credits; Adjustments and Tax Preference Items; Foreign Taxes; Other

EXHIBIT A-8 *(Continued)*

Form 1120S (1994)   Page **4**

Schedule L **Balance Sheets**	Beginning of tax year		End of tax year	
Assets	(a)	(b)	(c)	(d)
1 Cash		14,700		14,514
2a Trade notes and accounts receivable	98 400		33,700	
b Less allowance for bad debts		98,400		33,700
3 Inventories		126,000		298,400
4 U.S. Government obligations				
5 Tax-exempt securities		100,000		100,000
6 Other current assets (attach schedule)		26,300		26,300
7 Loans to shareholders				
8 Mortgage and real estate loans				
9 Other investments (attach schedule)		100,000		100,000
10a Buildings and other depreciable assets	204 700		204,700	
b Less accumulated depreciation	36 000	168,700	45,580	159,120
11a Depletable assets				
b Less accumulated depletion				
12 Land (net of any amortization)		20,000		20,000
13a Intangible assets (amortizable only)				
b Less accumulated amortization				
14 Other assets (attach schedule)		14,800		19,300
15 Total assets		668,900		771,334
Liabilities and Shareholders' Equity				
16 Accounts payable		28,500		34,834
17 Mortgages. notes. bonds payable in less than 1 year		4,300		4,300
18 Other current liabilities (attach schedule)		6800		7,400
19 Loans from shareholders				
20 Mortgages. notes. bonds payable in 1 year or more		161,300		215,530
21 Other liabilities (attach schedule)				
22 Capital stock		2,000		2,000
23 Paid-in or capital surplus		198,000		198,000
24 Retained earnings		268,000		309,270
25 Less cost of treasury stock		( )		( )
26 Total liabilities and shareholders' equity		668,900		771,334

Schedule M-1 **Reconciliation of Income (Loss) per Books With Income (Loss) per Return** (You are not required to complete this schedule if the total assets on line 15, column (d), of Schedule L are less than $25,000.)

1 Net income (loss) per books	106,270	5 Income recorded on books this year not included on Schedule K, lines 1 through 6 (itemize):		
2 Income included on Schedule K, lines 1 through 6, not recorded on books this year (itemize):	0	a Tax-exempt interest $ 5,000		5,000
3 Expenses recorded on books this year not included on Schedule K, lines 1 through 11a, 15e, and 16a (itemize):		6 Deductions included on Schedule K, lines 1 through 11a, 15e, and 16a, not charged against book income this year (itemize):		
a Depreciation $		a Depreciation $ 5,620		
b Travel and entertainment $ _Itemized statement attached_	16,350	7 Add lines 5 and 6		5,620 / 10,620
4 Add lines 1 through 3	122,620	8 Income (loss) (Schedule K, line 23). Line 4 less line 7		112,000

Schedule M-2 **Analysis of Accumulated Adjustments Account, Other Adjustments Account, and Shareholders' Undistributed Taxable Income Previously Taxed** (See instructions.)

		(a) Accumulated adjustments account	(b) Other adjustments account	(c) Shareholders' undistributed taxable income previously taxed
1	Balance at beginning of tax year	0	0	
2	Ordinary income from page 1, line 21	119,000		
3	Other additions	20,000	5,000	
4	Loss from page 1, line 21	(0)		
5	Other reductions	(42,500)	(850)	
6	Combine lines 1 through 5	96,500	4,150	
7	Distributions other than dividend distributions	65,000	0	
8	Balance at end of tax year. Subtract line 7 from line 6	31,500	4,150	

EXHIBIT A–9   Schedule K-1 (Form 1120S)

| SCHEDULE K-1
(Form 1120S)

Department of the Treasury
Internal Revenue Service | **Shareholder's Share of Income, Credits, Deductions, etc.**
▶ See separate instructions.
For calendar year 1994 or tax year
beginning _____ , 1994, and ending _____ , 19 | OMB No. 1545-0130

19**94** |

Shareholder's identifying number ▶	Corporation's identifying number ▶ *10* **448 7965**
Shareholder's name, address, and ZIP code John H. Green 4340 Holmes Parkway Metro City, OH 43704	Corporation's name, address, and ZIP code Strato Tech, Inc. 482 Winston Street Metro City, OH 43705

A Shareholder's percentage of stock ownership for tax year (see Instructions for Schedule K-1) . . . . ▶ **45** %
B Internal Revenue Service Center where corporation filed its return ▶ Cincinnati, OH
C Tax shelter registration number (see Instructions for Schedule K-1) . . . . ▶ ....
D Check applicable boxes: **(1)** ☐ Final K-1   **(2)** ☐ Amended K-1

		(a) Pro rata share items		**(b)** Amount	**(c)** Form 1040 filers enter the amount in column (b) on:
Income (Loss)	1	Ordinary income (loss) from trade or business activities . . .	**1**	53,550	See Shareholder's Instructions for Schedule K-1 (Form 1120S)
	2	Net income (loss) from rental real estate activities	**2**		
	3	Net income (loss) from other rental activities	**3**		
	4	Portfolio income (loss):			
	a	Interest	**4a**	1,800	Sch. B, Part I, line 1
	b	Dividends	**4b**	7,200	Sch. B, Part II, line 5
	c	Royalties	**4c**		Sch. E, Part I, line 4
	d	Net short-term capital gain (loss)	**4d**		Sch. D, line 5, col. (f) or (g)
	e	Net long-term capital gain (loss)	**4e**		Sch. D, line 13, col. (f) or (g)
	f	Other portfolio income (loss) *(attach schedule)* . . .	**4f**		(Enter on applicable line of your return)
	5	Net gain (loss) under section 1231 (other than due to casualty or theft) . . .	**5**		See Shareholder's Instructions for Schedule K-1 (Form 1120S)
	6	Other income (loss) *(attach schedule)*	**6**		(Enter on applicable line of your return)
Deductions	7	Charitable contributions (see instructions) *(attach schedule)* . .	**7**	10,800	Sch. A, line 15 or 16
	8	Section 179 expense deduction	**8**		See Shareholder's Instructions for Schedule K-1 (Form 1120S)
	9	Deductions related to portfolio income (loss) *(attach schedule)* .	**9**		
	10	Other deductions *(attach schedule)*	**10**		
Investment Interest	11a	Interest expense on investment debts	**11a**	1,350	Form 4952, line 1
	b	**(1)** Investment income included on lines 4a, 4b, 4c, and 4f above	**b(1)**	9,000	See Shareholder's Instructions for Schedule K-1 (Form 1120S)
		(2) Investment expenses included on line 9 above	**b(2)**		
Credits	12a	Credit for alcohol used as fuel	**12a**		Form 6478, line 10
	b	Low-income housing credit:			
		(1) From section 42(j)(5) partnerships for property placed in service before 1990	**b(1)**		Form 8586, line 5
		(2) Other than on line 12b(1) for property placed in service before 1990	**b(2)**		
		(3) From section 42(j)(5) partnerships for property placed in service after 1989	**b(3)**		
		(4) Other than on line 12b(3) for property placed in service after 1989	**b(4)**		
	c	Qualified rehabilitation expenditures related to rental real estate activities (see instructions)	**12c**		
	d	Credits (other than credits shown on lines 12b and 12c) related to rental real estate activities (see instructions)	**12d**		See Shareholder's Instructions for Schedule K-1 (Form 1120S)
	e	Credits related to other rental activities (see instructions) . .	**12e**		
	13	Other credits (see instructions)	**13**	2,700	
Adjustments and Tax Preference Items	14a	Depreciation adjustment on property placed in service after 1986	**14a**		See Shareholder's Instructions for Schedule K-1 (Form 1120S) and Instructions for Form 6251
	b	Adjusted gain or loss	**14b**		
	c	Depletion (other than oil and gas)	**14c**		
	d	**(1)** Gross income from oil, gas, or geothermal properties . .	**d(1)**		
		(2) Deductions allocable to oil, gas, or geothermal properties .	**d(2)**		
	e	Other adjustments and tax preference items *(attach schedule)* .	**14e**		

For Paperwork Reduction Act Notice, see page 1 of Instructions for Form 1120S.   Cat. No. 11520D   **Schedule K-1 (Form 1120S) 1994**

Source: "Tax Guide for Small Business, 1994," *Publication 334* (Washington, DC: Internal Revenue Service, revised November 1994), 226–27.

EXHIBIT A–9 *(Continued)*

	(a) Pro rata share items		(b) Amount	(c) Form 1040 filers enter the amount in column (b) on:
Foreign Taxes	**15a** Type of income ▶			Form 1116, Check boxes
	b Name of foreign country or U.S. possession ▶			
	c Total gross income from sources outside the United States *(attach schedule)*	15c		Form 1116, Part I
	d Total applicable deductions and losses *(attach schedule)* . . .	15d		
	e Total foreign taxes (check one): ▶ ☐ Paid ☐ Accrued . .	15e		Form 1116, Part II
	f Reduction in taxes available for credit *(attach schedule)* . . .	15f		Form 1116, Part III
	g Other foreign tax information *(attach schedule)*	15g		See Instructions for Form 1116
Other	**16a** Total expenditures to which a section 59(e) election may apply	16a		See Shareholder's Instructions for Schedule K-1 (Form 1120S).
	b Type of expenditures ▶			
	17 Tax-exempt interest income	17	2,250	Form 1040, line 8b
	18 Other tax-exempt income	18		
	19 Nondeductible expenses	19	7,358	See Shareholder's Instructions for Schedule K-1 (Form 1120S).
	20 Property distributions (including cash) other than dividend distributions reported to you on Form 1099-DIV	20	29,250	
	21 Amount of loan repayments for "Loans From Shareholders" . .	21		
	22 Recapture of low-income housing credit:			
	a From section 42(j)(5) partnerships	22a		Form 8611, line 8
	b Other than on line 22a	22b		

23 Supplemental information required to be reported separately to each shareholder *(attach additional schedules if more space is needed)*:

....

....

....

....

....

....

....

....

....

....

....

....

....

....

....

....

....

....

....

Index